The RELUCTANT cook

Dedication

For Jeannie, Steven and Janine for their inspiration and support.

And

for John.

This book accompanies the BBC Television series *The Reluctant Cook*, first broadcast on BBC2 from October 1988. The series was produced by Clare Brigstocke.

Published to accompany a series of programmes prepared in consultation with the Educational Broadcasting Council.

Food photography: James Jackson
Home economist: Allyson Birch
Stylist: Jacky Jackson

Line illustrations: Charles Front

Cover photography: S. Jeffrey Binns, Ivanhoe Studios Ltd
Cover illustrations: Anni Axworthy
Title artwork: Tony Spaul

The authors would also like to thank the following people: Nina Shandloff, our editor at BBC Books; Ruth Baldwin, the copy editor; Huw Davies, the book designer; Stacey Adams and Damaris Pitcher, who worked on the television series; Hilary Hardaker, who tested the recipes; our copy typist, Dee Cresswell; Ann White from Bejam, for the generous loan of a microwave oven; Sally Major for information on microwave cookery; Ian Greer of Sheffield; and Jenny Rogers and Claudia Roden for their advice and wisdom.

Published by BBC Books
A division of BBC Enterprises Ltd
Woodlands, 80 Wood Lane
London W12 0TT

ISBN 0 563 21414 7 (paperback)
ISBN 0 563 21424 4 (hardback)

Typeset in 10/11 Plantin by Phoenix Photosetting, Chatham
Printed and bound in Great Britain by Mackays of Chatham Ltd
Colour printed by Chorley & Pickersgill Ltd, Leeds

The RELUCTANT COOk

Kevin Woodford
&
Clare Brigstocke

BBC BOOKS

Conversion Tables

All these are *approximate* conversions, which have either been rounded up or down. Never mix metric and imperial measures in one recipe. Stick to one system or another.

Volume

Metric (millilitres)	Imperial (ounces)
15 ml	½ fl oz
25 ml	1 fl oz
50 ml	2 fl oz
75 ml	3 fl oz
125 ml	4 fl oz
150 ml	5 fl oz
	(¼ pint)
175 ml	6 fl oz
200 ml	7 fl oz
250 ml	8 fl oz
275 ml	9 fl oz
300 ml	10 fl oz
	(½ pint)
325 ml	11 fl oz
350 ml	12 fl oz
375 ml	13 fl oz
415 ml	14 fl oz
450 ml	15 fl oz
	(¾ pint)
475 ml	16 fl oz
500 ml	17 fl oz
550 ml	18 fl oz
575 ml	19 fl oz
600 ml	20 fl oz
	(1 pint)
1000 ml (1 litre)	1 pint 13 fl oz
1.5 litres	2½ pints

Weights

Metric (grams)	Imperial (ounces)
15 g	½ oz
25 g	1 oz
50 g	2 oz
75 g	3 oz
125 g	4 oz
150 g	5 oz
175 g	6 oz
200 g	7 oz
250 g	8 oz (½ lb)
275 g	9 oz
300 g	10 oz
325 g	11 oz
350 g	12 oz
375 g	13 oz
400 g	14 oz
425 g	15 oz
500 g	16 oz (1 lb)
750 g	1 lb 8 oz
1000 g (1 kilogram)	2 lb
1.25kg	2 lb 8 oz
1.5kg	3–3½ lb
2kg	4 lb

Length

Metric (centimetres)	Imperial (inches)
3 mm	⅛ in.
6 mm	¼ in.
1 cm	½ in.
2 cm	¾ in.
2.5 cm	1 in.
4 cm	1½ in.
5 cm	2 in.
6 cm	2½ in.
7.5 cm	3 in.
9 cm	3½ in.
10 cm	4 in.
13 cm	5 in.
15 cm	6 in.
18 cm	7 in.
20 cm	8 in.
23 cm	9 in.
25 cm	10 in.
28 cm	11 in.
30 cm	12 in.
33 cm	13 in.

Oven Temperature Guide

Centigrade	Fahrenheit	Gas Mark
110	225	¼
120	250	½
140	275	1
150	300	2
160	325	3
180	350	4
190	375	5
200	400	6
220	425	7
230	450	8
240	475	9

Imperial spoon measures are used throughout this book. These are *level* spoonfuls. If you have a set of metric spoons, use the following equivalents:

1 teaspoon = 5 ml
1 tablespoon = 15 ml

Contents

Introduction

What makes a person reluctant to cook?

Lack of experience? Well, this is a cooking manual, not a cookbook. Most cookbooks are written for people who already know how to cook. We assume no knowledge, and proceed from there.

The fact that they find it boring, or they lack the time? We won't guarantee that cooking will suddenly become fun after you have read this book, but we can help you organise your time better so that you can spend more time *out* of the kitchen than in it.

Lack of confidence? That's the hardest thing to remedy. Read on.

It can be infuriating to hear people wax lyrical about the joys of cooking when the idea of preparing food for a dinner party fills you with dread. This dread has largely developed because the goalposts have been moved. In this present culture gastronomy has been put on a pedestal. Knowing about and, better still, cooking good food is the new middle-class social skill of the 1980s. Restaurant food has improved enormously, people travel and eat abroad to a far greater extent and food is photographed in glossy magazines as lovingly, and as expensively, as fashion models. So, you may know exactly what you like to eat but haven't the first clue about how to make it at home. Moreover, the quality of prepared food has improved – quite elaborate ready-to-cook dishes such as Chicken Kiev now appear in supermarket chiller cabinets – with the result that you may feel embarrassed to present expectant guests with a meal that may not even match up to TV dinners.

With the huge choice of ingredients now available in many supermarkets, cooking has become more, not less, complicated. It has become a high-stress, high-anxiety activity for people who haven't yet acquired the knowledge, skill or confidence to produce successful meals.

If you've had failures, have slowly become disenchanted and are now totally intimidated by cooking, perhaps it's time to give it one last chance before you become completely resigned to being an absolute non-cook!

Consider this book as a tool to help you gain access at least to the *outer* sanctum of the Foodie Kingdom. If you love cooking, as we do, it's sometimes hard to put yourself in the shoes of a reluctant cook. But we've tried to remember the problems we used to have (and still do have! – *Ed.*) and have closely interrogated non-cooking friends and colleagues about their innermost cooking fears.

As a manual, this book has a learning curve, to use the current jargon. It's divided into three recipe sections, with extra information chapters stuck in between. The first section is absolute basics: how to crack open an egg; how to make a cup of tea; how to boil a potato. (Combine the three and you've made yourself a light supper!) If that sounds a little too much like teaching grandmother to suck eggs, it's meant to. If you're a grandmother who hasn't yet learned to suck an egg, you'll be grateful for the instructions. By the time you can manage all the recipes in Section One, confidence should be starting to sprout. With luck, cooking won't seem too bad after all.

If you're already an intermediate, you can progress straight to Section Two, where the real meat (pardon the pun) of the book lies – the respectable, I-can-put-a-decent-meal-on-the-table dishes. However, they all happen to be extremely easy, something our mothers never told us.

By now, confidence should be developing nicely. The real *coup* is to carry off successful entertaining – the kind you see in colour supplements, where groups of Beautiful People are gathered round a table groaning with sumptuous delights. At this point, you can tackle Section Three.

But first, let's get down to practicalities. This book is laid out conventionally but with more instructions than usual, especially in the first section. Make sure that you read about cooking techniques and terms (*see pages 8–12*) before starting out, and you'll save yourself confusion.

No precise measurements are given for salt and pepper because seasonings really are a matter of personal preference. This is especially important when it comes to salt, because over-salted food is a misery. Remember that you can always add more salt; it's less easy to take it out. Let people add salt to the food at the table. If you sprinkle lightly from a salt cellar, you don't risk tipping in too much at once. The term 'adjust the seasoning' simply means to add extra salt and pepper according to your taste.

Get a timer (this is also reiterated elsewhere in the book). It will pay for itself in the number of take-aways you *don't* have to buy to substitute for burnt dinners.

Serve food at the correct temperature. It takes co-ordination – and people sitting at the table at the right time – but the food will taste better. You'll notice that the words 'serve immediately' appear at the end of recipes. That's just to drive home the importance of giving your guests the food when it's at its best.

It sounds corny, but cooking is just as much of an art as it is a science. Once you understand the principles of cooking, you can feel free to bend – or even break – the rules. It can also work the other way around. No recipe can be absolutely guaranteed to work because there are so many variables: a temperamental oven, tough meat, a distracted cook. So, if something goes wrong, don't fling the book at the wall and vow never to set foot in the kitchen again. After all, you do have to eat . . . don't let a little thing like cooking defeat you.

We won't wish you luck. You won't need it!

Clare Brigstocke
Kevin Woodford
May 1988

Note: The authors accept no responsibility for panic attacks, tears, burnt offerings and severed friendships after inedible meals. However, they will take credit for visual delights, replete stomachs and praise from contented partners, relatives and guests.

Cookbook Decoder – Cooking Techniques and Terms

All cookbooks use a vocabulary that may not be obvious to a first-time user. This section gives a brief explanation of some terms that you'll need to understand before you start cooking.

What Does It Mean To 'Chop'

'Chop' is the catch-all verb used to describe cutting food into small pieces, which are relative to the size of the food itself. For example, if the instruction is to chop up a chicken breast, you would expect the resulting pieces to be larger than the chopped-up pieces of, say, a mushroom.

Always use as sharp a knife as possible, whether straight-edged or serrated. You will simply make a mess if the knife is blunt. Don't hold the food in the air while you cut it; it should be held firmly on a chopping board. Your fingertips should be curved under so that the fingernails and knuckles are protecting your fingertips, especially if you are chopping food into small pieces.

Chopping roughly. Again, this is dependent on the size of the food, but it means you don't have to take too much care, either because the food isn't going to be inspected (if it's in a sauce) or it's going to be cooked, then mashed up. 'Chopping roughly' also indicates that the resulting pieces need not be too small.

Chopping finely. This means cutting food into much smaller pieces than when chopping roughly. Usually the small pieces shouldn't be conspicuous in whatever sauce/batter/dough and so on they're being added to. In the case of herbs, 'to chop finely' means that you end up with infinitesimally small pieces which are sprinkled like sugar on a dish.

You can cut food into pieces of various shapes:
Cubes, which are square.
Dice, which are smaller cubes.

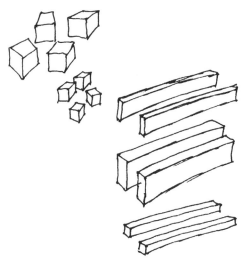

Slices, which may be thin or thick.
Matchsticks ('juliennes'), which are thin and square-sectioned.
Shreds, which are very thin and ragged.

See 'Salads' (*pages 43–45*) and 'Vegetables as a Side Dish' (*pages 57–79*) for how to chop vegetables.

How to Chop an Onion

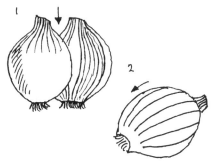

Peel the skin off the onion and cut it in half vertically, leaving a bit of root on each half. Now you are going to cut each half three-dimensionally.

Place one half-onion on a chopping board, cut side down, and grasp it firmly. Make thin cuts horizontally across towards the root but without cutting right through it. The root will hold the whole thing together.

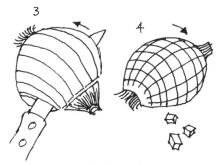

Now make vertical cuts from top to bottom, again without cutting through the root. Finally, make more vertical cuts at right angles to the first vertical cuts, working towards the root end. Neat small dice should drop off, with no tears expended. Repeat with the other half-onion.

How to Chop a Garlic Clove

The clove is one segment of a garlic bulb, encased in a thick papery skin. To remove the skin, place the clove on a chopping board

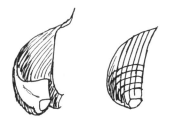

and hit it with the flat blade of a large knife. The skin should crack at one of the ends, making it easy to peel.

As when chopping an onion, slice the clove thinly in one direction horizontally, then vertically and finally across into very small dice. You may still end up with larger pieces than you want, however.

You can create a paste-like consistency by sprinkling salt over the chopped garlic and then mashing it firmly with the flat blade of a large knife. Do this until you get the consistency or have reduced the garlic pieces to the size you want.

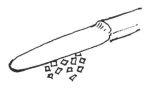

How to Chop Herbs

Herbs like parsley, coriander and rosemary have thick stems which need to be removed with a knife and discarded, leaving only the leaves. Wash the herbs and dry them on kitchen paper.

Hold the bunch of herbs in one hand, so that they are packed tightly together. Place this hand on a chopping board; only a small amount of the leaves should emerge from your hand.

Chop the herbs, with the sharp blade of a knife as close to your knuckles as possible.

As the herbs are chopped, move your hand down the bunch so that only a small amount of the uncut leaves is visible at a time and you have control over what is chopped.

If this is too much like hard work, you can buy a *mezza luna*, a very efficient tool for chopping, or a blender or food processor, or a purpose-made metal herb grinder.

What Does It Mean To 'Mix'?

You can combine ingredients together; the umbrella term is 'mixing', which usually means one of the following actions:

Stirring. Use a wooden or metal spoon to stir. It can be slow and gentle or faster and more vigorous. The action may be used to incorporate ingredients into each other or to stop the bottom of a sauce sticking over heat.

Beating. This is usually a vigorous action, done with a fork or wooden or metal spoon for incorporation of ingredients, or with a balloon whisk, electric hand mixer or rotary beater to change the texture of an ingredient (for example, egg whites or cream).

Whisking. Usually done with a fork or a metal whisk to change the texture of a single ingredient, as in beating (above) – an example is whisking raw eggs to combine the whites and yolks together evenly – or to combine different ingredients.

Blending. Again, a word with several meanings, depending on the circumstances. It may literally mean blending ingredients in a blender or food processor until smooth, or it could mean combining ingredients or mixtures of different consistencies smoothly together.

Folding. This is not to be confused with any kind of stirring action. A thin spatula or a metal spoon is used to mix ingredients into a batter which has just had air incorporated into it. The edge of the spoon or spatula 'cuts' through the ingredients. Hold the

spoon with the sharp edge pointing vertically upwards and scrape around the outside of the bowl. 'Cut' the mixture sharply through the middle, then scoop from underneath so that the mixture at the bottom of the bowl is brought up over fresh ingredients on the top.

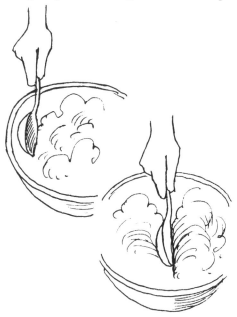

Greasing and Flouring Tins

Many mixtures, particularly when heated in an oven, will stick to the tin in which they have been cooked, making it very difficult, if not impossible, to turn out the finished result intact. Greasing or greasing and flouring tins will help prevent this.

If you intend only to grease, you can use either butter or a light, flavourless oil. Put ½–1 teaspoon butter, or a drop or two of oil, on a piece of greaseproof paper: the amount of grease you use depends solely on the size of the tin. Smear the butter or oil around the inside of the tin without missing an inch. The tin is now ready for use.

The addition of flour is extra insurance. After you have greased the tin, put in 1–2 teaspoons plain flour and, holding the tin in both hands, tilt it up and down and from side to side so that the flour sticks to the grease. Make sure that all inner surfaces are completely covered with a very thin layer of flour. You can grease and flour tins well in advance of use.

All recipes will indicate where greasing and flouring are needed.

10

What Does It Mean To 'Cook'?

The catch-all term 'to cook' means to 'prepare something to eat'. However, people often use the term as shorthand when they actually mean specific kinds of cooking. This can be very confusing when you're starting out. 'To cook', in this instance, means 'to transform food with the application of heat', which may be done in three ways: either on top of the cooker (also known as the hob or stove); in the oven; or under or on a grill (barbecue).

On Top of the Cooker

If food is immersed completely in water or other liquid, it can be:

Boiling

◊ The heating element is turned quite high, causing active bubbling.
◊ The food *cooks* rapidly when the liquid is boiling.
◊ Depending on the amount of heat, there is fierce, rolling, medium or gentle boiling.

Simmering

◊ The heating element is on low, causing the surface of the liquid to tremble; or with stronger simmering there are little bubbles.
◊ The food *cooks* gently and slowly when the liquid is simmering.

If food is simmering in a small amount of liquid, it is:

Poaching

◊ The heating element is turned down very low.
◊ The food *cooks* very slowly.

If food is suspended over boiling water, it is:

Steaming

◊ The food *cooks* in the steam produced by heating water to boiling point over a medium or high heat.

If food is being heated in a pan with oil or fat, it is:

Frying or Sautéeing

◊ The heating element is turned to medium or high, and there is a sizzling noise.
◊ The food *cooks* quite quickly, depending on the amount of heat applied.

Hobs

You will probably have either an electric or a gas hob. They are marked with gradations to indicate intensity of heat.

Most electric elements have five gradations:
1 is the lowest (simmer).
2 is medium-low (simmer to gentle boil).
3 is medium (medium bubbling).
4 is medium-high (medium to high boil).
5 is high (fierce boil).

These are fairly standard gradations, but hobs do vary, so you will have to learn the particular idiosyncrasies of your own.

Gas hobs simply have a naked flame of variable intensity. Gradations are marked, but they usually just indicate low and high, so you have to judge by the size of the flame and the effect it has on the food, or the medium in which the food is cooking. Many cooks prefer gas hobs because the control of the flame (and hence the heat) is more sensitive than that of electric hobs. You will have to judge for yourself what a low, medium or high flame looks like.

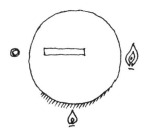

In the Oven

If food is surrounded by dry heat in an enclosed space, it is:

Roasting or Baking

The food *cooks* in dry heat.
The two terms have come to be almost interchangeable, although *roasting* is usually used for most meat and poultry while *baking* is used for cakes, pastry and bread.

Ovens

Ovens are heated either electrically or by gas. Older gas ovens have gradations or 'marks'. Newer ovens, both gas and electric, may be marked in degrees Fahrenheit or (now becoming most common) Centigrade. In this book, the recipes include all three – for example, 200°C (400°F, gas mark 6).

If the oven is fan-assisted, hot air is circulated around the oven evenly with a fan. In convection ovens, the hot air rises to the top. This means that in a fan-assisted oven, food cooks evenly; in a convection oven the upper half is hotter than the bottom half, so food cooks and browns at different speeds depending on where it is placed. This may be of assistance when you start baking cakes and bread, because you can move something from the bottom to the top of the oven if you want it to cook more quickly, or vice versa.

Pre-heating. As the term implies, this means heating the oven before the food is put in. It is very important to pre-heat if a recipe requires it, as the success or failure of a dish often depends on the oven being hot right at the start of cooking. Allow at least 5–10 minutes for pre-heating, depending on the idiosyncrasies of your oven.

Some cookbooks (not this one) assume that you'll pre-heat the oven without being reminded. But if you do forget to pre-heat, all may not be lost, provided you stick to the following rule: if the dish takes over an hour to cook (with the exception of roast meat or poultry), you can generally put the food in when you turn on the oven without any detrimental effects; but if the dish takes less than an hour to cook, don't put the food in until you've pre-heated the oven.

Under or On the Grill (Barbecue)

If food is subjected to intense heat on one side only, it is:

Grilling

The food *cooks* under or over dry heat.
The rate of cooking can usually be regulated only by moving the food closer to or farther from the heat source.

Grills

Some cookers are manufactured with grills located inside the oven itself so that you cannot grill and bake or roast at the same time. However, most grills are situated separately above the oven and come with their own grill pan and rack. You can usually adjust the distance of the pan from the grill by using one of two positions. You can also marginally adjust the actual heat intensity of the grill, though it is usually turned to full strength.

Equipment

Let's make the improbable assumption that you have a completely empty kitchen – that you're starting from scratch. Entering the kitchen section of a supermarket or a large department store can be bewildering if you don't know what you're looking for, or perhaps even looking at. A lot of cooking equipment, like cherry pitters or electric corkscrews, is either going to be used very rarely or doesn't really save time but just looks flash. Nonetheless, you will need some tools. They don't need to be expensive but they must do the job you need them to do: people have been put off cooking just because they had the wrong equipment which made the task harder, not easier.

We do not suggest that you spend a fortune in one go. If you're following this book, section by section, buy only the items you need for each level of difficulty, starting with a few essentials

Section One

Weights and Measures

Scales

Only really confident cooks can do without scales, and even then they are absolutely necessary for baking. Good spring-balanced modern scales, showing metric and imperial, which will weigh up to 2 kg (4 lb), should be sufficient. (If you cook a joint which weighs over 2 kg (4 lb) and you've thrown away the label showing its weight, you'll have to stick the meat on the bathroom scales!)

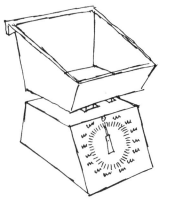

Measuring Cup

Again, get a cup, preferably glass, which measures both metric and imperial volumes. You'll find that if you buy two cups, you won't have to wash up so often during cooking. Measuring jugs are also useful simply because you can pour liquid out of them without spilling it.

Measuring Spoons

Kitchen spoons come in varying sizes and it's only when you use a set of measuring spoons that you can be confident of a consistent measure. You can only buy either metric or imperial spoons. You could get one set of each, but you'll find that the metric spoons are close enough in size to their imperial counterparts for you to use them for imperial measuring if necessary.

Knives

Cutting with bad knives is a misery and can completely ruin your attitude to cooking. A sharp knife should cut cleanly and be easy to use. The handle should feel heavy and correctly balanced in your hand, whatever the size. Some plastic-handled knives are just as good as, not to mention cheaper than, the famous foreign names. Make sure that the knife blade extends well into the handle and that it's firmly welded in. There should also be no sharp edges anywhere near where you grip the knife.

Overall, stainless-steel blades are more practical than carbon-steel because they are much easier to keep clean. Knives with straight edges should be sharpened as often as possible; small inexpensive sharpeners are just as effective as the traditional steels.

Start with three knives:

10–12.5 cm (4–5 in.) straight or serrated blade for slicing vegetables.
17.5–20 cm (7–8 in.) straight blade for cutting meat.
20–22.5 cm (8–9 in.) slightly serrated blade for slicing bread.

Chopping Boards

We definitely recommend wooden boards over plastic or laminate ones. If you buy only one chopping board, get a large heavy one, preferably made from one single piece of wood, that you can carve a roast on. You might want to use one side consistently for chopping onions and garlic as they tend to impart an indelible smell to any chopping surface. (Mark it with a felt-tipped pen in the corner.) It's very important to wash the board thoroughly, especially after cutting raw meat on it, as the cracks in the wood can harbour bacteria.

Saucepans

You will need three saucepans of differing sizes:
One small saucepan, 12.5–15 cm (5–6 in.) wide, big enough for one or two boiled eggs.
One medium saucepan, 20–22.5 cm (8–9 in.) wide, big enough for boiling four potatoes.
One large saucepan with a capacity of 3–4 litres (5–7 pints), big enough to boil pasta or a large amount of soup.

Saucepans can be made of different kinds of material – aluminium, stainless steel, enamelled cast iron or glass, with or without a non-stick coating – all of which have their advantages and disadvantages. Don't go out and buy a whole set at this stage, even if you do see a special offer. Start by trying out one relatively inexpensive pan of a particular type so that if you don't like it, you won't have seven mistakes staring you in the face.

Points to look for in a pan are as follows: the bottom should be fairly thick; the handle should be firmly welded on to the side; the pan should have a tight-fitting lid and the handle should not conduct the heat.

Frying Pans

Start with one large frying pan, 22.5 cm (9 in. wide), with a non-stick coating. At this stage it's most practical to buy a 'sauté' pan, straight-sided with a tight-fitting lid. Don't

spend too much money on it because the non-stick coating will eventually wear off. You can extend the life of the pan by using a non-scratch spatula when cooking and by making sure that you clean it gently with a non-abrasive cleaner. Non-stick pans are especially good for egg dishes which normally stick to conventional pans; and less fat is needed for cooking in a non-stick pan.

Other Containers

Metal Roasting Tin

Buy either an ordinary or non-stick shallow roasting tin measuring at least 22.5 × 32.5 cm (9 × 13 in.). It should have a fairly heavy bottom that won't buckle in high temperatures. A tin this size will be useful for baking as well as for roasting meat.

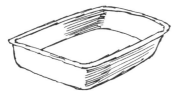

Shallow Casserole Dish

This is for use in the oven and in the microwave. It should be made preferably of ovenproof glass or earthenware and have a lid with an ovenproof handle. The casserole can be round, oval or square: a rectangular shape is the most useful for a conventional oven; round for a microwave. Ideally, it should be presentable enough to be taken straight from the oven to the table.

Mixing Bowls

At least two or three, of varying sizes, will always be useful in the kitchen, the largest big enough to double as a salad bowl, the smallest the right size to whisk two eggs in comfortably. Mixing bowls are inexpensive, whether made of glass or thick china.

Storage Containers

Thick plastic ones, with lids, are useful for storing left-overs in the fridge and can usually be put straight into the microwave.

Basic Implements

You will need the following:

Cutlery. A few ordinary kitchen knives, forks and spoons.

Vegetable peeler. Find one you feel comfortable using, whether it's the metal swivelling type or the firm-bladed kind. Some brands usefully combine a peeler with an apple corer.

Wooden spoons. Three of varying sizes.

Fish slice. A plastic one which won't scratch non-stick surfaces.

Rubber or plastic spatula. The best thing for scraping bowls clean.

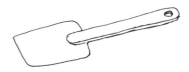

Scissors. The light, plastic-handled ones with the tightly-riveted sharp blades which are extremely good for cutting herbs, removing the skin from chicken and other myriad tasks.

Grater. A stout stable variety with four or five different surfaces.

Tin opener. Once you find one that works perfectly, guard it for the rest of your life!

Bottle opener and can piercer. As above!

Vegetable steamer. The least expensive ones are small, expanding metal baskets which fit inside saucepans. However, they only hold enough food for 1–2 people.

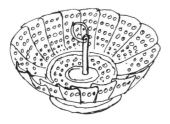

Juice squeezer. Made either of metal or plastic. More expensive ones have a little lipped cup to catch the strained juice.

Colander. A metal or enamel one won't melt like plastic, but their handles get hot; the choice is yours.

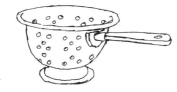

Sieves. Made of metal or plastic and useful for draining small amounts of vegetables; as a steamer over a pan of boiling water (metal only); and to sift flour extremely effectively. A tea strainer is also useful for sifting icing sugar finely over cakes.

Potato masher. Buy a good sturdy metal one.

Ladle. The easiest way to serve soup.

Pepper mill. Practically the most important piece of equipment you need. We recommend the wooden ones with an easy twisting action at the top. Beware some plastic mills whose threads can quickly wear out.

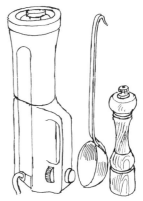

Blender or liquidiser. This may not seem like a basic piece of equipment but for certain cooking processes, like puréeing fruit and vegetables, it's easier than pushing the mixture through a sieve and cheaper than a food processor. Look for makes which are easy to clean, have a heavy base with a reasonably large motor and whose lids fit very securely.

Timer. A small inexpensive timer will guarantee more success than any amount of technical skill!

Section Two

Balloon whisk. It may look like something out of a restaurant kitchen but it performs functions that nothing else will: aerating eggs and cream, and preventing lumps from forming in sauces. Get a metal one whose spokes are firmly fixed in the handle. The most useful size is 25–27.5 cm (10–11 in.) long.

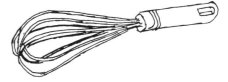

Omelette pan. It's not very easy to make omelettes in large pans. A real omelette pan is 17.5–20 cm (7–8 in.) in diameter and has rounded edges. The most useful kinds have non-stick coatings, though some people like to get cast-iron pans and 'wear' them in.

Lidded heavy metal casserole. Many stews start on top of the stove and finish in the oven, so you need a casserole dish that is flameproof with a thick bottom, and that has a good, tight-fitting lid with handles that won't scorch or melt. The best type is enamelled cast iron, of which there are one or two famous French brands. They are quite expensive but you'll find that buying one is a very good investment as it will last a very long time, even with a lot of wear.

Loaf tins. Buy thick metal tins, ordinary or non-stick, whose bottoms won't buckle with the heat. The most useful size holds a 500 g (1 lb) loaf. Most bread recipes make two loaves so buy two tins.

Cake tins. As with bread tins, buy thick round metal ones. The most expensive have a spring release or a flat blade which helps you turn out the cake, the least expensive are plain. For light layer cakes, buy two shallow (sandwich) tins measuring 17.5–20 cm (7–8 in.) in diameter. For fruit cakes, use a deeper, narrower, round tin (with a detachable bottom, if possible), 17.5 cm (7 in.) across.

Skewers. Metal skewers, both short and long, are always useful in the kitchen, from speeding up the cooking time of baked potatoes (simply plunge through the centre before placing in the oven), to fishing out rings that have fallen down the plug hole! Flat-sided skewers are the best for kebabs.

Ramekins. A fancy name for a small, round, straight-sided dish, the most useful size of

which is 7.5 cm (3 in.). As they're not expensive, whether made from glass or the traditional white earthenware, buy four or six: you can use them as serving dishes for mousses or fruit salads, or just to store left-over egg whites in.

Rolling pin. Although you can use a clean milk bottle, it doesn't do as good a job as an inexpensive, plain, wooden rolling pin. Make sure that the wood is completely smooth. Handles are not necessary.

Pie dish. Available in all sizes and varieties. The most useful is a glass one with sloping sides, 20–22.5 cm (8–9 in.) in diameter. Flan tins or earthenware flan dishes with vertical fluted sides can substitute for pie dishes.

Pudding basin. Although you can substitute a small round mixing bowl for an earthenware pudding basin, the traditional sloping shape is very attractive and they're not expensive. The most useful size is 850 ml (1½ pints).

Baking tray (or sheet). An invaluable item. The ones with non-stick coating are easier to use; buy two good heavy trays.

Square baking tin. Many recipes call for a shallow 20 cm (8 in.) square baking tin. It should be made of metal, with sturdy sides and bottom, either ordinary or non-stick. It can also be used for roasting potatoes.

Tartlet (or patty) tins. As the name suggests, these are sold for making tartlets, but they are also useful for small individual Yorkshire Puddings, buns and muffins. They are not going to be used every day but they are practical. Available in ordinary metal or with a non-stick coating, they should have twelve indentations. Measure the width of your oven before you buy one!

Electric hand mixer. This is the easiest and fastest way to whip egg whites and cream. As it's portable, you can use it in any of your mixing bowls.

Special Purchases

If you're a reluctant cook, you're not going to be terribly enthusiastic about spending a lot of money on kitchen equipment. There are a lot of electrical gadgets on the market, usually so highly specialised that you use them once and then forget about them. Electric sorbetières, waffle-irons, rice-cookers and woks fall into this category. Mind you, these are also the kind of things that one receives as wedding presents!

However, you may wish to consider the following:

Microwave Oven

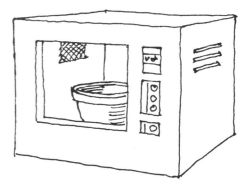

We're not recommending that you rush out and buy a microwave oven, especially if you already have a decent cooker. If you decide that you want one after reading pages 19–20, our advice is to buy a relatively straightforward variety with the highest wattage you can afford. The most practical microwave oven for someone who will be using it as an adjunct to a conventional cooker has a wattage of 650–700, a turntable, a defrost control and timer. That's all you really need – not the fancy browning elements, meat probe or computer timing devices. And make sure it comes with a good instruction manual!

Food Processor

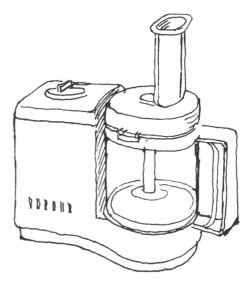

Our grandmothers all got along without food processors, but then they probably spent much more time in the kitchen than we do. There's no doubt that for many tasks – chopping, mincing, puréeing, grating – a food processor saves a huge amount of time. A good, long-lasting processor will have a heavy base and a sturdy plastic bowl. Try to see a demonstration before buying, if possible. Some makes come with a variety of additional gadgets, many of which you'll never use. Variable speed control is useful though not essential, but two or three slicing blades of varying thickness will come in handy. Try taking the bowl on and off before you buy – some are surprisingly awkward to handle, and also to wash. A good thing about food processors is that they rarely break down and they last for a long time.

Microwave Ovens

One in four households in Britain owns a microwave oven, so there's a chance that some readers of this book have one, even if it is used only to warm up cold cups of coffee. Using a microwave won't suddenly teach you how to cook, so if you don't already own one, you needn't rush out and buy one until you feel happy about cooking. You can function perfectly well without a microwave but there's no doubt that it can save a lot of time and washing up.

Putting aside the scientific explanations, microwaves basically cook food fast, usually much faster than conventional ovens, depending on the type of food. Microwaving is *wet* cookery, so what you can steam or poach, you can microwave. But straightforward microwave cookery (that is, using the basic oven without accessories like browning elements or meat probes) cannot give the flavour or the look of grilled or roasted food. You often end up with anaemic-looking and rubbery-tasting dishes. It's advisable, therefore, to concentrate on the really foolproof dishes – generally crisp vegetables and fish. (If later you want to extend your range and experiment, buy a cookbook that specialises in microwave cookery.)

Microwave instructions are given in this book only for those recipes which turn out as well as, or better than, when they are cooked conventionally. All timings are given for 650 watt ovens. If you have one with a lower wattage, you'll need to microwave the food longer – see the instruction manual for your particular model. In any case, do not feel that you must stick rigidly to the recommended timings as a lot depends on the shape of the food and your own brand of oven. It's useful to keep a note of the timings you find work for you so that you are not starting from scratch every time. Here are some general rules for microwaving:

1   When setting the timer, don't be generous. As food cooks so fast, always underestimate the time needed. You can easily reset the dial for more cooking time if necessary.
2   Always cook food in containers made of microwave-safe plastic, glass, earthenware or any other material that does not contain metal. If using earthenware, make sure that it doesn't have metal handles or any metallic decoration in the glaze.
3   Cook the food in round shallow dishes so that it can be arranged in one layer, or at least evenly.
4   Put thicker parts of the food, like cauliflower stalks, facing towards the outside edge of the dish, as that's where the heat tends to concentrate.
5   When cooking irregularly-shaped foods like vegetables, stop the microwave half-way through the cooking time (just open the door – don't press STOP, or you will mess up the timing), and re-arrange, stir or shake the food so that the heat reaches all parts of it evenly.
6   If the food itself doesn't contain much water, a little extra water may need to be added. Too much and the food goes soggy; too little and it may burn or dry out.
7   Most food needs to be covered so that it cooks in its own steam: use microwave-safe clingfilm, a roasting bag or even a plate – never aluminium foil. However, the steam must have a means of escape in order not to explode, so ensure that there is a little opening in the cover by piercing the clingfilm with a knife or rolling it back a very small distance from the edge of the container; by loosely tying the roasting bag; or by placing the plate not quite fully over the container.

What Can Go Wrong

The wrong choice of food. Don't cook eggs in their shells unless you want a spectacular explosion and a nasty mess. Foods which take a long time to cook, like stewing beef or dense vegetables, are not worth cooking in the microwave: stick to fish and crisp vegetables for the time being.

Over-cooking. At worst, food can sometimes collapse if it's cooked too long; at best it simply doesn't taste very nice.

Metal in the oven. Using metal in your microwave may damage it. This even applies to the little plastic-covered metal ties used to secure plastic bags, so avoid them.

Uneven cooking. If one part of the food is raw and another overcooked, you should have either stirred or re-arranged it half-way through the cooking, or laid it out more evenly in the container.

Time Saving

Defrosting. Most ovens have a defrost facility. When defrosting dense food, make sure that you stop the process every so often to separate individual items – for example, separate sausages as they defrost and turn the frozen edges towards the outside of the container. If you don't do this, the outside of the food will begin to cook before the inside has thawed. The microwave works better with smaller items, so let whole chickens or joints of meat defrost slowly in the fridge or some other cool place in the conventional way.

Reheating. This facility is a real godsend because you can reheat the food on the plate from which you intend to eat it and you don't risk drying out or burning it. You can also put more than one type of food on the plate. Simply cover the plate and microwave on HIGH for 1–2 minutes, then check the food to see if it needs longer. If you're entertaining and have cooked food earlier in the day, you can reheat it at the last moment with minimal loss of flavour and colour.

Extra cooking. If you've roasted or sautéed a chicken and underestimated the amount of time it needed so it's still pink inside, you can give it 3–5 minutes on microwave HIGH to cook it through quickly. This is a life saver for dinner parties!

Softening butter. A 30–45-second blast on microwave HIGH for butter straight from the fridge will soften it for spreading. Microwaving on HIGH 10 seconds will also be enough to make hard-frozen ice-cream just soft enough to serve.

Melting jam or honey. To soften jam or de-crystallise honey, put the jar, uncovered, in the oven and microwave on HIGH for 10–20 seconds. This method may also be used successfully to melt chocolate.

Freshening citrus fruit. Microwaving for 20–30 seconds on HIGH will make old, hard lemons and oranges yield more juice when squeezed.

Weights and Measures

Most cookbooks that you are likely to use, including this one, give actual measures for the ingredients. In many cultures, the notion of writing down cooking methods is unfamiliar. Recipes were passed down verbally through the generations and no new bride ever came to her groom unable to feed him! That's why many old cookbooks, or books from other countries, use terms like 'a knob', 'about a glass' (what size glass?) or 'until it's ready', the premise being that the cook already knew.

Cookbooks have evolved to suit their audience. The convention now is generally to give accurate measures, especially in baking where chemistry is important. In Britain, two sets of measurements are in use: metric and imperial. The latter is meant to be phased out eventually as we become more Europeanised. . . .

However, most schoolchildren learn metric as the norm and nowadays most ingredients are packaged and labelled with litres or kilograms, not pints and pounds. In this book the metric measurement is given first, the imperial second. You'll notice discrepancies like 75 g = 3 oz and then a big leap to 125 g = 4 oz. That's just to make measuring easier, so you don't have to deal with figures in fractions. As you can't get an exact equivalent, don't change from metric to imperial in mid-recipe or the proportions will be out. See page 4 for the measurement tables.

When it comes to flavourings we have, unusually, given measurements because, until you're confident about cooking, it's easier to follow someone else's taste as a guide. (These measurements are generally in imperial teaspoons or tablespoons, not the metric millilitres which are still slightly less common in sets of measuring spoons.) We have made an exception to this rule of salt and pepper, as personal taste in these seasonings varies so highly. Whether or not quantities are suggested, you must keep tasting as you cook, no matter how accurately you follow a recipe, otherwise you'll never develop your own taste. Also, the strength of the flavouring may vary from batch to batch, or it may depend on how long it's been hanging around your cupboard, so our suggested amount may not suit your ingredient.

Utensils for Measuring

Most plastic sets of scales have an adjuster to zero them. This is necessary because the scales drift out of alignment during use. Zero the scales before you start a recipe or you may end up with unforeseen results. This adjuster is very useful when you want to measure ingredients without getting the scales container dirty. If you want to weigh some butter on a piece of greaseproof paper, put the paper on the scales by itself. Zero the scales and then weigh out the butter. Alternatively, you can often remove the scales container altogether, allowing other containers to be used instead.

You may find it easier to measure out all dry ingredients first and place them in one, or separate, containers (depending on how they're being added to the dish). Then measure out the wet or greasy ingredients. This saves washing up the scales container between each ingredient.

Liquids in a measuring cup or jug need to be viewed with your eye level with the lines on the container. This usually entails crouching down uncomfortably. It's necessary because you can't accurately judge the measurement looking down on the cup. If you are measuring rice in the cup, shake it to level it out.

All measurements given in this book using sets of measuring spoons refer to *level* spoons. If in doubt, draw the straight edge of a kitchen knife across the spoon to discard any excess.

Organisation and Timing

Many people dislike cooking simply because they resent the number of hours spent in the kitchen. (Yet the time doesn't weigh so heavily if you're listening to something enjoyable on the radio – happy cooks are often radio addicts.) You can, however, save a surprising amount of time just by organising yourself.

In domestic science courses, budding cooks are taught to tie back their hair, wash their hands and lay all the utensils out neatly on the work-surface in the order in which they are going to be used. You needn't go that far, but the principle is a good one. The dish is less likely to go wrong, and you are less likely to panic, if you are reasonably methodical in the way you cook. We hate to lay down rules, but there's no harm in being sensible.

1   Get yourself an apron. No, this isn't a joke. An apron not only protects your clothes but provides you with a handy portable towel. If you spill melted chocolate all over your good clothes, you may waste precious cooking time trying to scrub it out.

2   Read the recipe before you start to cook. Doing this will tell you what ingredients you'll need and will alert you to all the pitfalls you may encounter in the method. You will kick yourself if you haven't noticed that part of the recipe needs to be started the day before!

3   Assemble, measure out and prepare all the ingredients before you begin cooking. This will prevent you from arriving at a point in the recipe which requires you to add ingredients quickly in order for the dish to succeed. An example of a recipe which can

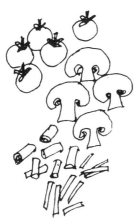

fail unless you follow this rule is crisp stir-fried vegetables: all the vegetables have to be chopped before you start to cook – you can't suddenly stop in the middle of cooking to start chopping, say, courgettes, because the first few vegetables will go soggy while waiting in the pan.

In the recipes in Section One of this book, the ingredients are simply listed and their preparation comes during the method at the most appropriate (and time-saving) point. In Section Two we itemise the ingredients with the type of preparation needed within the ingredients list (for example, '1 onion, finely chopped'), but also remind you during the method to prepare the ingredient. By the time you reach Section Three, we assume that you will follow the preparation directions as printed in the ingredients list.

4   Warm the plates. Serving hot food on hot plates is both practical and looks professional. Plates and serving dishes should go into a low oven – 110°C (225°F, gas mark ¼) – for 10–15 minutes before they're needed. However, you'll often find that the oven is being used simultaneously to cook the food at a much higher temperature which may crack the china. Putting the plates under a hot grill won't solve the problem because the heat comes from only one direction. A quick, safe way of heating plates is to fill the sink with very hot clean water and leave them to soak for 5 minutes. Then dry them quickly and serve.

5   Washing-up. You're either the type of person who doesn't mind a mess, or you're neat and tidy in every area in your life. If you have a small kitchen, it does make sense to wash up as you go along – that is, while the food is actually cooking, not in the middle of preparation. Even if you don't wash up, soaking pans before washing them will loosen the dirt. Egg-, flour- and potato-encrusted pans and bowls should be filled with cold water. Pans which have cooked meat, or which contain any amount of grease or fat, need to be soaked in hot, soapy water. Don't plunge a hot casserole dish straight from the oven into a sink full of water or it may crack.

A benefit of microwave cooking is that there is very little washing up.

One important aspect of organisation in the kitchen is the timing, especially when it comes to co-ordinating all the elements of a whole two- or three-course meal. Being organised (see above) will undoubtedly save you time. If you're not in a hurry and you're feeding only yourself or a friend, time may not be important. However, if you have to stick to a timetable or if you're entertaining guests more formally, you'll probably want to be able to give your guests, if not yourself, an estimated time for the meal.

1   Back-time from when you want to serve the meal. Decide when you want to eat the meal, giving yourself a sensible amount of time to prepare it. If you're trying a new recipe, make sure that you read it well in advance. Obviously, you make the most time-consuming dish first, and the one with the shortest cooking time last.

You may find it helpful actually to write down a timetable for yourself. In 'The Great British Breakfast' (*page 131*) and 'Sunday Roast Lunch' (*page 137*), you'll find examples of time organisation for these two tricky types of meal.

2   Save time internally. Most cooking processes don't need your active participation after you've done the initial preparation. For example, while the roast is in the oven you have plenty of time in which to prepare and cook vegetables. Many other recipes also contain hidden areas of 'fallow' time which can be put to good use. For instance, the time waiting for a pan of water to boil can be used to prepare other parts of the dish, or meal, or simply to lay the table. See page 195 for the best example of this – starting the pasta sauce when you put the pasta water on to boil. (Even more time can be saved if you boil a kettle and pour the hot water into the saucepan instead of starting cold water off in the pan.) The term 'meanwhile' used in the recipes obviously indicates that two activities can take place simultaneously. By carefully reading the recipe before you start to cook, you can identify any spare time.

3   Use a timer. Not only does this help you avoid burnt food, but the 'pinging' noise will rouse you to action. Otherwise, if a lot is happening in the kitchen, you can simply forget what's cooking where!

Basic Recipes

You've opened the book. You're hungry. And you've decided that you're going to give it a try. We get no prizes for guessing that you'll probably closet yourself alone in the kitchen, far from prying eyes, for your first few attempts at cooking.

In this section are the most basic recipes we hope you want to cook both to eat well – if not adventurously – and to serve to other people. As you progress through the book you will find yourself referring back to the cooking and preparation techniques in this section.

We've tried to be as clear as possible in the instructions. However, some of the vocabulary may not make sense unless you have read the 'Cookbook Decoder' (*see pages 8–12*), which explains cooking techniques and terms. Throughout the book, starting here, 'pepper' means black pepper, freshly ground, unless stated otherwise; 'vegetable oil' means sunflower or groundnut oil, for preference.

Snacks

Whether soft-boiled with toast soldiers, softly scrambled or as part of a good fry-up, eggs always seem to do as much for your mental state as for your physical well-being. Cooking eggs correctly can be a little difficult first time round, but the techniques are easily mastered.

Boiled Egg

This is easy, practically fail-safe survival food. You'll always succeed in boiling an egg – whether the resulting texture is as you like is another matter. Try these methods, and then play around with the timing. Don't forget: the variables are the size of the egg and its freshness. Most importantly, try to have your egg at room temperature before you start. A cold egg straight from the fridge will crack when it comes into contact with boiling water. Using a metal spoon to place the egg in the water helps to prevent cracking because the metal conducts the heat away from the egg. If you have to use an egg straight from the fridge, leave the spoon in the pan for a few minutes. Once an egg has cracked, there's not much you can do about it. However, the heat does coagulate the escaping white which will seal the crack. Water that is too hot, or overcooking, will make the egg rubbery.

If you like, you can prick the base of the egg with a needle to let the air escape; this will help prevent the shell from cracking.

Soft-boiled Egg

1   Try to take the egg out of the fridge at least 15 minutes before cooking it.
2   Put cold water into a small saucepan. Bring the water to the boil over a high heat. Then turn the heat down to medium-low.
3   Using a metal spoon, slip the egg into the pan.
4   Simmer the egg for 3½–5 minutes. The shorter time will result in a barely set egg, with both white and yolk still runny (some people like them like this!); about 4 minutes for a size 3 egg will result in a soft yolk but a set white; 5 minutes is for a larger egg. Only practice will tell you the right timing for your taste.
5   Lift the egg out of the water with a draining spoon and serve immediately.

Hard-boiled Egg

Cook in the same way as for soft-boiled, but allow 6–9 minutes. If you intend to use the egg in another recipe, plunge it immediately into cold water to prevent a dark ring from forming around the yolk. If you have cooked several eggs and find that you have too many, you can always use them in a salad or in a sandwich.

It's almost impossible to peel a hot hard-boiled egg without making a mess. Let it cool before attempting to shell it.

Scrambled Eggs

This is the point when you have to start taking the eggs out of their shells to cook them – a great leap forward in the learning process. Believe it or not, cracking an egg isn't as easy as 'cracking an egg'! To make the best scrambled eggs, cook them as gently as possible over low heat in a thick-bottomed pan – but don't use an aluminium pan, or the eggs will turn a horrid shade of green! How long you cook the eggs depends on how you like them. If you prefer them soft and creamy, cook them until they are still slightly runny (they will continue to cook in the heat built up in the pan, even off the cooker). The entire cooking time for 2–3 eggs should be no more than about 4 minutes. If you overcook the eggs, they will be positively leathery.

For 1

2 eggs
Small pinch each salt and pepper
1 tablespoon butter, preferably unsalted
Bread for toast

The first reason for using a small pan is common sense: the smaller the pan, the less time it will take for the water to boil; also, the less chance for the egg to bounce around and crack.

If necessary, you can stop the egg from cooking further by lightly bashing in the narrow end as soon as you take it out of the water.

If you accidentally muddle up your unshelled hard-boiled eggs with the raw eggs in the fridge, there's a simple way of distinguishing between the two. Spin them round on their side. Hard-boiled eggs spin round fast, raw ones much more slowly. This is because the yolk in a cooked egg is hard and doesn't slosh about in the suspension of a raw white.

For 2 people (or if you're hungry), use 3–4 eggs with 2 tablespoons butter.

1   Crack the eggs into a small high-sided bowl (that way you can easily retrieve them if something goes wrong!) The best way is to hold each egg in two hands and give it a quick gentle crack against the rim of the bowl. Insert your thumbs into the crack and, holding the egg over the bowl, pull the sides of the shell apart. If the thin skin inside the shell doesn't split open, keep trying. If any bits of shell do get into the bowl, scoop them out using a teaspoon.

2   Add the salt and pepper and mix thoroughly with a whisk or fork until you can scarcely distinguish the white from the yolk.

3   Heat half the butter in a thick-bottomed pan over a very low heat. When it has melted, tilt the pan until a film of butter completely covers the bottom.

4   Slowly pour in the eggs and start to stir with a wooden spoon. Don't be tempted to turn up the heat, even if the egg mixture doesn't seem to be setting. As it cooks on the bottom of the pan, gently scrape the scrambled mass up so that uncooked egg reaches the heated surface. As soon as the eggs are ready, take the pan off the heat.

5   While the eggs are cooking, toast the bread (*see page 134*).

6   Stir in the remaining butter and add a little extra salt and pepper if you like. Butter the toast.

7   Turn the scrambled eggs out of the pan on to the warm toast and serve immediately.

There is no substitute for butter here. Unsalted (sweet) butter has a better flavour and is less likely to burn.

An eggy pan is easier to clean if you put *cold* water in immediately and leave it to soak for at least an hour.

How to Separate Eggs

The two parts of the egg, each with its own unique properties, are often used separately in recipes. Sometimes you'll find that you need just the yolks, sometimes only the whites and sometimes both in the same recipe but added at different times or cooked in different ways. That's why you need to separate the egg from the yolk.

Usually a recipe calling for egg whites on their own requires them to be beaten. Egg whites with any trace of yolk remaining in them will not increase in volume, so it's important that you separate the eggs carefully. (And, of course, you want to avoid leaving behind broken pieces of eggshell, though they're much more easily fished out than a whole broken egg yolk.)

When separating an egg, have two bowls ready. Don't try to separate the egg directly into the food you're cooking as mistakes happen very easily. Don't separate an egg over a bowl already containing an egg white; if the yolk breaks, you'll have messed up the lot and will have to start again. Always separate an egg over an empty bowl and make sure that the white is 'clean' before adding it to others.

The yolk and white are connected by a little thread that can sometimes be very difficult to cut. Don't force it or the contents of the yolk will spill out: it's better to use a knife to cut it. (If you're thrifty, you'll want to make sure that you get all the white from the bottom of the shell; you can scoop out the remains with the tip of the finger.)

You can keep left-over yolks and whites in the fridge, covered with clingfilm. Yolks will quickly dry out, so use them up in scrambled eggs as soon as you can. Whites will last for a week or two but it's often harder to find an occasion to use them up.

Method 1 – Easy

The easiest way to separate eggs is to use a plastic separator. They come in different guises but the principle is the same. There is always some kind of gap for the white to slip through while the yolk is retained. Plastic egg separators usually have handles and hooks that enable them to be fitted over a bowl so you don't have to crack the egg with one hand while holding the separator with the other.

Method 2 – Traditional

This is slightly tricky but usually successful once you've got the hang of it. The theory is that you juggle the whole yolk between the two half-shells so that the white drops into the waiting bowl and you're left with the yolk in one of the shell halves.

Have two bowls ready. Crack the egg gently and pull the two halves apart, keeping the egg upright so that you know the yolk is in the bottom half of the shell. Transfer the yolk to the other half shell, letting some of the white fall into one of the bowls as the transfer takes place. Keep passing the egg from one shell half to the other until as much white as possible has dropped out. Put the yolk into the other bowl.

Method 3 – Messy but Sensuous

This method is not for the squeamish. In effect, your hand acts as the separator.

Have two bowls ready. Hold one hand, slightly cupped, over one of the bowls. Crack the egg gently with a knife, or on the rim of the bowl with the other hand. Open the eggshell and let the egg slowly fall into the cupped hand. By opening your fingers slightly you will let the white fall into the bowl between them and the whole yolk will remain in your hand. Put the yolk into the other bowl.

Croque Monsieur

This is the name they give in yuppie cafés to fried ham and cheese sandwiches. (It usually costs an arm and a leg too.) But if you serve your Croque Monsieur with a small green salad (*see page 46*) and a glass of wine, you could pretend you were in Paris.

It is important not to slice the bread too thickly or the heat will not get through to melt the cheese. This is where packaged white sliced bread works well.

Instead of frying the Croque Monsieur, you could toast it in a sandwich toaster (follow manufacturer's instructions).

Makes 2 sandwiches

4 slices white bread, buttered
4 thin slices Edam or Gruyère cheese
2 thin slices ham
2 tablespoons butter
1 tablespoon oil

A mixture of oil and butter helps prevent the butter from burning.

1   Lay a slice of cheese on a slice of buttered bread, place a ham slice on the cheese, top that with another slice of cheese and finish with another slice of bread. Repeat with the rest of the bread, cheese and ham, so that you have two thick sandwiches.
2   Cut the crusts off the bread and cut the sandwiches in half diagonally. Alternatively, if you have a scone cutter, calculate the best way of cutting right through the sandwiches in order to get the maximum number of rounds from each one. Eat the left-over bits while cooking the round bits!
3   Melt the butter in a frying pan over medium heat and, when it starts to froth, add the oil. Carefully fry as many sandwiches as will fit into the pan for 2 minutes on each side or until golden brown and oozing with melted cheese. Repeat with any remaining sandwiches. Serve immediately.

Welsh Rarebit

Photograph on page 50

Although this is a very easy recipe, it takes a little more time and a few more ingredients than ordinary cheese on toast. It is an authentic British recipe that tastes great. Because of the extra effort involved, it's worth making for more than just yourself. It's especially good as a late supper dish.

Any kind of beer is suitable, but the amount and type of mustard you use depends on how strong a taste you like.

You can add the mustard in powdered or made-up form.

You may store the finished sauce overnight (no longer) in the fridge if you wish. Be sure to cover it so that it does not dry out and form a skin.

For 4

4 tablespoons beer (optional, but the dish is not authentic without it!)
125 g (4 oz) Cheddar cheese
25 g (1 oz) butter
1½ teaspoons flour
75 ml (3 fl oz) milk
1 egg yolk (see page 26 for how to separate eggs)
Small pinch each salt and pepper
½ teaspoon English mustard
4 slices bread
1 tablespoon butter

1   Open a bottle of beer, measure the required amount into a small pan and put it to one side. Pour the remainder into a glass and drink it. Now you're ready to start.
2   Grate the cheese and set aside.
3   Bring the beer to the boil over a high heat and leave it boiling until only half the original volume remains. (This is known as a reduction).
4   Melt the butter over a low heat in a thick-bottomed pan.
5   Add the flour and mix well with a wooden spoon. Cook on a gentle heat, stirring constantly, for 2 minutes without browning the flour. (The result is known as a roux.)
6   Gradually add the milk and stir into the flour and butter mixture until you have a smooth sauce. Let the sauce simmer for 2 minutes.
7   Add the grated cheese and let the sauce cook for a further 2 minutes so that the cheese melts completely. You should be left with a smooth yellow cheese (mornay) sauce.
8   Remove the pan from the heat and add the egg yolk. Mix in quickly with a wooden spoon.
9   Add the beer to the cheese sauce. Season with the salt, pepper and mustard.
10 Leave the mixture to cool. As it cools it will thicken, making it easier to spread on the toast.
11 Toast the bread and butter it while it's still hot. Leave the grill on if you have cooked the toast under it; otherwise heat the grill to its highest setting.
12 Spread the cooled cheese mixture on the buttered toast. Put the toast in a heatproof dish and place under the grill until the topping is brown, watching it carefully as it can easily burn. Serve immediately.

Sandwiches

Sandwiches can make a perfectly respectable meal and appeal particularly to children. At worst, sandwiches fill you up; at best they bring out the joyous glutton in people. They also suit many different occasions. So, if you never learn to make anything but a good sandwich, you've got nothing to worry about.

Breads

The type of bread you use depends largely on what you like. It is true to say that the nicer the bread, the nicer the sandwich – so try out any new bread you see. Supermarkets now have lots, including Arab-style pitta bread, dark rye, French-type baguettes and Greek sesame loaves. But if you are limited to white sliced (which does make for neat sandwiches, even if the flavour of the bread is extremely bland and its texture pappy), fill it with something imaginative.

Guidelines for Making Sandwiches

1   Don't use bread straight from the oven as it will tear when you slice it.
2   A heavily serrated bread knife will cut the bread into mis-shapen pieces; use a lightly serrated knife. When slicing, use a sawing motion rather than a cutting one.
3   If you make a sandwich with a wet filling, like sliced tomatoes, or if the spread is wet, be sure not to make the sandwich too long in advance of eating it, or it will disintegrate.
4   If you have only stale bread, make a toasted sandwich with it (*see page 33*).
5   There is no need to cut the crusts off the bread unless you don't like them. Certainly dainty sandwiches – 'teatime at the Ritz' type – look better without crusts. They also look better if you quarter them in triangles. Save the crusts to make into dried breadcrumbs.
6   If you're making sandwiches in bulk and you want to use whole loaves of good bread, ask your baker to slice them for you.
7   To make lots of sandwiches at once, lay out the slices of bread on a flat surface in pairs as they come off the loaf so that the shapes will match up evenly.
8   Remember the most important point: *let the butter come to room temperature before you attempt to spread it.*

Simple Fillings

Peanut Butter. Popular combinations are peanut butter and jam (strawberry or raspberry, or grape jelly if you can find it) and peanut butter and mashed banana.

Cheese, or cheese and tomato, or cheese and pickle. Conventional wisdom dictates that slices of good hard British cheese like Cheddar, Leicester or Double Gloucester go well in brown bread, while soft cheeses like French Brie or garlic-flavoured Boursin are better in French baguettes. You go ahead and try what you want. Hard cheese slices more easily when it's chilled.

Cold meat and pâté. For many people, the only point of turkey at Christmas is to have the turkey sandwiches afterwards. Cold turkey, chicken, beef, ham and pork all make excellent fillings. The only meat that isn't very nice cold is lamb, which has an unpalatable greasy taste.

Most cooked meat you are likely to have at home that is suitable for sandwiches will come off a joint, and the longer it's been hanging around, the drier it will be. Therefore make sure that any left-overs stored in the fridge are well wrapped up, and if necessary moisten the sandwich with mayonnaise, chutney or mustard, or add moist vegetables like sliced tomatoes or cucumber. A good tip is always to put shredded lettuce in meat sandwiches to help combat dryness. Season the filling with salt and pepper.

You can buy pre-cooked meat from delicatessens but it's usually fiendishly expensive. Sandwiches made with left-over meat from joints are something to look forward to, like eating fruit and vegetables when they're in season. Ham is the only exception to this rule because it's consumed less commonly as a home-cooked roast than as bought-in ready-to-eat slices. You can buy cured ham – *prosciutto crudo*, of which Parma ham is a variety – as an expensive treat, or the more readily available cooked ham. Ham sliced for you off the joint, honey-flavoured or sugar-cured, is wonderful; those little wet vacuum-sealed plastic packs contain ham that is less than wonderful. If you go for the latter, you may find that it needs plenty of the afore-mentioned camouflage.

Pâté sandwiches often stick to the roof of your mouth. Again, lettuce or other salad vegetables are a good addition. As with everything, there are good and bad pâtés. Keep on trying until you find one you like.

Prepared fish. Smoked salmon is fine, if you like it and can afford it. One tip is to ask your fishmonger to sell you the cheaper scraps. Smoked salmon is traditionally served on the thinnest possible slices of buttered brown bread with the crusts cut off. Don't forget to squeeze a little lemon juice on the fish. The great New York favourite, which makes a very impressive brunch, is smoked salmon and cream cheese on a bagel – extremely nice, even if it sits in your stomach like a lead weight. Remember: spread the cream cheese on first, then add the smoked salmon. The scraps are especially good for this.

You can buy prepared fish pâtés, like smoked mackerel and trout. Cheaper still are tinned sardines, mashed into a paste on their own or with cream cheese.

Vegetable fillings. Cucumber or cress sandwiches are often served as a savoury at a formal tea before the 'sweet', perhaps to make it seem more like a complete meal. They are quintessentially British and nice to serve to visiting foreigners! The secret is paper-thin slices of good brown bread (not pre-sliced packaged) and, believe it or not, white pepper instead of black. Keep the sandwiches covered with a clean teatowel until you are ready to eat them so that the edges of the bread don't dry and curl up.

Sandwiches Requiring a Little More Time

Tinned salmon and tuna. Of course, you can put the contents of the tin straight on to the bread, but we recommend a little more finesse. Try to buy the fish preserved in brine rather than in oil, as it's much less greasy and fattening, and always pour off the brine and drain the fish well before using it. With salmon, you may feel happier removing the skin and bones, though they are so soft that when you mash the salmon with a fork they disappear.

Put the drained fish into a small bowl. Add enough good-quality mayonnaise (not salad cream!) to make the mixture soft but not wet. Mix well with a fork. Slice 2–3 spring onions into thin rounds, depending on their size, and add them to the bowl. (Alternatively, substitute ½ small onion, chopped very finely.) Season with salt and pepper and a squeeze of lemon juice.

Spread mayonnaise on the bread, then a thick layer of the prepared mixture, top with a lettuce leaf or two and cover with the other slice. A 200 g (7 oz) tin of fish will make three thick sandwiches or four less greedy ones.

Hard-boiled egg. You need one hard-boiled egg for one sandwich, though you can make two eggs stretch to three sandwiches, and so on exponentially! Hard-boil the eggs as described on page 25, and cool before shelling. Chop the eggs finely and put them in a bowl. As in the preceding recipe, add mayonnaise and spring onions or ½ small onion. Mix thoroughly and season with a small pinch each of salt, pepper and cayenne.

Pan Bagna

Photograph on page 49

This is a classy name for a big doorstep of a Provençal peasant sandwich. Because of the number of ingredients, it's not worth making just one at a time. Pan bagna is great for picnics because by the time you eat it, it will be juicy and full of flavour. Make pan bagna with big crusty rolls (no one can manage more than one) and use only olive oil.

For 2 people

2 crusty white bread rolls, or ½ French baguette
2 tablespoons olive oil
1 tomato, sliced
Small pinch each salt and pepper
A few cucumber slices
½ green pepper, sliced
2 spring onions, sliced
1 hard-boiled egg, thinly sliced
½ 200 g (7 oz) tin tuna, drained and flaked
4–8 black olives, stoned and halved (optional)

Cut the bread rolls in half and sprinkle the olive oil on to the cut sides. Alternatively, cut the baguette in half and then slice open each piece. On the bottom halves lay first the tomato and season with salt and pepper, then arrange the cucumber, green pepper and spring onions evenly on that and finish with the egg slices, flaked tuna and olives. Cover with the top halves of the rolls. If you make the sandwiches in advance, wrap them in clingfilm or they'll leak.

Toasted Sandwiches

You can substitute toast for fresh bread in most of the preceding sandwich recipes. However, here are some sandwiches which are traditionally toasted.

BLT. This always sounds mysterious in American movies, but it's simply bacon, lettuce and tomato. Allow 2–3 bacon slices and 1 small tomato per sandwich. Grill or fry the bacon as described on page 133 and drain it well on kitchen paper. Slice the tomato. Toast 2 slices of brown bread and spread mayonnaise on them. Place the bacon slices on one piece of toast, then the tomato slices. Season the tomato with a small pinch each of salt and pepper and cover with a lettuce leaf or two and the other slice of toast.

Toasted cheese made in a sandwich maker. Sandwich makers are the kind of gadget you receive as a wedding present – in other words, they are not used very often. But they do make good toasted cheese sandwiches because they seal the filling while toasting the bread. Cheese, or cheese and ham, are the best to try because the cheese melts deliciously.

Simply cut the crusts off two pieces of buttered bread. Lay a thin slice of cheese – Edam, or Gruyère for preference because it melts well – on top of one of the pieces of bread. Top it with a slice of cooked ham if you like. Place the second slice of bread over this and press down well. Insert into the sandwich maker and cook according to the manufacturer's instructions.

Club sandwich. This is the king of butties, made by placing a filling of shredded lettuce, grilled bacon, slices of hard-boiled egg, mayonnaise and slices of cooked chicken or turkey, seasoned with a small pinch each of salt and pepper, between two slices of hot buttered toast and pinioning them with toothpicks. Obviously, you make it only when you have all the ingredients to hand, because it's not worth buying and cooking a chicken specially for it!

Bookmaker sandwich. This is simply a steak sandwich – actually a real luxury. It's good to eat accompanied by a bottle of beer while watching some boring TV sports programme with the lads.

For 1

Cook a small minute steak as described on page 87. While it's cooking, toast 2 slices of white bread, preferably crusty enough to soak up the meat juices. Butter the toast and spread a little French mustard on it. Stick the steak between the slices; cut in half if you're a wimp.

Open Sandwiches

These are served in Scandinavian households, where the predominant ingredient used is some kind of preserved fish like rollmop herring or caviar, or in this country as canapés for fussy entertaining. They're not really worth the effort for serious eating because the topping tends to fall off larger slices of bread unless it's glued on with aspic.

Soups

Soup Stock (from a Cube)

No serious cook admits to liking – much less using – stock cubes. But very few home cooks have huge quantities of chicken or beef stock bubbling on the stove or stashed in the freezer. Stock cubes do have a particular taste that isn't like real stock, they are full of chemicals and too much salt, but they are convenient. So, until you're ready to make real stock, go ahead and use them – after you have read the warnings below.

There are different brands of stock cubes, some with a more 'real' taste than others. Give them all a try, and always use half the amount of cube the package recommends. Use them mostly for soups in which there are going to be stronger flavours that will mask the 'false' cube taste. Finally, try the vegetable stock cubes, powders and pastes; they seem to have less of a synthetic flavour. You can buy vegetable stock powder in bulk, which is cheaper. Don't buy lamb stock cubes: you'll probably never have the need to use them.

To make 600 ml (1 pint) stock

1　Boil a kettle of water.
2　Put ½ stock cube, or 1 teaspoon stock powder, in a measuring jug.
3　Pour on the boiling water up to the 600 ml (1 pint) mark.
4　Stir with a wooden spoon until the cube or powder has completely dissolved in the water.

Alternatively, dissolve 2 teaspoons of Marmite, Bovril or other proprietary essence in 600 ml (1 pint) boiling water to make meat stock.

Chicken Soup

Adding wholesome vegetables and lemon juice goes a long way towards disguising the stock cube element. Serve the soup with crusty bread – wholewheat to be virtuous – and you'll fool yourself into thinking that the soup's home-made (well it is, after all!).

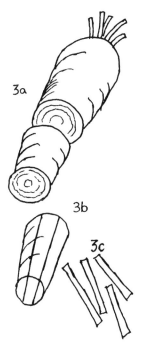

3a

3b

3c

For 4

1 litre (2 pints) water
1 chicken stock cube
1 carrot
1 stalk celery
50 g (2 oz) vermicelli or Chinese egg noodles
Small pinch each salt and pepper
Squeeze lemon juice

1   Make chicken stock with the water and the cube, as described on page 35.
2   Wash the carrot and celery, and trim the ends. Peel the carrot if it is old.
3   Using a sharp knife, cut the vegetables evenly into little batons as follows: first cut them into 5 cm (2 in.) lengths; then cut across each section into three, making flat pieces; finally, cut each piece lengthways into thin strips.
4   Put the stock into a saucepan and bring to the boil over the highest heat.
5   When the water boils, put in the vegetables and the noodles.
6   Bring the soup back up to the boil, then turn the heat down to medium so that it is bubbling gently.
7   Cook the soup for 8 minutes. Taste the noodles to see if they're cooked. They should be firm, not soft to the bite, with no hardness or rawness.
8   Taste the soup. Season with pepper and salt if necessary. Squeeze in some lemon juice. Taste the soup again and add more lemon juice if needed.

Take care when seasoning soup made with a stock cube: it may already be salty enough.

Italian Chicken and Egg Soup

Photograph on page 253

This is a simplified version of a soup called *stracciatella*. If you use at least one or two fresh ingredients, you can happily use chicken cube stock without its being detectable. You can use ready-grated Parmesan cheese and even packet dried breadcrumbs, but you must use fresh parsley to succeed with this soup. Serve the soup with extra grated Parmesan and a lemon cut into wedges.

For 4

1 litre (2 pints) water
1 chicken stock cube
½ bunch parsley
2 eggs
3 tablespoons grated Parmesan cheese
2 tablespoons dried breadcrumbs
Small pinch each salt and pepper
Lemon wedges to serve

1   Make chicken stock with the water and the cube as described on page 35.
2   Heat the stock in a large saucepan over a medium-high heat.
3   Meanwhile, chop the parsley finely (*see page 9*).
4   Break the eggs into a small bowl. Add the parsley, cheese, breadcrumbs and a small pinch of pepper to the eggs. Using a fork, beat until all the ingredients are thoroughly combined.
5   When the stock is boiling gently, turn the heat down to low.

It's important not to let the soup boil once you have added the eggs, or they will go rubbery.

6   Pour the egg mixture slowly into the stock. Stir gently to break up the egg into little strands, leaving no great chunks of cooked white.
7   Taste the soup and add a small pinch of salt if necessary, then give it a final quick stir and ladle it out immediately, making sure that the breadcrumbs have not sunk to the bottom of the pan.
8   Serve with extra Parmesan cheese sprinkled on top and lemon wedges to squeeze into the soup.

Tomato Soup

Photograph on page 49

This soup can be made with fresh or tinned tomatoes. You get two different flavours but they're equally good (and you can't say that when comparing most tinned vegetables with their fresh counterparts). It's only worth making soup from fresh tomatoes if they're absolutely ripe and full of flavour; if it's midwinter and fresh tomatoes are expensive and tasteless, use a tin instead.

When making the stock, you can substitute vegetable stock powder for the chicken stock cube, or simply use water on its own.

For 4

1 litre (2 pints) water
1 chicken stock cube
500 g (1 lb) fresh or 397 g (14 oz) tinned tomatoes
2 carrots
1 small onion
50 g (2 oz) butter or margarine
1 teaspoon sugar
1 tablespoon tomato purée
Small pinch each salt and pepper

1 Make the chicken stock with the water and the cube as described on page 35.
2 Roughly chop the tomatoes, discarding as many of the seeds as you can.
3 Wash the carrots, trim the ends and peel them if they are old. Cut roughly into small pieces.
4 Peel the onion and trim the top and base. Chop roughly into small pieces.
5 Put the butter in a large thick-bottomed saucepan and place it over a low heat until melted.
6 Add the chopped carrots and onion and cook, covered, for 3–4 minutes over a low heat.
7 Add the tomatoes with the sugar and the tomato purée, stir and cook, covered, for 2 minutes.
8 Add the chicken stock and turn the heat up so that the soup comes to the boil.
9 Turn the heat down to low, keeping the pan covered, and let the soup cook gently for approximately 20 minutes.
10 Taste the soup to make sure that the vegetables are cooked and soft. Season with salt and pepper.
11 If you have a food processor or blender, pour the soup into the bowl (do it in two batches) and blend or process it into a purée. Then pour it through a sieve if you like a smoother texture. Otherwise, pour the soup through a wide-meshed sieve and mash the vegetables through it.
12 Pour the soup back into the saucepan and warm to just below boiling on a medium heat. Serve immediately, stirring as you pour it out to prevent the purée from sinking to the bottom of the pan and leaving only liquid at the top.

You can keep back a tablespoon or two of the cooked vegetables and add them to the soup after the purée stage to give texture to the soup.

Alternatives

Tomato and Rice Soup

Make this with either fresh or tinned tomatoes. Add 2 tablespoons of plain white uncooked rice to the soup when you put in the stock. Taste the rice to make sure that it is completely soft before serving.

Tomato and Pepper Soup

Use either fresh or tinned tomatoes. Select a small red or yellow pepper, remove the stem and seeds and cut the flesh into small pieces. Add the pepper to the carrots and onion to be cooked in the butter.

Curried Lentil Soup

This soup can be turned into an Indian Lentil Dal by using only half the amount of water. Simmer until most of the water has evaporated, leaving a thick stew, and add extra lemon juice to taste. Dal is best made using individual spices rather than curry powder.

Red lentils cook very fast and break down into a nice thick soup which needs no puréeing before serving. They also act as a good vehicle for a lot of spices. You can use either a good proprietary curry powder or the more authentic individual ingredients (ginger, cumin and cayenne).

For 4

250 g (8 oz) red lentils
1 litre (2 pints) water
1 clove garlic
2.5 cm (1 in.) cube fresh root ginger or 1 teaspoon ground ginger
2 teaspoons ground cumin
¼ teaspoon cayenne
Small pinch each salt and pepper
½ lemon

1   Put the lentils in a sieve and rinse them under cold running water to wash off the dust. Remove any small stones and other debris.
2   Put them in a large saucepan and cover with water. Stir to keep the lentils from sticking together.
3   Bring to the boil over the highest heat. When the lentils are boiling, turn the heat down to medium-low so that they are simmering very gently. Cover and cook for 20 minutes.
4   Meanwhile, peel the garlic and chop it finely (*see page 9*).

5   Peel the root ginger, if using, and chop it finely.
6   When the lentils have cooked for 20 minutes, add the garlic, ginger, cumin, cayenne, salt and pepper to the soup. (If using curry powder, substitute 2 teaspoons of this for the ginger, cumin and cayenne.)
7   Cook for another 20 minutes or until the lentils have almost completely dissolved.
8   Squeeze the juice from the lemon and add it to the soup.
9   Taste the soup and add extra salt, cumin or lemon juice as necessary. Serve immediately.

Carrot Soup with Yoghurt

This is an example of a simple soup where the thickening is provided simply by putting the cooked vegetable through a sieve, blender or food processor, giving bulk and texture. You can use either water or chicken stock made from a cube (*see page 35*).

Here a thick-bottomed pan is called for. This is because the vegetables are 'sweated' – cooked gently in a little butter and in their own moisture to release their flavour. In a thin-bottomed pan the vegetables are more likely to burn, even over a very low heat. If you don't have a thick-bottomed pan (for example, one made of enamelled cast iron), make sure that you stir the vegetables frequently.

For 4

750 g (1½ lb) carrots
75 g (3 oz) onions
50 g (2 oz) butter
1 sprig fresh thyme or ½ teaspoon dried thyme
½ bayleaf
1¼ litres (2¼ pints) hot chicken stock or boiling water
Small pinch each salt and pepper
4 tablespoons plain yoghurt

1   Wash the carrots, trim the ends and peel them if they are old. Cut the carrots into thin rounds.
2   Peel the onions and chop them finely (*see page 9*).
3   Heat the butter in a thick-bottomed pan over low heat until it has melted.
4   Add the onions, carrots, thyme and bayleaf and cook, covered, stirring occasionally, for 10 minutes.
5   Slowly add the hot chicken stock or water. Turn up the heat to high until the mixture boils.
6   Turn the heat down to medium-low and cook, uncovered, for approximately 20 minutes, or until the vegetables feel completely tender when pierced by a knife.
7   Blend or process, or pour through a sieve into a clean saucepan. Season with salt and pepper.
8   Warm the soup through over a medium heat, stirring so that the vegetable purée is evenly distributed. Serve in individual bowls and swirl in 1 tablespoon yoghurt.

Leek and Potato Farmhouse Soup

Potato and water serve as the base for many vegetable soups. The potato breaks up when it's cooked, giving texture to the soup so that you don't need to thicken it.

For 4

750 g (1½ lb) potatoes
350 g (12 oz) leeks
125 g (4 oz) butter
1 litre (2 pints) boiling water or chicken stock made with a cube (*see page 35*)
Salt and pepper
1 bouquet garni
125 ml (4 fl oz) single cream (optional)
Chopped chives (optional)

A bouquet garni is a mixture of herbs, wrapped in muslin or sealed in a small paper sachet. It is used to flavour stocks, soups and stews. You can buy them ready-made, and discard after use.

1   Peel the potatoes and dice finely. Wash the leeks thoroughly, trim and dice finely (*see page 79*).
2   Heat the butter in a thick-bottomed pan over a low heat. When it's melted, add the potatoes and leeks and cover. Cook over the lowest heat for 2–3 minutes, shaking the pan occasionally so that the vegetables don't stick.
3   Gradually add the water, and season with salt and pepper – as potatoes are quite bland, you may need more seasoning than you normally use. Bring to the boil and remove any scum that rises to the top with a large metal spoon. If you don't remove the scum, the soup may taste gritty.
4   Add the bouquet garni and turn the heat down to medium-low. Simmer the soup until all the vegetables are cooked and soft. This should take 10–20 minutes, depending on how finely you have diced the vegetables – taste them after 10 minutes.

If you like a smoother texture, either take out half the vegetables at stage 5 with a slotted spoon and process or blend them to a purée, or leave them in the soup and mash them with a fork or potato masher.

5   Remove the bouquet garni.
6   Season the soup to taste with more salt and pepper if necessary and add the cream, if using. Warm the soup through and serve with the chopped chives sprinkled on top.

Variation: Potato and Watercress Soup

Wash 1 bunch (or 1 bag) of watercress and chop finely, discarding any slimy bits. Follow the main recipe to the end of stage 3, then add the watercress, keeping aside some of the better leaves for garnish. Add the bouquet garni, return the soup to the boil and simmer for 10–20 minutes or until the vegetables are soft. Put the soup through a blender or food processor, or push through a sieve. Reheat the soup with the cream on a low heat until it's hot but not boiling. Float the reserved watercress leaves on the soup after serving into bowls.

Salads

As most salads are usually made from raw vegetables, this is one area where you don't have to face the terror of cooking. And, since so many restaurants serve interesting salads as starters or main courses, you also don't have to feel that you're feeding yourself or your guests with 'rabbit food' (an insulting term that should be excised from our vocabulary). For the foreseeable future at least, salads are trendy!

The green and mixed salads in this section can be served as side dishes or as starters. We also give two salads which can be served on their own as light meals or snacks.

The vegetables described below are found in most supermarkets; speciality grocers sell a wider variety, but you are likely to do all your shopping in one place and will not necessarily have access to Cypriot or Chinese grocers.

Do wash vegetables thoroughly before eating them. A few slugs probably won't harm you, nor will a little grit. But little is yet known about any harm that prolonged exposure to the pesticides coating the outside leaves of most vegetables might bring; and lead, which can contaminate vegetables grown or displayed for sale on or near busy roads, is known to have injurious effects.

Salad leaves

Round lettuce. The cheapest and most common lettuce, this doesn't have much flavour but it is good mixed with other salad leaves. Its outer leaves are usually a little tough and discoloured and it goes slimy, particularly at the stem end, if it's left completely sealed in the plastic bag you often buy it in. To help prevent this, try to ensure that there is plenty of air surrounding the lettuce within the bag – you could also invert it so that more air gets to the stem end.

Cos lettuce. Shaped like a rugby ball with long leaves, this lettuce is moist with a good flavour and lasts a long time. It usually costs more than a round lettuce but is worth the extra money. In a salad the leaves need to be broken up as they are a little unwieldy.

Iceberg lettuce. This is an American import that is spreading perniciously throughout the land. Despite its extraordinary lack of flavour and high moisture content, it's favoured by grocers because it keeps well. Like French Golden Delicious apples, it should be used only in emergencies!

Curly endive. Looking like a great head of frizzy hair with a yellow centre, this is very attractive in salads, but unless you like its bitterness you should use it in small quantities in combination with other leaves. It's expensive, but it lasts a long time. Another lettuce called **frisée** resembles curly endive but it has a mild flavour.

Batavia. Like curly endive, this has a slightly bitter flavour and should be used sparingly.

Mâche. Also called lamb's lettuce, this is very expensive and is best used to decorate dishes, in the same way that you might use watercress.

Radicchio. The designer leaf, used in combination with green salad leaves for its attractive presentation and because it also has a bitter taste. Expensive but classy.

Oak leaf lettuce. Another pretty leaf which dresses up a salad. Unlike radicchio, it has a delicate flavour.

Chicory. This vegetable is often eaten cooked. It has a slightly sharp taste when eaten raw. Its leaves are pointed and look very attractive decorating the outside of a salad.

Watercress. This peppery-tasting leaf enlivens any green salad. It's also more commonly found than many of the leaves mentioned above, so it's a good standby party salad vegetable.

Preparing Salad Leaves

Trim the root end (where applicable) and carefully pull the leaves apart. Discard any blemished, tough or slimy outer leaves. Handle delicate leaves like watercress and mâche gently as they discolour if bruised.

As salad leaves are hard to dry, try not to drown them when you wash them. You can either wipe leaves with moist kitchen paper, or if you have a salad spinner, put the leaves in the basket and run cold water through it.

It's important to dry leaves thoroughly. Salad dressing won't cling to wet leaves, and they also turn to slime quickly if they are left moist. Dry the leaves in a clean teatowel, or spin dry in a salad spinner. They will keep in a loosely sealed plastic bag in the fridge. But don't leave them anywhere near the freezer compartment; half-frozen salad is worse than slimy salad.

Other Raw Vegetables for Salads

One way to make a salad look appealing is to include vegetables cut into interesting shapes. Some vegetables dictate the way you cut them, with others you can play around. Various ways of preparing raw vegetables are given below.

Carrots. Choose small young carrots for salads if possible. If they are very fresh, they will just need washing, trimming and a gentle scraping, not a full-blown peeling. Cut into rounds, batons (called 'julienne' in the trade) or diagonal slices. Grated carrots are slightly old-fashioned in a mixed salad, though they are fine served on their own sprinkled with vinaigrette (*see page 48*) or as part of an hors d'oeuvre (they are also very wet).

Celery. You buy celery by the 'head' – a bunch of stalks growing out of a crunchy base. The leaves are traditionally cut off and used for flavouring in cooked dishes; you may wish also to cut off the white flatter bottom of each stalk, as the long creamy-white or green upper part is more attractive for salads. Lay the stalk on a board and slice thinly across, producing neat little half-moon shapes.

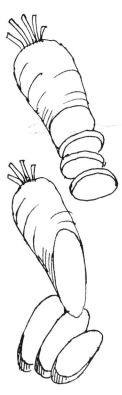

Cucumber. If you're not going to peel it – and there's no reason to, except that the peel gives some people indigestion – scrub the cucumber well to remove any waxy covering (sometimes applied to preserve it). Cut off the stem end. You can score the entire length of the cucumber with a small knife so that you can get attractive scalloped slices, or cut it into lengths or wedges.

Peppers (sweet). These may be green, red or yellow. Wash and dry them and cut across into rounds, slice into thin strips or dice. Make sure that you discard all the seeds and white membrane from the inside. Peppers have a strong flavour which can overpower a delicate salad, so use them with discretion.

Radishes. Wash and dry thoroughly (they can become waterlogged). Remove the root with a small knife and scrape the stem end. If the radishes are really small, you can add them whole to a salad; otherwise cut them across into rounds or into little batons.

Spring onions. There are practically no circumstances under which you'd put ordinary onions in a salad – they taste too strong. However, spring onions, if they are cut into small enough rounds, add a delicate pungency. The green part is milder than the white. Trim off the root, and any discoloured outside skin, wash and slice into rounds.

Tomatoes. Unless you are going to make a tomato salad, choose small tomatoes; try to avoid imported tasteless ones which come from outside the Mediterranean area. Always wash them well. In summer, whole cherry tomatoes can go straight into salads. Larger tomatoes should be cut into quarters or eighths for a salad in a bowl; or sliced for a salad on a plate (*see page 229*).

Fresh herbs. As you can now buy fresh herbs in supermarkets, there's no excuse not to use them in salads, especially as they can transform these dishes from the mundane to the outstanding. You will have to experiment with them to discover what combinations you like. Parsley and chives, generally, go with everything; basil has an affinity with tomatoes, as do oregano and marjoram; strong-tasting vegetables like celery usually overwhelm herbs. Nothing impresses people like cutting a few stalks of chives over a green salad with a pair of scissors just before you eat it!

Green Salad

With the advent of salad leaves in pretty pinks and copper tones, a green salad is no longer strictly green. But it usually is mostly salad leaves with perhaps a few cucumber, green pepper or celery slices thrown in for good measure. The leaves should be torn gently, not cut with a knife, and tossed in a large bowl. If you are entertaining, a mixture of salad leaves is nice, but don't overdo it: three different varieties is enough, including, if possible, one of the sharper-tasting leaves. A few fresh herbs, chopped finely, are better in a plain salad than great chunks of vegetable.

As for salad dressings, if we say it once, we'll say it a thousand times throughout this book – yes, you can buy them (at a price) but given that they are so easy to make yourself and you can control what's in them, do try making your own. The composition of salad dressings provokes great arguments among chefs but it comes down to what you like and can afford. See page 48 for the standard vinaigrette recipe plus variations.

Unless you're a vegetarian or a slimmer, you're not likely to want to eat a green salad on its own as a main course. It's usually served before (American-style), with (British-style) or after (French-style) a dish or meal. If you're serving more than one person, it's easier to make a salad in one big bowl rather than in little individual bowls.

Choose a large wide bowl – white always looks good. With your hands, break the washed and dried leaves into the bowl. Just before serving, pour over the salad dressing and mix well so that every leaf is coated with it. You may find that using your hands to do this is more effective than any other method. Your aim should be to avoid having some leaves completely drenched with dressing, some bone-dry and a puddle of dressing at the bottom of the bowl. A word of caution here: don't overdo the dressing. Start off with a few teaspoons, mix that in well and then add more bit by bit. You can't de-dress a salad, and a wet salad is pretty disgusting. Make sure that you dress the salad just before it gets eaten, because salad leaves go soggy very quickly. For this reason, try not to dress more salad than you need, because you can't really eat slimy salad the next day.

It is also important not to keep the undressed salad for too long before dressing it or the leaves will wilt. You can cover it with a teatowel or piece of kitchen paper soaked in cold water and wrung out. This will keep it fresh for at least an hour.

Mixed Salad and Mixed Salads

Mixed Salad and Mixed Salads are two different things. The first is similar to a green salad but it simply contains a greater variety of ingredients with more texture and colour. For example, to a salad-leaf base (usually a bland lettuce) add tomato quarters, carrot chunks, whole radishes, sliced spring onions and any other vegetable you like. You might wander round your supermarket and pick up a courgette, a small fennel bulb or a kohlrabi and try a bit of it in your salad. Just be sure that you know what's edible raw and what isn't (that is, *not* aubergine or potato). The same rules for dressing a green salad apply to this one.

Mixed Salads are what you often get in a café in France as a starter. They are nothing startling; it's just that the French present commonplace vegetables rather well. The main thing is that they don't mix the ingredients together. They also put the salad on a plate rather than in a bowl so that you can use slices of certain vegetables – tomato, for example. All the vegetables are simply moistened with a little vinaigrette (*see page 48*).

Salad Dressings

The gist of the great salad dressing debate is basically the oil-to-vinegar ratio; whether to add anything other than oil, vinegar, salt and pepper; and whether to use vinegar at all. Reputations have risen and fallen, fortunes have been made and unmade in the exercising of this conflict.

If you are starting out, however, there are some guidelines. Unless you can't afford anything else, don't use 'vegetable oil' or, worse still, 'cooking oil' because they are often a concoction of different oils. If you like a light oil that doesn't taste too strongly, try safflower or sunflower. Corn oil has too dominant a flavour. Real connoisseurs use olive oil, which can have a strong taste.

You may have heard a lot of talk about virgin and extra virgin olive oil. Until you become an expert taster (and there are people around who are olive oil experts in the way that others are wine experts), choose the type whose flavour you find most pleasing. It is true that extra virgin is more 'authentic', but even your basic supermarket virgin olive oil, made with olives from more than one country, still tastes like the real thing and won't contain petroleum byproducts. The oils made from other nuts and seeds, like walnut or hazelnut, are expensive but make an interesting change.

As for vinegars – there are a lot on the market, but the same principles apply. Don't use cider, malt or distilled vinegar for salads. A good rule of thumb is: if it goes on fish and chips, it doesn't go on salads! Buy wine vinegar, red or white. If you want to try the fancier vinegars – raspberry, sherry, herb – go ahead.

Try making the basic vinaigrette below to start with. Then vary the ratio of oil to vinegar, then try adding other ingredients. Perhaps you'll soon have your picture on salad dressing bottles in shops all over the world and be making a fortune from it like Paul Newman!

French Dressing (Vinaigrette)

Makes enough for a medium salad (for 2 people)

You can double or quadruple the ingredients. In addition the mixture keeps well. Freshly squeezed lemon juice can be substituted for the vinegar.

4 tablespoons olive oil
½–1 tablespoon wine vinegar
Salt and freshly ground black pepper

Put all the ingredients in a screw-top jar. Put the lid on and shake furiously until the oil and vinegar are well mixed. Don't be surprised when the oil and vinegar separate after you've left the dressing for a while: just mix it again.

Additional ingredients

Add one of the following to the basic vinaigrette mixture – or all of them together! If you use yoghurt, mayonnaise, cream or milk, you need to use up the salad dressing in one meal as it will turn rancid if kept.

1 teaspoon French mustard or ½ teaspoon ready-prepared or powdered English mustard.
Fresh or dried herbs, particularly tarragon.
Crushed garlic.
1 teaspoon plain yoghurt, mayonnaise, cream or even milk.

Opposite: Pan Bagna (page 33) and Tomato Soup (page 37).

Overleaf (left): Welsh Rarebit (page 28).

Overleaf (right): Grilled Chicken Breast (page 80) with Garlic, Lemon and Parsley Butter (page 86) and French Beans (page 66).

Mayonnaise

We're not going to suggest that you make your own mayonnaise. Finish this book, and then you'll be ready to try it. But there are good mayonnaises in the shops (they are usually labelled 'French' or 'real' and contain egg) which can be doctored. They are nice to stir into the Mixed Salads (*see page 47*).

To 4 tablespoons prepared mayonnaise add one of the following:

2 teaspoons chopped fresh herbs
1 teaspoon good French mustard
1 teaspoon tomato ketchup
1 teaspoon chopped capers and 1 teaspoon chopped gherkins
1 teaspoon anchovy essence
1 teaspoon chopped tinned anchovy fillets

You can also mix equal quantities of plain yoghurt and prepared mayonnaise for a lighter (and cheaper) alternative.

Potato Salad

Potatoes have become a 'prima donna' vegetable. And this dish has helped, because there can't be many people who don't like a good potato salad. It's especially useful to serve to large groups of people: it can be made in advance and is inexpensive and easy. You can also put all sorts of things in it, from German sausage to pickled herring.

However, if it's the middle of winter and there are no new potatoes, you can still make the salad using red, waxy potatoes. They're better than white because they are less likely to fall apart when you cook them.

The herbs must be fresh and not dried: don't make this dish unless you can get fresh herbs. Mint makes a delicious addition to or substitute for the chives and parsley.

For 4

250 g (8 oz) small new potatoes
50 ml (2 fl oz) good-quality mayonnaise
1 tablespoon chopped fresh chives
1 tablespoon chopped fresh parsley
Small pinch each salt and pepper

Opposite: Shallow-fried Fish Fillets (page 106) and Microwaved Broccoli (page 72).

1 Wash the potatoes and scrub them well. (New potatoes do not need peeling.)
2 Boil the potatoes whole (*see page 58*), drain them as soon as they are cooked (or they will absorb water and make a soggy salad) and leave to cool slightly.
3 Cut into quarters and put in a large bowl (you will need plenty of room to mix the salad).
4 Add the rest of the ingredients and mix carefully until the potatoes are completely bound in the sauce.
5 Transfer to a clean dish or carefully wipe the sides of the bowl clean. Serve at room temperature.

Coleslaw

This is a quick stand-by salad using inexpensive ingredients which are readily available. It's not an exciting salad, but it can be very nice. This is an easy version. If you don't have mayonnaise, don't be tempted to use salad cream instead!

Savoy or red cabbage can be substituted for a white cabbage: prepare it in the same way.

For 4

½ head medium white cabbage
3–5 carrots
4 tablespoons good-quality mayonnaise
1 teaspoon French mustard
Pinch each salt and pepper
Sunflower oil

1 With a sharp knife, cut the woody stem out of the cabbage and discard. Shred the rest as finely as possible.
2 Trim the carrots. If they are old, peel and then wash them. Otherwise, wash and scrape them lightly. Grate them coarsely.
3 Put the shredded cabbage and grated cabbage in a bowl and mix them together.
4 Add the mayonnaise, mustard, salt and pepper to the vegetables and mix thoroughly.
5 If the mayonnaise is very thick and makes the vegetables clump together, add 1 teaspoon of oil and mix again.
6 Serve at room temperature.

The following two salads can be served on their own because they both contain protein in the form of cheese. (This is one of the few bits of nutritional advice you'll find in this book.)

Greek Salad

If you're feeling nostalgic about Greek holidays, you can drink Retsina wine (an acquired taste) and serve Greek sesame bread with this salad.

Greek feta cheese is available in most supermarkets now, usually packed in water – hence the need to drain it before use. You could use another cheese, but then it wouldn't be a Greek salad! The use of 'ordinary' onion here is an exception to the rule about using only spring onions in salads. However, try to find mild onions, like red ones or a big Spanish one, in which case you need only half. Lettuce is not an essential ingredient of the salad, but may be used as bulk.

Greek olives are, of course, best for this salad; they have a distinctive bitter taste. Otherwise, any other black olive, pitted or unpitted, will do. Only oil is used to dress the salad – the combination of flavours is so strong that you don't need any vinegar.

For 4

250 g (8 oz) feta cheese
2 tomatoes
1 green pepper
1 small onion
½ cucumber
8 lettuce leaves (optional)
12 black olives
2 teaspoons dried oregano
Salt and pepper
8 teaspoons olive oil

1   Lay the feta cheese on kitchen paper to drain, then cut into 1 cm (½ in.) cubes.
2   Wash and dry the tomatoes and slice thinly.
3   Wash and dry the pepper and cut into thin rounds, discarding the seeds and white membrane inside.
4   Peel the onion, trimming away the top and base, and cut into thin rounds.
5   Wash and dry the cucumber and cut into 1 cm (½ in.) chunks.
6   Wash and dry the lettuce leaves, if using, and tear into smallish pieces.
7   In four small bowls lay a bed of lettuce, if using.
8   Put the sliced tomatoes in the bowls, followed by the well-separated rounds of green pepper, sliced onion and cucumber chunks.
9   Lay the cubed feta and olives on top of each salad.
10 Sprinkle the bowls with dried oregano and a small pinch each of salt and pepper.
11 Just before serving, sprinkle the olive oil on top.

Israeli Salad

This is a messy-looking but delicious strong-tasting salad that's good for using up left-overs. The recipe uses a combination of ingredients that are popular in Israel – lots of fresh vegetables and dairy products.

If you don't have vinaigrette already made up (see page 48), mix in 4 tablespoons oil – preferably olive – combined with 1 tablespoon lemon juice or wine vinegar.

With all the ingredients, but especially in the case of the herbs and garlic, you'll find that you may like different proportions from the ones suggested here. Keep trying until you get the taste that suits you. Remember that the olives, cheese and capers all contain salt, so taste the salad before seasoning it.

For 4

Optional extras: chopped tinned dill pickles, capers, chopped celery

½ lettuce
2 medium tomatoes
½ cucumber
3 spring onions or ½ small onion
12 black olives
50 g (2 oz) cottage cheese
25 g (1 oz) any hard cheese, such as Cheddar
2 boiled potatoes
4 tablespoons vinaigrette
1 teaspoon mixed dried herbs, including oregano
Salt and pepper
1–2 cloves garlic
2 hard-boiled eggs
Plain yoghurt and wholemeal toast to serve

1 Wash and dry the lettuce. Tear into rough pieces.
2 Wash and dry the tomatoes and cucumber and cut them into irregular chunks.
3 Slice the spring onions thinly into rounds. If using ½ small onion, slice it into thin rounds and then cut the rounds in half.
4 Put all the vegetables into a large wide salad bowl.
5 Add the olives and cottage cheese and mix well.
6 Grate the cheese and mix it into the salad.
7 Cut the boiled potatoes, peeled or unpeeled, into cubes and mix into the salad. At this point, add any of the optional extras.
8 Stir the vinaigrette well into the salad. Stir in the mixed herbs and season with salt and pepper.
9 Peel and chop the garlic finely. Mix into the salad.
10 Shell and quarter the eggs. Use them to decorate the top of the salad.
11 Serve at room temperature with yoghurt and toast.

Vegetables as a Side Dish

Cooking Vegetables

Although thousands of vegetable dish recipes exist, most people cook vegetables very simply, especially if they are to accompany a meat or fish dish. And, for most vegetables, the simplest cooking method is often the best way of bringing out their flavour. So there's no shame in boiling or steaming nice fresh vegetables. (Old tired-out vegetables are another matter; they usually need some form of camouflage.) In this section basic cooking instructions are given for all the common inexpensive vegetables. In the next section are more difficult vegetable recipes; here we don't use more than one cooking method at once. Where microwaving is suitable for particular vegetables, brief instructions are given.

Boiling

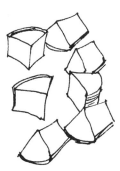

Boiling is one of the easiest and most common ways to cook vegetables. Here are a few guidelines:

1   You don't have to peel the vegetables before boiling, so long as you wash them first. Often they taste better unpeeled, they are better for you – and it's less work.
2   When cutting a vegetable up for boiling (or for any form of cooking), remember that the smaller the pieces, the faster it cooks. The only drawback is that small pieces of vegetable can get waterlogged (especially potatoes).
3   It's long been the custom to add salt to the water in which vegetables are boiled. This is not actually necessary. Decide after you taste the cooked vegetable if you want to salt it or not.
4   As soon as you add the vegetables to the water, it will stop boiling. Wait for the water to come back to the boil, then lower the heat. Don't just put the vegetables in and walk away, because the water will soon boil over.
5   It can be faster to boil an electric kettle and pour the boiling water over the vegetables, bringing the water back to the boil on top of the cooker.
6   Taste the vegetable during cooking to decide how crunchy or soft you like it. When it's cooked, drain the water immediately; don't let vegetables sit in hot water as they'll continue to cook and go watery or soft.

Potatoes

Potatoes have come out of the closet. For a start, they are not the calorie-ridden menace many people assume. And they are extraordinarily versatile. You can eat them as a snack, as a main course or as an accompaniment. They soak up sauces and go into salads. They're bland enough to combine with other flavours and interesting enough to be eaten naked, cold and boiled as a midnight snack (everyone's secret vice). In the following recipes allow 500 g (1 lb) old potatoes for 3 people or 500 g (1 lb) new potatoes for 4 people.

Boiled Potatoes

The best potatoes for boiling are new ones, the smaller the better. They don't need peeling, just gentle washing. Of the older, main crop potatoes (the ones hanging around for months after they've been dug up), choose a red-skinned variety for boiling, or a good all-rounder like King Edward – many other white varieties turn into a slushy mess when they're boiled. Potatoes are also more likely to disintegrate if they've been cut in pieces, so buy small-to-medium ones for boiling so you can leave them whole.

In fact, this is the only thing that can really go wrong. Every time you let water enter a potato – by cutting it in half or by testing it with a knife – there's more chance of it becoming waterlogged. Obviously, you'll need to test the potatoes when you start cooking for the first time. Try to learn to judge the time needed to cook a potato by its size: the bigger it is, of course, the longer it needs.

1   Wash the potatoes. There's no need to peel them unless you're fussy. However, if there are any 'eyes', sprouting bits or blemishes, cut them away. It is also particularly important to remove any green areas as these signal the presence of toxins. If the green goes right through the potato, throw the whole tuber away.
2   If the potatoes are very big, cut them into even-sized pieces. Otherwise leave them whole.
3   Choose a pan big enough to hold the potatoes in one layer with the water just covering them.
4   Bring the water to the boil over a high heat. When it's boiling, add the potatoes. After the water has come back up to the boil, turn the heat down until the water is just bubbling and simmer the potatoes gently for about 20 minutes. If you cook them too quickly, this will encourage any propensity they have to break down in the water and become mushy.
5   Check if the potatoes are done by inserting a thin knife. If there's any resistance, cook a little longer.
6   Carefully drain off the water, place the potatoes in a warmed serving dish, add a knob of butter and serve at once.

Mashed Potatoes

A floury variety like Maris Piper is best for mashed potatoes. To speed up the cooking process you can cut the potatoes into small pieces. Peel them or not, as you prefer – but remember that it's easier *after* cooking (hold them in an oven glove so that you don't burn yourself) and you won't need a peeler to do it.

Plain yoghurt or soured cream may be substituted for the milk or single cream added in stage 4. You can also add chopped fresh herbs such as chives and parsley, in which case omit the nutmeg.

1 Prepare the potatoes as in the preceding recipe for Boiled Potatoes up to the end of stage 5. Drain off the water.
2 Return the drained potatoes, still in the pan, to a medium heat in order to dry them out briefly. Give the pan an occasional shake to prevent the potatoes from sticking to the bottom.

Don't put the potatoes in a blender or food processor. The starch in them comes out and makes them gluey.

3 Now mash them. You can push them through a sieve, or squash each one with a fork and mix together, or use a purpose-made potato masher. Make sure that you get all the lumps out!
4 Add 25 g (1 oz) butter for each 500 g (1 lb) of potatoes, plus a little milk or single cream if you wish, and mix well. The consistency of the potatoes depends on your personal choice.
5 Season, if necessary, with a little salt, pepper and grated nutmeg.

Roast Potatoes

You may need to turn the potatoes more than once if they are cut in uneven sizes. You may also find that their outside layer sticks to the pan when you try to turn them over, and you can avoid this by using a metal spatula to get right under each potato. Otherwise, leave the stuck bits stuck. The potatoes will crispen again and you've got the crispy stuck bits to look forward to – remove these from the pan by scraping vigorously, *after* you have transferred the potatoes to a warmed serving dish.

Any variety of potato is suitable for this cooking method. Just make sure that you cut the potatoes into even-sized pieces so that they all cook at the same rate. Most people eat roast potatoes with a joint of meat (see page 137 for timing the meal), and it seems a treat to eat them on other occasions. But when you do cook them without the joint, you won't have the meat fat and juices to cook them in, so you will have to use a fat which does not burn at a high temperature – lard or vegetable oil, not butter or margarine.

1 Pre-heat the oven to 230°C (450°F, gas mark 8).
2 Put a pan of cold water on a high heat and let it come to the boil.
3 Wash the potatoes and peel them. Cut them into even-sized pieces about 5–6 cm (2–2½ in.) thick.

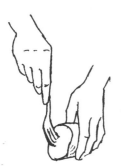

4   Boil them over medium-high heat for about 6 minutes. (This is known as par-boiling.)
5   Meanwhile, put 75 g (3 oz) lard or 6–8 tablespoons vegetable oil into a metal roasting tin big enough to hold the potatoes in one layer. Place it in the oven to heat up.
6   Drain the potatoes and return them to the pan. Place the pan over a medium heat and shake it so that the potatoes dry out completely – otherwise the fat will spit badly when you put them in it.
7   Score the cut edges of the potatoes with a fork to help the outsides crispen during roasting.
8   Put the potatoes in the roasting tin and spoon the hot fat all over them. Season with a little salt and pepper. Put the tin on a shelf in the top of the oven where it is hottest.
9   Cook for 45 minutes, spooning the hot fat over the potatoes from time to time. After about 20 minutes, turn them over to brown the other side.
10 Test to see if the potatoes are done by inserting a knife. They should be soft inside and crisp outside.
11 Drain on kitchen paper and serve immediately.

Roasting Without Par-boiling

To cut down on cooking time and to make sure that they cook evenly, in the method given above the potatoes are par-boiled before roasting. If you prefer, you can omit the par-boiling stage and cook them in the oven from the beginning. To do this, dry the potatoes thoroughly after washing, heat the fat in the tin (as described in stage 5), score the potatoes with a fork (stage 7) and cook as described for 1 hour or more, turning them after 30 minutes.

Jacket (Baked) Potatoes

This is probably the easiest way to cook potatoes. Nothing can go wrong – unless you forget about them completely. They are nice on their own or with a variety of toppings, and make a very cheap and healthy meal.

To speed up cooking, plunge a metal skewer through the centre of the potato. This conducts heat to the centre of the potato. Don't use skewers in microwave ovens!

1   Make sure you select average-sized potatoes of roughly equal size, regular in shape and with smooth unblemished skins.
2   Pre-heat the oven to 230°C (450°F, gas mark 8).
3   Scrub the potatoes absolutely clean and dry them. Make a cross-shaped incision deep into each one.
4   Place them on a baking tray which has first been sprinkled with salt (this stops them from sticking) and place in the hot oven for about 1 hour.
5   To see if the potatoes are cooked, hold one of them in a clean cloth and squeeze gently. If it's cooked, it will give easily and a star shape will form from the incision.
6   Gently squeeze each cooked potato in order to create the star effect. This allows you to put the filling inside neatly.

You can eat a potato cooked in this way with butter or margarine, and seasoned with a little salt and pepper, as a side dish to a meal, or add one of the following fillings to make it a meal in itself:

Yoghurt and chives. Add 1 tablespoon chopped chives to 3 tablespoons plain yoghurt per potato.

Garlic, Lemon and Parsley Butter (see page 86).

Coleslaw (see page 54).

Garlic and black pepper cream. Combine 3 tablespoons double cream with ½ clove garlic, finely chopped, black pepper and a little salt per potato.

Sour cream or fromage frais, seasoned with salt and pepper.

Bolognese sauce (see page 194).

Microwaved jacket potatoes

The rumour about microwaved baked potatoes is that they're fast but taste horrible. Well, that's half right. If you've got an ordinary microwave oven, you can try cooking a jacket potato in it and see what you think. Prick the potato and microwave on HIGH for 4–6 minutes.
    However, if you have a more sophisticated microwave oven with a conventional oven element, this will cook a baked potato quickly and leave it tasting just as good as if it had been cooked slowly. Prick the potato and cook on HI-SPEED for 12 minutes.

Sauté Potatoes

Potatoes suitable for boiling are also suitable for this dish.

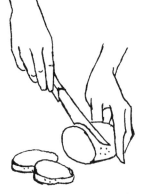

The temperature is very important. If the fat is not hot enough, the potatoes will immediately soak it up and become greasy; if it's too hot, they'll burn. You can test it by putting a little square of fresh bread in the fat. If it turns a golden brown colour in a few seconds, the fat is ready to receive the potatoes.

If you salt the potatoes while they're still cooking, they'll stick to the pan.

1   Scrub even-sized potatoes, allowing 1–2 per person depending on the size of the potatoes. Do not peel them.
2   Boil them as described on page 58. Let them cool, then peel them.
3   Slice the potatoes into 6 mm (¼ in.) slices.
4   Put 1 teaspoon of fat (lard or vegetable oil) per potato in a large frying pan (non-stick for preference) over a medium-high heat.
5   Heat the fat until its surface ripples slightly. Do not let it get so hot that it smokes.
6   Add the slices of potato in one layer – they must not overlap – and fry. Turn each piece over with a fish slice or palette knife at regular intervals so that they brown evenly. You may need to add more fat to the pan.
7   When they are golden brown, remove from the fat and drain on kitchen paper. Sprinkle on a little salt and serve immediately.

Carrots

The carrot is one of those vegetables, like Brussels sprouts and beans, which are traditionally overcooked. Of course, it's down to your own taste, but vegetables do lose their flavour and nutritional value if they are cooked for hours on end. They are really best cooked *al dente* – that is, slightly undercooked, so that they retain a little bite as opposed to being mushy. Whether you're buying small carrots with the feathery tops still attached or the larger coarser variety, they should be firm and bright in colour.

Boiled Carrots

You can use older carrots for boiling but you may want to peel them if the skin looks tough and battered.

Allow 500 g (1 lb) for 4 people

1   Fill a saucepan with cold water and bring to the boil over a high heat.
2   Meanwhile, wash the carrots and cut off the tough root and stem end. Peel them if you want.
3   Cut the carrots into any shape you like (*see page 8*).
4   Put the carrots into the boiling water, return to the boil and cook over a medium heat for 5–15 minutes, depending on the size of the pieces.
5   Taste to see if they are done. Drain immediately and serve.

Glazed Carrots

This is a slightly more interesting way of cooking carrots. It's a good method for older carrots, which may have lost some of their flavour.

For 4

500 g (1 lb) carrots
Pinch salt
Pinch sugar
25 g (1 oz) butter
2–3 parsley stalks (optional)

1   Trim, peel and wash the carrots and slice into even-sized pieces.
2   Place the carrots in a pan with the salt, sugar and butter and just cover with cold water.
3   Cover with a tight-fitting lid and bring to the boil.
4   Lower the heat to medium, cover and cook, checking frequently, until the carrots are done.
5   Meanwhile, wash the parsley, if using, and chop it finely.

6   Remove the lid from the pan and drain off any remaining water. Put the pan back on to the stove and turn up the heat to high. Shake the pan over the heat for 1–2 minutes. This will give the carrots a lovely shiny appearance.

7   Serve immediately with chopped parsley sprinkled on top.

Microwaved Carrots

Microwaving is a good way of cooking carrots cut into small pieces, like matchsticks (julienne strips) or thin rounds.

Put the carrot pieces into a microwave dish and cover. For 500 g (1 lb) carrots add 2 tablespoons water. Cover and microwave on HIGH for 10 minutes. Stir or shake during the cooking.

Turnips and Swedes

Turnips are small, and white and pink in colour. Swedes are larger, with a brown skin and orange flesh, and have a stronger flavour. Both should be hard, with unwrinkled skins.

Turnips and swedes both need to be peeled before cooking; the older-looking the vegetable, the tougher and thicker the peel will be. Turnips also need to be 'topped and tailed' (that is, the root and stem end should be removed). Swedes take a very long time to cook as they are very dense, so cut them into 2.5–5 cm (1–2 in.) pieces. You'll need a good stout knife and lots of muscle for this.

To boil turnips or swedes, follow the recipe for Boiled Carrots on page 62.

Turnips or Swedes Cooked in Foil

This is the simplest of dishes, because you can leave it to cook unattended. Also, if you overcook the vegetables by a few minutes, it won't matter. They take a long time to cook, but the result is deliciously tender with an intense flavour.

1 large or 2 small turnips or ½ medium swede per person
Oil or butter
Salt and pepper

1   Pre-heat the oven to 200°C (400°F, gas mark 6).
2   Wash the turnips and top and tail them. If using swedes, peel them and cut them into quarters.
3   Grease the vegetables with a little oil or butter, then season them with a little salt and pepper.

4   Wrap them tightly in foil so that no steam can escape.
5   Bake them in the middle of the oven for at least 30 minutes for the turnips and up to 1 hour for the swedes, depending on size. They are done when they 'give' slightly if squeezed.

Glazed Turnips or Swedes

For 4

500 g (1 lb) turnips or swedes
25 g (1 oz) butter
Pinch each salt and sugar
Chopped parsley to garnish (optional)

Cook in the same way as for Glazed Carrots (*see page 62*).

Mashed Swede and Potatoes

There must be some olde English or Scottish name for this, like 'bashed tatties and neeps', to give it a bit of historical or cultural interest. In any case, it tastes just fine.

For 4

250 g (8 oz) swede
250 g (8 oz) potatoes
50 g (2 oz) butter or margarine
Salt and pepper

For example, cut the potatoes into four and the swedes into six or eight. This is to ensure that the two vegetables cook in the same time, given that swedes take longer to cook.

1   Peel and wash the swede and potatoes. Cut the swede into smaller pieces than the potatoes.
2   Put the vegetables in a saucepan and cover them with cold water. Bring to the boil, then turn the heat down to medium so that they boil steadily for 15–20 minutes, or until cooked.
3   Put a skewer through them to make sure that they are soft. Turn the heat off and drain away the water.
4   Return the vegetables to the pan and mash them together, adding the butter to make them into a smooth purée (or a lumpy one, if you prefer).
5   Add salt and pepper to taste, and serve immediately.

Cauliflower

Cauliflower is another vegetable that has suffered from overcooking. Choose one that's free from blemishes and that feels heavy when you pick it up. If you buy one that's been trimmed of leaves, it will cost more, but on the other hand you pay for the leaves if you buy an untrimmed one; so try to find an untrimmed cauliflower with not too much foliage and plenty of curd (as the white part is known).

Boiled Cauliflower

You can either boil a cauliflower whole or separate it into florets. The problem with the former method is finding a lidded pan big enough. The problem with the latter method is that the stem is harder than the floret, so when the floret is cooked, the stem is hard, and when the stem is cooked the floret is mushy. It is therefore better to cook cauliflower whole if you can, immersing the stem, which needs more cooking, in boiling water and allowing the florets to cook in the resulting steam.

Allow 1 large cauliflower for 4 people

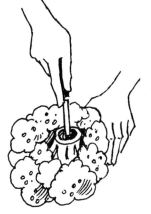

If steam seems to be escaping from the covered pan, place a piece of foil over the open pan to seal it. Then replace the lid tightly.

Cauliflower loses its heat very quickly. Have a warmed bowl ready which is large enough to contain the body of the cauliflower.

1   Choose a pan with a lid that will hold the cauliflower and put 5 cm (2 in.) water in the bottom. Cover the pan and bring the water to the boil over a high heat.
2   Meanwhile, trim the stem of the cauliflower and remove all the outer leaves.
3   Hollow out the stem with a vegetable peeler or small sharp knife.
4   Wash the cauliflower well in salted water: this will flush out any insects hidden in the crevices. Re-wash in plain cold water. Cut away any brown or damaged parts.
5   Put the cauliflower in the pan, stem down, and bring the water back to the boil. Turn the heat down to medium-high so that the water is rolling but not boiling violently. Cover tightly with the lid and cook for about 20 minutes or until the cauliflower is done.
6   Test the cauliflower to see if it is cooked. Both the stem and the florets should be tender but not too soft. Drain and serve immediately.

Steamed Cauliflower

Steaming is a better method of cooking for cauliflower florets – when you want to cook only a one-person portion. In any case, the most common vegetable steamers (the little baskets described on page 16) will not hold a whole cauliflower.

Allow 1 small or ½ medium cauliflower for 2 people

1 Wash the cauliflower and trim away the leaves and any brown or damaged parts.
2 Cut away the woody stem.
3 Very carefully separate the florets.
4 If the florets are big and their stalks thick, cut them neatly in half lengthways, keeping each half attached to the stalk – it will fall to pieces otherwise.
5 Put 2.5 cm (1 in.) water in the bottom of a pan large enough to hold the steamer. Bring the water to the boil over a high heat.
6 When the water is boiling, put the florets in the steamer basket. Try to keep the stems pointing to the centre; otherwise, try to keep the florets piled up with the stems closest to the water.
7 Turn the heat down to medium-high. Cover the pan tightly and steam the cauliflower for 4–6 minutes, or until cooked. Check occasionally to make sure that the water has not boiled away and top it up if necessary.
8 Test the cauliflower to see whether it is done. Serve immediately.

Microwaved Cauliflower

This is a very good way of cooking cauliflower florets because they don't go soggy. Prepare the florets as described in the recipe for Steamed Cauliflower (above).

Put 500 g (1 lb) cauliflower in a microwave dish and add 3 tablespoons water. Cover and microwave on HIGH for 10 minutes, shaking or stirring during the cooking.

Beans

All beans are inedible raw, but taste at their best cooked *al dente*. French or Kenya beans are now usually served whole, as they retain their flavour better. Larger beans such as runner beans are usually cut into smaller pieces. They should all be bright green in colour and firm, without wrinkles, when you buy them.

Boiled French Beans

This method also applies to the small Kenya beans.

Allow 250 g (8 oz) for 4 people

1 Put 5 cm (2 in.) cold water in a pan and bring to the boil over a high heat.
2 Meanwhile, carefully trim the tops and the tails of the beans using a sharp knife.
3 Wash the beans.

4   Put the beans in the boiling water, return to the boil and cook over a medium-high heat for about 7–10 minutes, depending on their size, or until they are done.
5   Test the beans to see if they are done. They should not taste raw, and should be tender but firm. Drain them and serve with a knob of butter on top, or with lemon wedges.

Boiled Runner Beans

Allow 250 g (8 oz) for 4 people

1   Put 7.5 cm (3 in.) cold water in a pan and bring to the boil over a high heat.
2   Meanwhile, wash the beans and remove the 'string' down each side with a sharp knife.
3   Cut the beans into diagonal pieces about 1 cm (½ in.) thick, or into thin strips 5–7.5 cm (2–3 in.) long.
4   Put them into the boiling water and cook for 7–10 minutes, depending on the size of the pieces, or until they are done.
5   Test the beans to see if they are done, as for French beans. Drain them and serve immediately with a knob of butter or lemon wedges.

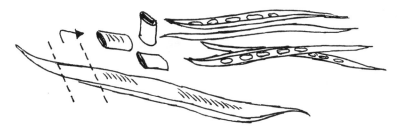

Microwaved Beans

Beans can be microwaved whole or in pieces. Again, French beans are best left whole, runner beans best cut up.
    Prepare the beans as described above. Put 500 g (1 lb) in a microwave dish with 3 tablespoons water. Cover and microwave on HIGH for 12 minutes, stirring or shaking during the cooking time.

Sweetcorn

Fresh sweetcorn should be firm, with plump kernels. It has a short season and is best eaten on the cob as a starter or as part of a light meal. Otherwise, if you fancy sweetcorn kernels as a vegetable, buy frozen corn and follow the directions on the packet.

Allow 1 cob per person as a starter

1 Choose a pan large enough to hold the sweetcorn. Fill with cold water and bring to the boil over the highest heat.
2 Meanwhile, remove the leaves and all the 'silk' attached to the corn. Trim the stem end.
3 When the water has come to a rolling boil, add the corn and bring the water back up to the boil. Boil steadily over a medium-high heat for 10–15 minutes, depending on its freshness: the older the corn, the longer it takes.
4 Test one kernel of the corn by prising it off the cob. It should be quite soft. Drain and serve immediately with butter and salt.

You get very messy when eating sweetcorn off the cob. Provide your guests with wooden toothpicks and plenty of warm water and towels.

Peas

Peas, sweetcorn and spinach are the only frozen vegetables we recommend using regularly. In the case of peas, the frozen variety often tastes better than the tired-looking pale green pellets sold past their prime. Anyway, really fresh peas never make it into the pot: they are always wolfed raw straight from the pod. Frozen ones are easier to prepare, usually cheaper and more easily available. To cook them, simply follow the directions on the packet, adding a sprig or two of fresh mint for extra flavour. However, here's how to cook good fresh peas.

Boiled Fresh Peas

Choose pods that are bright green, not dull or discoloured.

Allow 1 kg (2 lb) – unshelled weight – for 4 people

1 Bring a pan of water to the boil over a high heat.
2 Meanwhile, gently squeeze the pods open and remove the peas. Rinse them.
3 Place the peas in the boiling water, return to the boil and cook for about 10–20 minutes, depending on their age. You can add a sprig of mint to improve the flavour.
4 Taste the peas to see if they are done. Drain and serve immediately.

Variation

To make the peas slightly less commonplace, here's an easy trick. Return the hot drained peas to the pan and place over a low heat. Add 25 g (1 oz) butter and ½ teaspoon caster sugar. Stir the peas gently until the butter and the sugar are melted and the peas are well coated. Serve immediately. This works equally well with fresh or frozen peas.

Tomatoes

Tomatoes are used a lot in cooking, but mostly in sauces. They are rarely served as a vegetable in their own right, except to accompany a cooked breakfast or mixed grill. For grilling choose firm – not over-ripe – tomatoes, big or small, but don't choose the elongated Italian plum tomatoes you sometimes find in shops: they are suitable only for sauces.

Grilled Tomatoes

Allow 500 g (1 lb) tomatoes (or 4 large tomatoes) for 4 people

Vegetable oil for greasing
1–2 teaspoons butter
Salt and pepper
Chopped parsley (optional)

1   Pre-heat the grill to its highest setting.
2   Grease a baking tray with a drop of vegetable oil.
3   Wash the tomatoes and remove the stem end using a small sharp knife. Cut in half across the middle.
4   Place the tomato halves, cut side up, on the tray.
5   Put a dab of butter on each tomato half and season with a little salt and pepper.
6   Turn the grill down to medium. Place the tomatoes under the grill and cook for 5–10 minutes, depending on their ripeness (very soft ones will burst if overcooked) and how soft you like them.
7   Garnish with parsley if using, and serve immediately.

Stuffed Herbed Tomatoes

Photograph on page 187

Do not use tomatoes that are too ripe for this recipe as they will fall apart when they cook. Choose ones that are firm but not hard. Allow 1 large tomato per person as a first course, or 1 smaller tomato as a vegetable garnish for a main course.

For 4

4 tomatoes
2 cloves garlic
½ bunch parsley (optional)
50 g (2 oz) dried breadcrumbs
1 tablespoon mixed dried herbs (which must include either oregano or marjoram)
Salt and pepper
Olive oil
2 tablespoons grated Parmesan cheese (optional)

Dried breadcrumbs are made from very dry stale bread, crushed with a rolling pin or pulverised in a blender or food processor.

1   Wash the tomatoes and remove the stem end. Cut the tomatoes in half across the middle.
2   Using a spoon – with a little help from a sharp knife – scoop out the insides of the tomato halves, leaving the outside 'walls' intact. Discard as many of the tomato seeds as possible and chop the remaining pulp finely. Set aside.
3   Finely chop the garlic and the parsley if using.
4   Place the garlic, parsley, breadcrumbs, dried herbs, salt and pepper and tomato pulp in a mixing bowl and combine well. The mixture should be moist enough to form into a ball without falling apart.
5   Pre-heat the grill to its highest setting.
6   Place one spoonful of the mixture into each of the eight tomato halves. If any mixture is left, divide evenly among the tomatoes. Using a small spoon, put a few drops of olive oil on the top of each tomato half. Sprinkle with the Parmesan cheese, if using.
7   Place the tomatoes on a grill rack. Turn the grill down to medium and set them under it. Cook until the tops are browned and the tomato skins feel soft when you prod them. Serve immediately.

Brussels Sprouts

The Brussels sprout is a much-maligned vegetable which suffers the indignity of being perenially overcooked. Go ahead, try them crunchy! And instead of putting butter or margarine on them, flavour them with a squeeze of lemon juice for a change. Only buy firm, green sprouts, avoiding any with discoloured outer leaves.

Boiled Brussels Sprouts

Allow 500 g (1 lb) for 4 people

1   Bring a pan of water to the boil over the highest heat.
2   Using a sharp knife, trim the stems of the sprouts and remove the discoloured outer leaves.
3   Place the sprouts in the boiling water, return to the boil and cook for 7-10 minutes, depending on their size and your preference. If you don't like them crunchy, cook them a little longer, remembering that they should still be bright green when you eat them.
4   Drain the sprouts and serve immediately.

Steamed Brussels Sprouts

If you want to help the sprouts cook more quickly, cut a cross about 6 mm (¼ in.) deep in the stem end of each one.

1   Prepare the sprouts as described in the recipe for Boiled Brussels Sprouts (above).
2   Put 2.5 cm (1 in.) water in the bottom of a saucepan.

Place the steamer inside, cover and bring the water to the boil.
3   When the water is boiling, put the sprouts into the steamer in one layer, if possible. Cover tightly.
4   Steam for 8–10 minutes, or until they are cooked. Check half-way through to make sure that the water has not boiled away and top up if necessary. Turn the sprouts if they are not in one layer.
5   When the sprouts are done, serve immediately with lemon juice squeezed over them.

Microwaved Brussels Sprouts

Like other vegetables, sprouts keep their freshness and colour when cooked in this way. There's the added bonus that you don't have the cooking smell.

Prepare the sprouts as described in the recipe for Boiled Brussels Sprouts. Put 500 g (1 lb) sprouts into a microwave dish with 3 tablespoons water. Cover and microwave on HIGH for 8 minutes, stirring during the cooking time.

Broccoli

The purple or dark green calabrese, a variety of broccoli, tastes the same and is treated in the same way. The florets should still be green, not beginning to yellow.

As with cauliflower, the only trouble with cooking broccoli is that the florets cook faster than the stems. Steaming or microwaving overcomes the problem as you can arrange the broccoli according to where the heat is greatest. The best and easiest accompaniment for broccoli is a squeeze of lemon juice.

Boiled Broccoli

Allow 500 g (1 lb) broccoli for 4 people

1   Bring a large pan of water to the boil over the highest heat.
2   Wash the broccoli and scrape off the little leaves growing on the sides of the stem.
3   Separate the florets of broccoli from each other using a knife. Cut 6 mm (¼ in.) off the tough stem end.
4   Put the broccoli into the boiling water.
5   Let it come to the boil again, then turn it down to a medium boil.
6   Cook the broccoli for 5 minutes, then pierce the stem with a knife. If the knife goes through easily, the broccoli is done; if it doesn't, continue cooking for a few more minutes, then test again.
7   Drain and serve immediately. Like cauliflower, broccoli loses its heat quickly, so be sure to have a warmed serving dish ready for it.

Steamed Broccoli

Some people peel the broccoli stems when the broccoli is a little old and tired-looking. This is rather fiddly and only worthwhile if you are entertaining. If the broccoli is old and you need to cook the stems for much longer than the flower heads, cut off the stems completely and put them on to boil first, then drop in the flower heads 2–3 minutes later.

1   Prepare the broccoli as described in the recipe for Boiled Broccoli on page 71.
2   Put 2.5 cm (1 in.) water into a large saucepan. Place the steamer inside and bring to the boil over the highest heat.
3   When the water is boiling, put the broccoli pieces in the steamer with stems pointing towards the middle and as close to the water as possible.
4   Cover tightly and boil at a medium heat for 3 minutes. If necessary, rearrange the florets so that all the stems cook evenly (the floret tips will take care of themselves).
5   Cook for another 2 minutes. Test the stems by piercing with the tip of a knife to see if they are cooked. If the knife goes through easily, the broccoli is done; if it doesn't, continue cooking for a few more minutes, then test again.
6   Serve immediately.

Microwaved Broccoli

Photograph on page 52

Prepare the broccoli as described in the recipe for Boiled Broccoli. Put the broccoli in a microwave dish with their heads pointing towards the centre. Spinkle over 2–3 tablespoons water, cover and microwave on HIGH for 10 minutes. Turn the broccoli over half-way through cooking.

Courgettes

Courgettes are often cooked to death, leaving them unpleasantly oozing water. Because of their high water content, most cooking methods, especially boiling, make them go soft and mushy. The three basic methods below preserve what little flavour plain cooked courgettes have. Make sure that you don't overcook them: if in doubt, give them too little rather than too much time.

Steamed Courgettes

Allow 500 g (1 lb) courgettes for 4 people

1   Top and tail the courgettes and wash them thoroughly. Cut into whatever shapes you like. However, ensure that the pieces are all the same size.
2   Put 2.5 cm (1 in.) water in a saucepan. Place the steamer inside and cover. Bring the water to the boil.

3 Put the courgette pieces into the steamer in one layer if possible. Cover tightly.
4 Steam for 3–4 minutes, or until cooked – they should still be slightly firm when you take them to the table. Serve immediately with chopped herbs sprinkled on top if you feel so inclined.

Sautéed Courgettes

In order to cook the courgettes quickly without letting their water escape, you need to fry them at a fairly high heat. Therefore you need to use oil, which will not burn at a high temperature – sunflower (or any other vegetable oil) or olive.

1 Prepare the courgettes as described in the recipe for Steamed Courgettes.
2 Heat 3 tablespoons oil in a frying pan. When the surface of the oil ripples very slightly, add the courgettes.
3 Fry over a medium-high heat, stirring constantly with a wooden spoon, for 4 minutes or until the courgettes are cooked but still slightly firm. This isn't difficult after you've practised it a few times. You may need to adjust the flame on the gas a bit to make sure that the courgettes don't burn as you cook them quickly. If they cook at too low a temperature, they turn soft and the water comes out.
4 Season with a little salt and pepper and serve immediately.

Garlic Sautéed Courgettes

Photograph on page 254

It's important to chop the garlic because if it is crushed in a press it's likely to burn in this recipe.

This is similar to the recipe above but with much more flavour. Do try to use olive oil as it makes a big difference to the taste.

For 4

500 g (1 lb) courgettes
2–4 cloves garlic
3 tablespoons olive oil
Salt and pepper

1 Prepare the courgettes as described in the recipe for Steamed Courgettes, cutting them into little wedges.
2 Peel the garlic and chop finely with a knife.
3 Put the olive oil in a large frying pan and turn the heat up to medium-high. When the oil starts to smoke slightly, add the garlic, stir it round quickly in the hot oil once, then immediately add the courgettes.

In this variation the courgettes cook a little longer than in the basic recipe for Sautéed Courgettes because the garlic needs time to lose its raw taste.

4   Stir the courgettes over the heat for about 5 minutes or until very small patches of brown appear on them. Taste a piece, and if it's very slightly soft but still crunchy, the courgettes are done.
5   Season with a little salt and pepper and serve immediately.

Microwaved Courgettes

Cut the courgettes into even-sized sticks, rounds or wedges. Place them in a microwave dish without water, cover and microwave on HIGH for 5 minutes, shaking well during cooking. Drain well before serving.

Cabbage

There are five types of cabbage you are likely to come across. Dutch white cabbage looks like a pale green, tightly packed football; ordinary English cabbage has dark green leaves; Savoy has crinkly dark green leaves; Chinese cabbage is elongated with a firm white base and pale green crinkly foliage; while red cabbage looks burgundy-coloured and cooks up purple! The first three taste relatively similar, with a familiar cabbage flavour. Chinese cabbage has a delicate taste and needs very little cooking. It's usually served raw in salads, or sautéed Chinese style. Red cabbage, however, is a real treat: it has a rich flavour and is a good winter vegetable.

Boiled White, Green or Savoy Cabbage

Allow 500 g (1 lb) cabbage for 4 people

1   Put 5 cm (2 in.) cold water in a pan and bring it to the boil.
2   Remove any discoloured outer leaves from the cabbage and discard.
3   Cut the cabbage into four and cut out the woody centre stalk and discard.
4   Shred the cabbage (*see page 54*) and wash it well.
5   Put the cabbage in the boiling water. Bring it to the boil again, then turn the heat down slightly so that the cabbage is cooking in bubbling water. Cook for 10–15 minutes or until done – green and Savoy cabbage will probably take less time than the harder white variety. Turn the cabbage half-way through if there's a large quantity in the pan and it's not cooking evenly. Taste to see that it is done (it tastes much better if it isn't overcooked).
6   Season with salt and pepper and serve immediately.

Braised White, Green, Savoy or Chinese Cabbage

1   Prepare the cabbage as described in the recipe for Boiled Cabbage above.
2   Place the cabbage in a thick-bottomed pan with 50 ml (2 fl oz) water and 1 tablespoon butter or margarine. Cover the pan tightly.
3   Bring to the boil, making sure that the fat has melted completely. Turn the heat down as low as possible and cook, covered, for 10–15 minutes or until done, remembering that green, Savoy and Chinese cabbage are likely to need less time than the harder white variety. Check occasionally to make sure that the water hasn't evaporated. If it has, add some more, a few tablespoons at a time.
4   When the cabbage is cooked, season it with salt and lots of black pepper and add some more butter if you like. Serve immediately.

Braised Red Cabbage

Red cabbage needs much longer cooking than other types, plus the addition of vinegar to bring out its rich flavour. If you cook it in the oven, you don't have to keep watching it. This dish also tastes just as good reheated.

Allow 500 g (1 lb) red cabbage for 4 people

1 tablespoon butter
3 teaspoons white or red wine vinegar or cider vinegar
Salt and pepper

1   Pre-heat the oven to 150°C (300°F, gas mark 2).
2   Prepare and shred the red cabbage as described in the recipe for Boiled Cabbage.
3   Place the cabbage in a thick-bottomed ovenproof saucepan with 50 ml (2 fl oz) water and 1 tablespoon butter or margarine. Cover the pan tightly.
4   Bring to the boil on top of the cooker, making sure that the fat has melted completely. Turn the cabbage over, ensuring that it's completely moistened with the butter and water.
5   Cover tightly and transfer to the oven. Cook very slowly for 1½–2 hours, stirring and adding extra water if it begins to dry out.
6   Ten minutes before the end of the cooking time, add the vinegar and stir in well.
7   Drain off any excess water, season with salt and pepper and serve immediately.

You may not have a pan that can go in the oven as well as on the hob – for example, it may have a plastic handle. If this is the case, put the cabbage in an ovenproof casserole and set aside. Melt the butter with the water in a small pan over a low heat, pour it over the cabbage and mix well. Cover and place in the oven.

Spinach

However much fresh spinach you buy, there never seems to be enough after you've cooked it. That's because it contains so much water that it reduces by at least half over heat. So allow at least 250 g (8 oz) per person.

Look for spinach that's not tired-looking, whether it's the large coarse leaves, or the small delicate ones. Ideally, the leaves should be bright green and crinkly. Make sure that you wash them thoroughly as they're usually full of grit.

Braised Spinach

Spinach can absorb lots and lots of butter. We have moderately suggested 50 g (2 oz) here, as some people want to live to a ripe old age . . .

1 kg (2 lb) spinach
50 g (2 oz) butter or margarine
¼ teaspoon ground nutmeg or 4 gratings fresh nutmeg (optional)
Salt and pepper

1   Put a large pan of cold water on high heat.
2   While it's coming to the boil, remove the thick stems of the spinach and wash the leaves in three changes of water. This is best done with the sink full of water and the leaves floating in it.

If you don't have a pan big enough to contain all the leaves, put in half and they'll immediately wilt in the water, leaving enough room to add the rest.

3   Put the spinach in the boiling water, return to the boil and simmer for 4 minutes if the leaves are large and tough, 2 minutes if they are small and more delicate.
4   Drain the spinach and plunge into a bowl of cold water. (This is known as refreshing – it helps vegetables to retain their vivid colour.)
5   Over the sink, squeeze the excess water out of the spinach rather as you would wring out the washing. This is the best way of removing as much water as possible.
6   Melt the butter in a large frying pan over medium heat.
7   Separate the spinach leaves a little and put them in the frying pan. Cook over a low-medium heat for about 2 minutes, stirring constantly so that the spinach does not colour.
8   Stir in the nutmeg and a little salt and pepper. When the spinach is hot and has absorbed the butter, serve it immediately.

Creamed Spinach

Vegetable purées are no longer the preserve of infants; they are becoming very fashionable in expensive restaurants. The preferred consistency is thick enough to spoon up – thicker than that of a sauce – but the choice is yours. The recipe for Fillet of Beef with Ginger and Garlic on a Bed of Creamed Spinach (*see page 241*) calls for the spinach to be thick enough to hold its form on a plate.

You can use frozen chopped spinach for this dish, even though it has lost some of its fresh taste. Defrost the spinach and add it to the melted butter at stage 4. It will take a bit of cooking, stirring continuously, to evaporate all the water.

For 4

1 kg (2 lb) spinach
50 g (2 oz) butter
150 ml (5 fl oz) single cream (or less, to taste)
¼ teaspoon grated nutmeg (optional)
Salt and pepper

1   Prepare the spinach as in the recipe for Braised Spinach (opposite) up to the end of stage 5.
2   Put the blanched spinach leaves in a blender or food processor and blend until they become a smooth purée.
3   Put the butter in a frying pan and melt over medium-low heat.
4   Pour the purée into the frying pan and cook, stirring, until any liquid has evaporated and the spinach is quite thick.
5   Pour in the cream and stir well. Let it cook for 1 minute. If you like its consistency, season with the nutmeg, salt and pepper and serve immediately. If you like a thicker consistency, cook the spinach a few minutes longer.

Onions

There are three types of white onion you're likely to come across: the common white onion, sold in its brown skin; the mild-tasting Spanish onion with a flat base, usually sold peeled; and the large Bermuda onion. The last two are better for cooking as a vegetable in their own right as they are not as sharp in flavour as the white onion, even when they are undercooked.

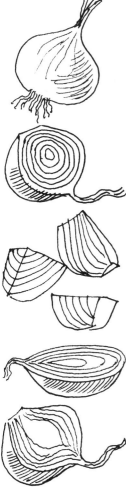

Braised Onions

For 4

500 g (1 lb) onions
2 tablespoons olive oil
Salt and pepper

1   Cut the onions in half and then peel them. Cut off the stem and root ends and discard. Cut the onions into chunks.
2   Put the onions into a thick-bottomed saucepan and add the oil and 1 cm (½ in.) water. Season with a little salt and pepper. Bring to the boil, then turn the heat down to low. Cover tightly with a lid and cook for 20 minutes, checking occasionally to make sure that the water has not evaporated. If it has, add some more.
3   When the onions are soft, take off the lid, turn up the heat to medium-high and cook, stirring constantly, to evaporate all the water. Serve immediately.

Fried Onions

Frying seems to be most people's favourite way of cooking onions, but it's regarded as more of a garnish for meat than as a vegetable dish in its own right. The thing to remember is that the more slowly the onions cook, the sweeter they'll be.

For 4

1 kg (2 lb) large onions
125 ml (4 fl oz) vegetable oil
Salt and pepper

If the onions begin to dry up, you can add a bit of water from time to time if you want a soft texture. Otherwise, you'll get a crisper burnt texture and taste if you cook them in the oil alone. Remember that the slow browning will make a mess in the frying pan unless you use a non-stick one.

1   Cut the onions in half lengthways. Peel them, discarding the stem and root ends, and slice them thinly.
2   Heat the oil in a large frying pan (preferably non-stick) over medium heat.
3   Add the onions to the pan and cook slowly, stirring frequently, until nicely browned and soft. This will take at least 15–20 minutes. Season with a little salt and pepper.
4   Drain on kitchen paper before serving.

Leeks

Leeks are a great British – sorry, Welsh – vegetable that should be eaten on their own more often. Watch out that you don't overcook them as they can become slimy.

Steamed Leeks

For 4

1 kg (2 lb) leeks or 1 medium leek per person
Salt and pepper

1   Put 2.5 cm (1 in.) water in a saucepan and place the steamer inside. Cover the pan and bring to the boil.
2   Chop the root end away from the leek and discard any discoloured outside leaves. Cut the leeks in half lengthways and wash well under running water. Make sure that you wash all the sand and dirt away.
3   Cut the halved leeks in slices.
4   Place the leek slices in the steamer, cover the pan tightly and steam for 10–15 minutes or until soft.
5   Season with a little salt and pepper and serve immediately.

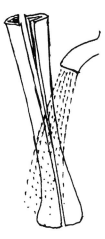

Braised Leeks

As with braised onions this method brings out leeks' sweetness.

For 4

1 kg (2 lb) leeks
50 g (2 oz) butter or margarine
Salt and pepper

1   Prepare and slice the leeks as described above.
2   Put the leeks in a thick-bottomed saucepan with half the butter, a little salt and pepper and 1 cm (½ in.) water. Cover tightly and bring to the boil.
3   Turn the heat down to low and simmer for 10–15 minutes or until the leeks are soft. Check to make sure that the water has not evaporated, and if it has, add a little more.
4   Taste a piece of leek to see whether it is done. If so, drain the leeks on a piece of kitchen paper. Then replace them in the pan with the remaining butter and return them to a medium heat. Stir until well coated with the butter and warmed through. Check the seasoning and adjust if necessary. Serve immediately.

Chicken

When you first begin cooking, chicken is cheaper to make mistakes with than most meat; it's also easier to get right. People who are interested in health (most of us, at least from time to time) appreciate that chicken is a good form of protein because it's relatively low in fat – discounting, of course, all the fat you might want to cook it in!

We'll assume that you're most likely to buy your meat in a supermarket or a butcher's shop and that you don't go down to the farm and get the farmer to sell you a fowl, freshly slaughtered and uneviscerated (the technical term for 'ungutted').

Although chicken is both cheaper than most red meat and extremely adaptable in cooking, there are two problems associated with it. It doesn't contain much fat, so when it cooks it dries out very quickly. Therefore don't overcook it with a dry heat. On the other hand, it has to be thoroughly cooked to avoid salmonella poisoning, which is quite common and very unpleasant. Getting the balance right between undercooking and overcooking needs a bit of practice.

The easiest cut of chicken to deal with is also, as you might expect, the most expensive: the boned chicken breast, also known as a *suprême* (pronounced 'soo-prem'). You may find it too expensive to buy on a regular basis, but it's good to start practising on as it takes such a short time to cook. Chicken breasts are dear because of the labour involved in taking the breast bone out. Conversely, a whole chicken is the cheapest per pound to buy. But if you don't fancy buying a whole one and cutting it up yourself, buy chicken pieces, unless you're going to serve Roast Chicken (opposite).

Grilled Chicken Breast

Photograph on page 51

Chicken breast is the cut that is most likely to dry out under the grill, so the trick is to keep the meat moist. You can use either butter or olive oil: they give two different but equally good flavours.

Successful grilling depends on balancing the heat of the grill with the distance of the meat from the source of heat. If you can't adjust the grill rack, you have to fiddle with the heat. Remember that you don't want a fierce heat on a breast that's barely 2.5 cm (1 in.) from the grill. So it's either a hot grill with the meat a good 7.5 cm (3 in.) from the actual heat source, or a medium heat with the chicken closer to the heat source.

The basic cooking method is given below, plus some serving ideas. Once you get the hang of cooking the breasts, you'll find that lots of different flavours go well with this cut of chicken.

For 4

4 boned chicken breasts
50 g (2 oz) butter or 4 tablespoons olive oil
Salt and pepper

1　Pre-heat the grill to its highest setting.
2　Wash the chicken breasts and dry with kitchen paper.
3　In a small frying pan melt the butter, if using, over a low heat.

If you don't grease the tray or rack, the chicken will stick to it and tear when you try to lift it off.

4　Grease the grill rack.
5　Place the chicken breasts on the rack. Then brush them with the butter or oil, season with a little salt and pepper and place the rack under the grill.
6　Let the chicken cook for 15–20 minutes on each side, brushing frequently with oil or butter.
7　Test the chicken breasts to see if they are done by piercing the flesh right through with a skewer or a thin-bladed knife. The juices which ooze out should be clear with no trace of blood. Do not undercook the chicken!
8　Serve with one of the following garnishes poured over:

Melted butter with a squeeze of lemon juice (to which you could add a pinch of paprika or a few chopped chives).

Plain yoghurt and chopped parsley seasoned with a little salt and pepper.

Garlic, Lemon and Parsley Butter (*see page 86*).

Roast Chicken

The thought of cooking a roast chicken is one of those things that often terrifies reluctant cooks. This is understandable – if something goes wrong, it's a pretty tangible failure, not to mention an expensive one. And usually you've got at least one hungry person waiting for the meal, only to be told that you're popping round the corner for a take-away. Actually, few things are simpler than roasting a chicken. The recipe below gives only very basic instructions; recipes for gravy, bread sauce and timings for a traditional Sunday Roast Lunch are given on page 138, and a recipe for Sage and Onion Stuffing is on page 93. It's a good idea to get in some practice on the main dish before attempting the whole complicated meal.

First, select the bird. For 4 people, choose a 1.5–1.75 kg (3–3½ lb) chicken, fresh or frozen. Signs of freshness are a plump breast, firm flesh, white unbroken skin with a bluish tinge and a pliable breastbone (give it a tweak!).

Supermarkets and butcher's shops nowadays sell both battery chickens (produced on the assembly line) and free-range ones. If you prefer to eat a chicken which has lived a happy life – relatively speaking – and whose flesh usually tastes more 'chickeny', and you can afford the higher price, choose a free-range bird. Alternatively, eat battery chicken

If you are cooking for more than 4 people, try a capon (a large chicken). Follow the method for Roast Chicken but allow 20 minutes per 500 g (1 lb) plus an extra 20 minutes. If you find yourself stuck cooking for more than 8 people, choose a young turkey and allow 20 minutes per 500 g (1 lb). Make sure that you read the section entitled Sunday Roast Lunch (*see pages 137–40*) for tips on timing.

during the week and reserve the free-range one for entertaining on the premise that your guests have highly developed palates. You can also base your choice on how much you're going to disguise the chicken with other strong flavours.

All chickens sold in the shops are completely gutted. Some may still have a little plastic bag containing the giblets (heart, liver, kidneys and neck) shoved in the cavity. Make sure that you *remove it first* before cooking the bird whole! If you are going to make a stock or gravy (*see page 138*), keep the giblets for this purpose.

If using a frozen bird, you must defrost it thoroughly first. This is best done by leaving it for 24 hours in the fridge. Place it on a plate as it will exude a lot of liquid which always seeps out of the plastic wrapping.

For 4

1 × 1.5–1.75 kg (3–3½ lb) chicken, defrosted if frozen
50 g (2 oz) butter, margarine or chicken fat
Salt and pepper

1   Pre-heat the oven to 220°C (425°F, gas mark 7).
2   Wash the chicken under cold running water inside and out. Dry it thoroughly with kitchen paper.
3   Rub the outside of the chicken with half the fat.
4   Season the chicken inside and out with salt and pepper.
5   Place the chicken breast uppermost in a roasting tin. Put the rest of the butter or fat on top of the chicken.
6   Place the roasting tin in the oven and cook for 15 minutes. Then reduce the oven temperature to 200°C (400°F, gas mark 6), turn the chicken on to its side and cook for a further 30 minutes. During the cooking time, spoon the juices that have collected in the bottom of the pan all over the chicken. (This is known as basting.)
7   Now turn the chicken over on to its other side with a fork and cook for a further 35–45 minutes. Again, baste the chicken from time to time.
8   To check that the chicken is completely cooked, stick a fork through the thigh at the end nearest the body and tilt the fork slightly to enlarge the holes. The juices that run out should be clear with no traces of blood. If the juices are slightly pink, place the chicken back in the oven for another 5–10 minutes and then retest.
9   Once the bird is cooked, remove it from the oven and place it on a warmed plate. Let it 'rest' for at least 10 minutes. This makes it easier to carve.
10 Poultry requires some sectioning as well as carving. The legs are cut into two – the thigh and the drumstick. Find the ball-and-socket joint which connects the leg to the body. Stick the point of the knife straight into the joint and cut through it. (If you're lucky, you might be able to find

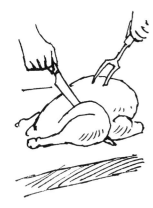

the gap between the ball and socket, which makes separation even easier.)
11 Separate the thigh and drumstick by cutting through the joint where it bends. The wings can also be cut off at the joint. You can leave the breast on the bird and simply slice down along it.

Chicken Pieces

Cheaper than chicken fillets and smaller than whole chickens are chicken pieces with bones in them – breasts, thighs or drumsticks. They are also very easy to cook, though they take longer than boned fillets (any poultry with a bone in will always take longer to cook).

In the following two recipes you can use either leg or breast meat; just remember that breasts take a shorter time to cook and dry out more easily.

Tandoori Thighs

This is a very easy way to enliven chicken. We recommend only very few commercial products, but tandoori powder produces a very good taste.

You can buy prepared tandoori powder in a tin. It's mixed with plain yoghurt, smeared on the chicken and left for many hours to marinate, so you need to plan the dish a day in advance. The amount of powder and yoghurt to use is given on the tandoori powder tin. The result is not quite like the tandoori chicken at an Indian restaurant – domestic ovens can't get the same heat – but it's still pretty good.

Serve it with a good chutney, plain Boiled Rice (*see page 116*) and a Green Salad (*page 46*). Alternatively, it can form part of an Indian meal (*see page 218*).

Photograph on page 135

For 4

Tandoori powder mix
Plain yoghurt
4 chicken thighs

1 In a deep bowl, mix together the powder and the yoghurt until completely blended.
2 Take the skin off the chicken completely. Wash the chicken and dry it well with kitchen paper. Make deep scores with a sharp knife almost to the bone so that the marinade can penetrate into the flesh.

3   Put the chicken pieces in the tandoori mixture and turn them over several times, making sure that they are completely coated.

4   Cover the bowl with clingfilm or a large plate and place in the fridge overnight, or for a minimum of 6 hours.

5   Pre-heat the oven to 180°C (350°F, gas mark 4).

6   Grease a roasting tin. Place the chicken pieces in the tin and pour over any mixture left in the bowl. Put the chicken in the oven and cook for 20 minutes.

7   It's difficult to tell if the chicken pieces are done by testing with a fork in the usual way, as the red of the tandoori mix masks any blood that may be present in the juice that you release. If in doubt, overcook rather than undercook. Once cooked, serve immediately.

Maryland Chicken

Maryland Chicken is like fried chicken but without the frying, with a crisp breadcrumb coating and tender inside.

For 4

4 chicken pieces
8 tablespoons flour
Salt and pepper
1 egg
Dried breadcrumbs
4 tablespoons grated Parmesan cheese (optional)

1   Pre-heat the oven to 200°C (400°F, gas mark 6).

2   Wash the chicken, and dry it with kitchen paper.

3   Scatter the flour on a large plate. Sprinkle a little salt and pepper on it and mix well.

4   Roll the chicken pieces in the flour so that they are completely coated. When you have finished, do them all over again. (The double coating of flour helps to seal in the juices.)

5   Using a fork, beat the egg with a little water and put in a shallow dish big enough to hold a chicken piece. Mix together the breadcrumbs and the grated Parmesan cheese (if using) and put on another plate.

6   Dip the chicken, one piece at a time, into the egg to coat it completely, then roll it in the breadcrumbs so that it's covered. Do the same with the rest of the pieces.

7   Grease a roasting tin. Place the chicken pieces on the tray and put it in the oven.

8   Cook for at least 20–30 minutes, depending on the size of the pieces. To check whether the chicken is cooked, pierce the flesh with a knife or skewer. If the juices run clear, it's ready. Serve immediately.

In the USA, cooks put the flour, salt, pepper and chicken in a paper bag, close the bag completely and shake until the chicken is well coated – hence the American fast food preparation with the brand name 'Shake 'n Bake'.

Meat

There's no doubt that meat is the easiest thing to cook – though by no means the cheapest – to get your protein. In this section the meat is divided up according to type. No exotic cuts are included, just the ones your local supermarket is most likely to have.

You may go to a butcher and see a huge variety of meat and simply not know what to buy. Don't worry, the butcher is there to advise you – all in the name of making a sale, of course. You will usually find, if you ask the butcher what cut he or she recommends for a particular method of cooking, that the more expensive it is, the less time it takes to cook. That's why stewing steak (cooking time about 2 hours or more) is much cheaper than a sirloin you shove under the grill for a few minutes.

If you're confused as to what you've dug out of the freezer because its label has fallen off, here's a bit of advice. If it's basically flat, with or without a bone, you can grill it or fry it (see Section Two of this book for other methods). If it's a big lump, you bung it in the oven and roast it. Presumably you can recognise mince!

This section is concerned with the most common cuts of meat, starting with those that cook most quickly, and ways to cook them.

Beef Steaks

Allow 125–175 g (4–6 oz) per person

Rump. A really meaty, tasty piece of beef which tends to need chewing well and in return yields excellent flavour.

Fillet. A tender steak, usually very expensive, which needs careful cooking as it doesn't contain much fat and therefore has a tendency to dry out.

Sirloin. Always a good bet. It's a piece of meat with enough fat running through it to keep it moist without being greasy. It has lots of flavour and enough 'chewiness' to make it interesting to eat without it being a chore.

Minute steak. A thinly pounded-out sirloin steak. It cooks very quickly.

You can either grill or fry steaks. The former is a better method for thin cuts of meat and it's healthier; the latter is more appropriate for thicker cuts.

How to Grill Steak

Only time and experience will equip you with the ability to cook steak to the degree that you like. You can grill a tomato and a few mushrooms at the same time if you wish (*see pages 69 and 133*).

1   Pre-heat the grill to its highest setting.
2   Season the steak with salt and freshly ground pepper.
3   Smear 1 teaspoon vegetable oil over both sides of the steak.
4   Put the steak on the grill rack. Place the rack under the grill 7.5 cm (3 in.) from the heat source. When the top has browned, turn it over and cook on the other side. It will take 3–5 minutes on each side. The trick is to cook the inside of the steak to the colour you like it without burning the outside. This will take practice and you may have to experiment with either turning the heat down or moving the grill rack down when the outside of the steak is sufficiently coloured.
5   Serve immediately with a lemon wedge or the Garlic, Lemon and Parsley Butter described below.

Garlic, Lemon and Parsley Butter

Photograph on page 51

Here is an easy butter to serve with steak or chicken. Prepare it before you start cooking the meat. It's easiest if you have the butter at room temperature.

For 1

1 tablespoon butter
1 teaspoon lemon juice
1 sprig parsley
½–1 clove garlic
Small pinch each salt and pepper (optional)

1   Put the butter in a bowl. Add the lemon juice and mash it in with a fork until well blended.
2   Wash the parsley, dry it on kitchen paper and chop it finely. Add it to the butter and mix it in well.
3   Peel the garlic clove and chop it finely or put it through a press. Add it to the butter and mix well.
4   Season with salt and pepper, if using, and form the butter into a neat shape with a spoon.
5   Serve the butter on top of the hot steak.

If you want to have this butter on hand in bulk, make up a larger quantity and freeze it as described below. You can then cut off slices and serve them as you need them.

125 g (4 oz) butter
Juice ½ lemon
2 tablespoons chopped parsley
2–3 cloves garlic, finely chopped
Salt and pepper

1   Prepare the butter as described above and roll it on a clean surface into a sausage shape with your hands.
2   Place the butter in the centre of a sheet of aluminium foil. Bring the edges of the paper together lengthways to wrap up the butter and twist the ends.
3   Place in the freezer until needed.
4   To serve, unwrap the parcel and slice the butter into 1 cm (½ in.) slices. Rewrap the remaining butter and put back in the freezer.
5   Place one round of butter on each steak to melt.

How to Fry Steak

1   Season the steak with salt and freshly ground black pepper.
2   Heat 1 tablespoon vegetable oil (or equal quantities of oil and butter for a more delicious flavour) in a frying pan over a medium-high heat until it is smoking slightly. If you use a non-stick pan, you need less fat. Make sure that the fat is hot enough before you put the meat in the pan: if you don't, the fat will be absorbed by the meat, making it greasy instead of sealing it.
3   Put the steak in the pan and cook for 2–4 minutes on one side or until browned. Turn it over and cook the other side. As with a grilled steak, you have to balance the heat of the pan so that the outside of the meat browns without burning while the inside cooks.
4   Serve immediately with a wedge of lemon, some Garlic, Lemon and Parsley Butter (opposite) or Sauce Lyonnaise (see below).

Sauce Lyonnaise

Here is an easy, rich-tasting sauce to go with pan-fried beef steak. Keep the steak warm while you make the sauce. Remember: don't wash the frying pan you cooked the steak in, as you will need the pan juices to make the sauce.

For 4

250 g (8 oz) onions
1 tablespoon French mustard
600 ml (1 pint) hot beef stock made with ½ stock cube
Salt and pepper
1 glass red wine (optional)

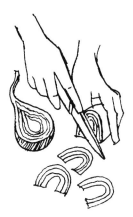

1   Before frying the steak, cut the onions in half lengthways. Peel them, discarding the stem and root ends, and cut into thin slices.
2   The pan you cooked the steak in should contain the fat and juices which exuded from the meat. Place the pan over

a medium heat and fry the onions in it. Cook the onions for 3–5 minutes so that they become soft but not too browned.

3   Add the mustard and mix it in well.

4   Pour the beef stock into the pan. Stir well to mix with the onions.

5   Season with a little salt and pepper, remembering that the stock will already be quite salty.

6   If you have a bottle of red wine already open, pour a glass into the pan. Turn the heat up to medium-high and boil, stirring constantly, until about half the liquid has evaporated and the sauce has thickened and become a little syrupy.

7   The steak will have given off more juice while keeping warm. Pour this into the pan and cook 1 minute longer.

8   Pour the sauce over the warm steak and serve immediately.

Lamb and Pork Chops and Gammon

Allow 1 large or 2 small lamb chops/1 medium-to-large pork chop/125–175 g (4–6 oz) gammon per person

There are three types of lamb chops suitable for fast cooking methods: cutlets, small and neat, which come from the bottom of the loin; larger coarser-tasting chops from the top of the loin; and leg chops or steaks, which are a bit of a chew but cheaper than the first two.

The best pork chops suitable for quick cooking are taken from the loin. Don't be tempted to buy pork leg chops or steaks as they are far less tender than loin chops.

You can grill and pan-fry lamb and pork chops using the same method as for beef steaks. Garnish with grilled tomatoes and mushrooms (*see pages 69 and 133*).

Grilled Gammon

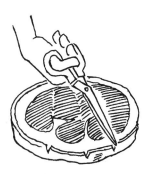

A gammon steak, another readily available cut which is suitable for fast cooking, is really a thick slice of meat from the back leg of bacon. If it still has the rind (skin) on it, snip through the rind in several places to prevent it curling up when cooking.

For 1

125–175 g (4–6 oz) gammon steak

1   Pre-heat the grill to its highest setting.

2   Put the gammon on a greased grill rack and place under the grill. Cook the gammon for 3–5 minutes on each side or until it is browned. Serve immediately.

Roasting Meat

Like roasting chicken, roasting meat is much less difficult than it looks. Once mastered, it's very hard to get wrong.

Only good-quality meat is suitable for this method of cooking. You're most likely to buy your joint from the supermarket or the butcher. Most supermarkets pack and label their meat for roasting; these joints should be easy to carve. If you buy your meat from a butcher, ask him or her to prepare the joint for roasting – for example, you may want the bone removed for even easier carving.

No matter which type of meat you're roasting, the same rules apply:

1   Always try to place the joint on a trivet or on a bed of root vegetables in the roasting tin. The joint should be dry-roasted all the way round, not braising its bottom in a pool of juices and fat.
2   Always pre-heat the oven. Put the joint into a hot oven (see below), let it seal (brown) for 10–15 minutes and then reduce the oven temperature slightly.
3   Season the joint with salt and pepper.
4   Baste the joint regularly to prevent it drying out (pork is the exception to this rule).

Many people fiddle about with foil, or three or four different oven temperatures during the cooking time. However, if you put the joint into an oven pre-heated to 220°C (425°F, gas mark 7), then turn down the heat after 15 minutes' cooking to 200°C (400°F, gas mark 6), and leave the temperature alone for the rest of the time, it will cook nicely whatever type of meat it is.

The amount of time required to cook a joint will depend on the type of cut, the weight and the shape. Below are some guidelines, but don't be afraid to experiment. To check whether meat is cooked, stick a fork into the deepest part of the joint and look at the colour of the juices which come out. *If you're cooking pork, make absolutely sure that there is no blood whatsoever in the juices.*

Obviously, the length of time you cook a joint will also depend on your taste: the darker and more well done you like your meat, the longer you need to cook it. The only meat you must cook thoroughly is pork; otherwise you can eat your meat as rare as you please.

The cooking times for meat roasted as described above – that is, started off briefly at 220°C (425°F, gas mark 7), and finished at 200°C (400°F, gas mark 6) – are:

Beef   15 minutes per 500 g (1 lb)
Pork   25 minutes per 500 g (1 lb) plus an extra 25
         minutes
Lamb   20 minutes per 500 g (1 lb) plus an extra 20
         minutes
Ham   25 minutes per 500 g (1 lb) plus an extra 25
         minutes

Roasting vegetables under a joint is a very easy way of cooking them as you can put them in with the meat and then forget about them. Choose carrots, parsnips, potatoes or swedes, or a selection of all of these. Peel and trim them and cut into even-sized pieces.

The Best Cuts for Roasting

Roast Beef

Beef should be lean, bright red meat with small flecks of white fat throughout. Recommended cuts for roasting are:

Rib. This traditional joint may be bought on the bone, or boned and rolled.

Sirloin. Situated in the middle of the animal's back, this lies between the rib cage and the rump. It is sold in a single piece for roasting either on or off the bone.

Topside. From the rear upper part of the back leg, this is leaner than the two cuts described above, with less marbling of fat. It is also therefore less juicy, so keep it well basted during roasting.

When you try roasting beef for the first time, don't worry about cooking Yorkshire Pudding, roast potatoes or any of the other paraphernalia that makes the traditional roast dinner so complicated. During the time that the roast is 'resting' (a waiting period after it is taken out of the oven, which makes it easier to carve), just boil a few vegetables like beans and potatoes. As you become less panic-stricken, add another item to the meal (try gravy first). Always remember to count time back from the moment you carve, not from the moment you take the roast out of the oven. The Yorkshire Pudding which follows this recipe is also an easy accompaniment to try once you feel confident about cooking the meat. It can go into the oven when the meat comes out to 'rest'.

Remember that it makes sense to cook a little more meat than you need because a larger joint dries out less easily and you can always use the left-over cold meat in sandwiches.

For 4

1 × 1.5–2 kg (3–4 lb) joint beef
Large pinch each salt and pepper
Root vegetables for roasting (optional)

1   Pre-heat the oven to 220°C (425°F, gas mark 7).
2   Calculate the cooking time according to the weight of the joint (*see page 89*) – you may need to weigh it if it is not pre-packed with the weight given on the label.
3   Wash the joint and dry it thoroughly with kitchen paper.
4   Rub the salt and pepper into the joint.

If you don't have any of these things, you can still cook a joint, but the bottom of the joint will get more browned and can become tough. Of course, some people like these bits! If you're cooking a joint with a bone in it, try to position the joint with the bone side down.

5   To cook the meat properly, put a trivet (or grill rack or similar rack) or a selection of peeled root vegetables in the bottom of a roasting tin.

6   Sit the joint firmly on top of whatever you've prepared so that it won't topple off.

7   Place the roasting tin in the oven and cook for 10–15 minutes.

8   Then turn the heat down to 200°C (400°F, gas mark 6). Cook for the length of time recommended for the weight.

9   During the cooking, baste the meat – spoon some of the juices in the pan over it to keep it moist.

10 At the end of cooking, feel the meat with your finger or the back of a spoon. It should be springy, not soft to the touch.

11 Lift the meat out of the pan using large spoons so that you don't pierce the flesh. Place on a large warmed plate, or on a wooden board placed on a tray – whatever the container, it must have a lip to hold the juice that will leak from the meat as soon as it leaves the oven.

12 If you have roasted vegetables under the joint, drain them on kitchen paper, then put them in a bowl in the oven – turned down to 170°C (325°F, gas mark 3) – to keep warm.

13 Let the meat 'rest' for 15–20 minutes before carving (*see page 140*).

Yorkshire Pudding

Yorkshire Pudding is very easy and your guests will be impressed that you've gone to the trouble of making it. The batter for Yorkshire Pudding is best made a few hours before you want to cook it. Even better, make the batter the night before and then it becomes one less thing to worry about. The puddings need to be put in the oven to cook 15 minutes before you're ready to serve the beef, so you can put them in while the beef is 'resting'.

Makes 4 large or 6 small puddings

125 g (4 oz) plain white flour
½ teaspoon salt
1 egg
250 ml (8 fl oz) milk
25 g (1 oz) vegetable oil or fat from the roasting tin

1   Sift the flour and salt into a large bowl.

2   Make a well in the centre of the flour. Crack the egg into this and pour in half the milk. Beat hard until the mixture becomes a smooth paste.

3   Slowly add the rest of the milk, beating all the time. The batter should be smooth and quite thin. Try to get rid of any lumps.

4   Alternatively, put the egg and milk in a food processor or blender and process or blend until well mixed. Then add the flour a little at a time, blending each time. Leave the mixture to 'rest' for at least 30 minutes, much longer if possible.

5   Pre-heat the oven to 230°C (450°F, gas mark 8).

6   Put a little oil into each of six Yorkshire pudding tins.

7   Place the tins in the hot oven to heat the oil and leave for about 10 minutes, or until the oil is very hot and spitting slightly.

8   Using a ladle or a measuring cup with a lip, pour equal quantities of the batter into each tin. Place the tins in the middle of the oven if possible, with plenty of space above, as the puddings rise and could stick to the top of the oven if they are on the uppermost shelf.

9   Cook for about 15 minutes, or until the puddings have swelled and are golden brown on top. (They will sink as they are taken out of the oven.)

You can either buy tins with four indentations which are sold specifically as Yorkshire pudding tins or, if you want a larger number of smaller puddings, you can use tartlet tins (in which case the cooking time will be shorter). If you're cooking a roast at the same time, do spoon some fat from around this into the Yorkshire pudding tins: it will give more flavour to the puddings, and it's cheaper.

Roast Pork

When choosing a fresh piece of pork, make sure that the skin (rind) is smooth, the fat firm and not flabby and the meat pale pink with a fine texture.

Here is a selection of cuts suitable for roasting:

Leg. This is the back leg of the pig. It is a lovely joint full of flavour with a well-developed texture. A whole leg weighs about 5 kg (10 lb), but you can buy half-legs in supermarkets and a butcher will cut a leg in half for you.

Shoulder. This is the front leg. Although it has plenty of flavour, it tends to be more chewy. Buy it bone-free.

Spare rib. This is the area above the shoulder – the neck and the top of the back. It has an abundance of flavour to match the amount of fat it contains. Be sure to cut off as much of the fat as you can see before you cook it.

Loin. This is the section of meat that runs lengthways down the back of the pig from the spare rib to the beginning of its tail, and widthways from the backbone half-way down the rib cage. It is a very tender joint which cooks and carves easily.

Many people enjoy pork crackling, the skin that becomes crisp when roasted. Remember not to baste the joint during cooking or you'll end up with soggy crackling.

In any case, you do not need to baste because the thick layer of fat beneath the skin will keep the meat moist as it cooks. Serve with Sage and Onion Stuffing and Apple Sauce (*see below and page 94*), both of which can be made while the roast is cooking.

It is possible to catch parasitic worms from underdone pork so, for your health's sake, *never undercook pork*.

For 4

1 × 2–2.5 kg (4–5 lb) joint pork
Large pinch salt

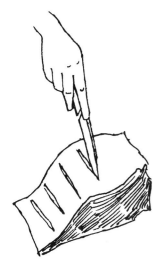

1   Pre-heat the oven to 220°C (425°F, gas mark 7).
2   Calculate the cooking time according to the weight of the joint (*see page 89*) – you may need to weigh it if it is not pre-packed with the weight given on the label.
3   Wash the joint and dry it thoroughly with kitchen paper.
4   Score the rind with a sharp knife.
5   Rub salt all over the rind, especially in the cuts in the skin.
6   Place the joint, rind uppermost, on a trivet (or grill rack or similar rack) in a dry roasting tin.
7   Place the tin in the upper third of the oven where the heat is greatest. (Adjust the rack if necessary.) This is to make sure that the crackling gets crisp.
8   After 15 minutes, turn down the oven to 200°C (400°F, gas mark 6).
9   Cook, without basting, for the remaining time. If the crackling looks as if it might burn during this period, move the meat lower down the oven.
10 Test the joint to see if it is thoroughly cooked by inserting a fork. If the juices run clear and you can see no trace of blood anywhere, take the joint out.
11 Let the joint 'rest' for 10 minutes before carving (*see page 140*).
12 Serve with the crackling (cut into strips), if desired.

Sage and Onion Stuffing

This is the traditional stuffing for pork; it also goes with roast chicken or turkey. If you cook the stuffing separately in a baking tin it minimises the chances of undercooking the meat.

The breadcrumbs are made by grating a loaf of bread with a grater or by processing it in a food processor.

½ small onion
2 tablespoons butter, margarine or fat from roasting tin
125 g (4 oz) fresh white breadcrumbs
Pinch dried sage or 2 finely chopped fresh sage leaves
Large pinch each salt and pepper

1 Chop the onion finely.
2 Put the fat in a small pan and melt it (if necessary) over a low heat.
3 Put the onion in the fat and cook for 3–5 minutes or until soft but not brown.
4 Add the rest of the ingredients and mix thoroughly. Be cautious when adding the sage as it has a strong flavour – put it in a little at a time until the stuffing has the taste you require.
5 Grease a small baking tin. Put the stuffing in the tin and smooth it down. Place it in the oven 15 minutes before the joint is due to be served. The stuffing is ready when it is firm and the top is browned.

Apple Sauce

Of course, you can buy apple sauce ready-made, but it is very easy to prepare at home. If you've been given a bag full of cooking apples in the autumn or you've gone wild at a pick-your-own farm, you'll be grateful to have something to do with them! In fact, some people buy a joint of pork simply because they have so many apples hanging about. Tart cooking apples, of which Bramley is a common variety, are the best to use. If you use an eating apple, don't add too much sugar.

500 g (1 lb) cooking apples
1 tablespoon butter or margarine
1 tablespoon sugar, or to taste
2 tablespoons water

If the lid doesn't fit tightly, put a piece of kitchen foil on top, then jam the lid down over it. If you don't have a lid at all, cover tightly with foil, then place a plate on top. The point is that none of the steam should escape.

1 Peel and core the apples. Cut them into quarters.
2 Put the apples, butter, sugar and water into a saucepan with a tight-fitting lid.
3 Put the pan on a low heat and allow to simmer gently for 10 minutes. Check from time to time to make sure that the apples are not burning or sticking to the bottom. If the liquid has evaporated, add a little more water.
4 The apples are cooked when they have completely broken down into a mush and no liquid remains. Taste for sweetness and add more sugar if necessary.
5 Serve the sauce as is, rough and ready, or push it through a sieve to break up the lumps. You can also process or blend it to achieve a smooth texture.

Roast Lamb

When buying lamb, look for meat that is dull red in colour with an even distribution of surface fat. Lamb is very fatty, like pork, but it's the fat that makes the meat juicy when cooked. Therefore do trim away excess fat (the enormous blobs), but leave the fat that's immediately under the thin paper-like skin.

Here is a selection of the easiest cuts for roasting:

Leg. This is the back leg of the animal. You can usually buy it in supermarkets boned or unboned – boned joints are easier to carve.

Loin. This is the portion of the back between the rib cage and the bottom of the spine. A single loin may be bought with the bone in, or boned and rolled.

Shoulder. The lamb's front leg, which is best bought boned and rolled as it's easier to carve.

Lamb is most often served plain or with Mint Sauce (*see page 96*). If the flesh has been flavoured with garlic or rosemary, it won't even need the sauce. Serve it with roast or boiled potatoes and other vegetables of your choice. Try to eat the entire joint at one sitting, as, being very fatty, it is not as pleasant when cold.

For 4

1 × 2–2.5 kg (4–5 lb) joint lamb
2 cloves garlic or 3 sprigs fresh rosemary (optional)
Oil
Large pinch each salt and pepper

1   Pre-heat the oven to 220°C (425°F, gas mark 7).
2   Calculate the cooking time according to the weight of the joint (*see page 89*) – you may need to weigh it if it is not pre-packed with the weight given on the label.
3   Wash the joint and dry thoroughly with kitchen paper.
4   If using garlic, peel each clove and cut lengthways into three long slivers. Make six incisions in the lamb flesh and push the garlic slivers in as far as they will go. If using rosemary, make incisions between the flesh and the skin and push in the rosemary sprigs.
5   Rub the skin with oil and sprinkle salt and pepper all over.
6   Place the joint on a trivet (or grill rack or similar rack) in a roasting tin.
7   Place the tin in the middle of the oven.
8   Cook for 15 minutes, then turn down the heat to 200°C (400°F, gas mark 6).
9   Cook for the remaining time. You don't need to baste lamb.

10 Test to see if it is done by pressing the meat with the back of a fork. If the juices which run out are pink, the lamb will be slightly pink: if you like it this way, remove it from the oven now. If you prefer your lamb well done, cook it until the juices run clear when you test the meat.
11 After taking the joint out of the oven, let it 'rest' for 10 minutes before carving (see page 140).

Fast Mint Sauce

Mint sauce, like apple sauce, is easily bought, but if you've got fresh mint in a pot or in the garden it's also easily made.

1 small bunch fresh mint
1 teaspoon (or more) caster sugar
75 ml (3 fl oz) white wine vinegar

1   Wash the mint and chop it finely.
2   Put it in a jar with a tight lid, or in a jug. Add the rest of the ingredients. Put the lid on the jar and shake hard, or stir well if using a jug.
3   Taste the sauce. If it's too acid, add a little water or more sugar. If it's too sweet, add some more vinegar.

Mince

The term 'mince' usually refers to minced beef, though you can also buy minced pork and lamb, which are more usually found in Continental dishes. Real purists will actually buy meat and mince it themselves so that they know exactly what has gone into their mince and can control its fat content. Many supermarkets sell ordinary mince, which is fairly cheap, and lean minced beef which, as its title indicates, comes from the leaner cuts of beef. Of course, it's more expensive. If you're not worried about money, use the latter. A vast amount of fat leaks out of ordinary mince when it's fried. It's not particularly good for you and it also makes the dish very greasy.

Hamburgers

Supermarket freezer cabinets are full of ready-made hamburgers, and if you like the taste of them, go ahead and cook them. Just don't expect us to tell you how, because we wouldn't eat them!

With a little time and effort (sounds familiar?) you can produce home-made hamburgers which taste 1000 per cent better than store-bought ones. They are also cheaper, you can freeze them, and they're not made from the nasty bits of the cow some of us would prefer not to think about.

The hamburgers may be either grilled or fried. Grilling is healthier as you do not need to add extra fat.

Makes 4

½ small onion
1 sprig parsley (optional)
250 g (8 oz) minced beef
125 g (4 oz) fresh breadcrumbs
2 tablespoons cold water
1 tablespoon margarine or soft vegetable fat
1 small egg
Salt and pepper
4 hamburger buns (optional)

1   Peel the onion, discarding the root and stem ends, and chop it finely.
2   Wash and dry the parsley and chop it finely (*see page 9*).
3   Put the minced beef into a large bowl and add the breadcrumbs, parsley and water. Using your hands (the best way), mix it into a mass so that the beef breaks up and is completely amalgamated with the breadcrumbs.
4   In a small pan melt the fat over a medium heat and add the chopped onion. Cook it gently for about 5 minutes or until the onion is translucent and soft but not coloured.
5   Add the onion to the hamburger mixture and combine well. Beat the egg in a small bowl, add to the mixture and mix thoroughly with your fingers until you can no longer distinguish any egg in the mixture. Season with salt and pepper.
6   Divide the mixture into four equal pieces and shape them into hamburger patties, about 7.5 cm (3 in.) across. If the mixture is a bit sticky, dust the palms of your hands with a little plain flour. These patties can be stored in the fridge, covered, but don't leave them for longer than one night.
7   To grill the hamburgers pre-heat the grill to its highest setting. Put the hamburgers on the grill rack and place it under the grill. Turn the grill down to medium. Cook the hamburgers on each side for 3–4 minutes or until completely browned. Make sure that they are cooked all the way through by pressing each one and checking that the juice which runs out is clear of blood.

Serve on toasted buns, if you like, with a variety of garnishes (lettuce, sliced tomato, fried onion slices – *see page 78* – ketchup, American-style relish and mustard are all traditional). Alternatively, you can serve the hamburgers without buns. Try pouring Sauce Lyonnaise (*see page 87*) over them.

8   If you want to serve the hamburgers in buns, toast the buns under the grill after you've turned the hamburgers over to cook the second side. Watch the buns carefully, as they burn very easily.
9   To fry the hamburgers, heat 1 tablespoon oil in a frying pan over medium heat. (If you have a non-stick frying pan you don't need any oil.) Cook the hamburgers on each side for 3–4 minutes or until browned.

Shepherd's Pie

For 4

1 stick celery
1 medium carrot
1 onion
2 tablespoons oil or cooking fat
500 g (1 lb) minced beef
2 tablespoons tomato purée
2 tablespoons flour
250 ml (8 fl oz) beef stock made from a cube (*see page 35*)
Salt and pepper
500 g (1 lb) potatoes
2 tablespoons butter

If you have left-over cooked potatoes, you have a good excuse to make this. Otherwise, you can boil the potatoes while the meat mixture is cooking. Make sure that you have an ovenproof dish deep enough to contain both a layer of meat and a layer of potatoes before starting out.

1   Wash the celery. Trim and peel the carrot and onion. Dice all three vegetables finely.
2   In a medium saucepan, heat the fat over a medium heat. Add the chopped vegetables and cook, stirring with a wooden spoon, for 2–3 minutes.
3   Add the minced beef and break it up with the wooden spoon. Cook the meat, stirring constantly, until all of it loses its pink colour.
4   Add the tomato purée and mix it in well. Then add the flour and mix well. Make sure that all the fat has been absorbed by the flour. Cook the mixture, stirring, for a few more minutes to cook the flour thoroughly.
5   Slowly add the stock, a ladleful at a time, stirring between each addition. Once all the stock has been added, season sparingly with salt and pepper – remember that the stock cube already contains a lot of salt.
6   Transfer the mixture to a clean pan. Turn the heat up so that the mixture bubbles gently. Leave it to cook, uncovered, for 20–25 minutes. It will thicken as the liquid evaporates. Check from time to time that the mixture isn't sticking to the pan and burning. If it is, add a little water, stir well, and keep stirring occasionally.
7   Wash the potatoes, peel them if you like (now or after boiling – *see page 58*), and cut them into quarters. Put them in a saucepan with enough water to cover them. Place the pan over a high heat. When it boils, turn the heat down and simmer the potatoes for 15–20 minutes or until soft.

If using cold left-over potatoes, melt the butter in a pan before adding the potatoes.

This dish can be reheated very successfully in a microwave oven. Cover and reheat on HIGH for 4–5 minutes or until it is hot all the way through.

8   When the potatoes are cooked, drain them and return them to the pan. Mash them by pushing them through a sieve or by using a fork or potato masher, getting rid of all the lumps. Add the butter and mix thoroughly.
9   Pre-heat the oven to 200°C (400°F, gas mark 6).
10 The meat mixture should be very thick by now. Spoon it into a deep ovenproof dish. Cover it with the mashed potatoes. Place the dish in the oven.
11 Heat through until the top is brown. Serve at once.

Fish

It's hard to get many people to eat fish, let alone cook it. Here's the sales pitch:

Myth	Fact
It's full of bones.	Some fish have lots, others very few. It depends entirely on the cut. Most fish steaks have no bones apart from the large central portion of spine. Fillets should not have any at all, though in practice the odd one sometimes remains.
It smells.	Again, it depends on the fish and how you cook it. Steaming, poaching or microwaving fish leaves hardly any smell.
It tastes too fishy.	Oily fish like herring and mackerel do have a strong taste. But the white fish have a very delicate flavour and are good for combining with other ingredients.
It's too messy.	Only if you gut and scale fish yourself, which is unnecessary as you can buy it ready-prepared.
It's too expensive.	Fish is not expensive when you consider how little is wasted.

Other plus points with fish are that it's very healthy; it takes only a short time to cook; and there are many more varieties of fish than there are of meat, so you're sure to find something you like.

Buying Fresh Fish

Most supermarkets have a wet fish counter and also sell cleaned, packaged portions, so there's no excuse not to try fish. However, if you do have a fishmonger nearby, you should go there instead as he or she will usually have more time to give advice and to prepare the fish in the way you want.

Pre-packaged supermarket fish, of course, looks easier to handle because it's been cleaned, gutted and scaled. But a fishmonger will also do all that for you for free, once you've chosen your fish. For the beginning of your fish-cooking career, you should arrive home with either fish fillets (without bones) or fish steaks (which usually contain only the spine in the way of bones).

Fresh fish looks and feels slightly slimy. The eyes should be clear and bulging and the flesh springy when you prod it. (If buying pre-packed fish, you can do this through the packet.) If you buy it at the supermarket, check that the sell-by date is still valid, as fish does not keep. Otherwise, smell it. Basically, if it stinks, don't buy it. If it smells of the sea, it's OK. Frozen fish fillets contain a lot of water.

Fish can be divided up into two main shapes, for simplicity's sake: round and flat. You can get both fillets and steaks from each shape but round fish give you thicker steaks and flat fish give you less bony fillets.

Below is a list of some of the most common fish and the forms in which they are most usually available. You should find these the easiest forms on which to start practising your culinary skills.

Allow 125–175 g (4–6 oz) per person

Cod – steaks and fillets
Haddock – fillets
Plaice – fillets
Sole, lemon and Dover – fillets
Trout – whole fish
Salmon – steak

The best thing about cooking fish is that it's easy and fast. In this section only grilling, steaming, microwaving and shallow-frying are covered.

You'll notice in this section (and in other recipe books) that the fish are interchangeable, which should help you when you go shopping. If you are looking for a particular type of fish steak, you can usually buy any variety and the recipe will work just as well. The same goes for fish fillets. That's because groups of fish have similar textures, so they are treated in the same way.

Grilled Fish Steaks

Grilling in this instance refers to fish cooked under the grill of an oven, not on an outdoor grill (see pages 219–21 for information on barbecues). You can use any fish steak for this recipe – the cheaper whiting, cod or haddock, or the more expensive halibut, salmon or swordfish.

Fish steaks are much more filling than you might think, because the flesh is dense. Make sure that you cook them all the way through: the thicker they are, the longer they take to cook. A thick steak will take *more* than twice as long as one half its thickness: see the chart below for suggested timings. Watch that the fish doesn't burn. If the top is getting brown too quickly, set the rack at a greater distance from the heat source. You can omit the flour and simply brush melted butter on both sides. If you use oil instead of butter, choose a light olive or a good-quality vegetable oil.

Grilling Times for Fish Steaks

Thickness of fish steak	*Grilling time (turning over at half-time)*
1 cm (½ in.)	4 minutes
2.5 cm (1 in.)	10 minutes
3.5 cm (1½ in.)	12 minutes
5 cm (2 in.)	15 minutes

Opposite: Spaghetti with Tomato Sauce (page 114).

For 4

4 × 125–175 g (4–6 oz) fish steaks
2 tablespoons plain flour
Salt and pepper
3 tablespoons butter or oil
Lemon wedges to serve

1 Wash the steaks and dry them on kitchen paper. Leave the skin on as it holds the steaks together.
2 Put the flour on a plate. Sprinkle salt and pepper on the flour and mix all together with the back of a fork.
3 Pre-heat the grill to its highest setting.
4 If using butter, put it in a small frying pan and melt it over a very low heat. When it's melted, take it off the heat and set it aside.
5 Coat the fish steaks completely with the seasoned flour by laying first one side, then the other, in the flour. Make sure that the flour adheres to the fish, but shake off any surplus. Place the steaks on a clean plate.
6 If using melted butter, dip the fish steaks into the frying pan, making sure that both sides are completely coated. If using oil, pour it into a saucer, then dip the steaks in.
7 Put the steaks on the grill rack and place under the grill.

If there is any butter left in the frying pan, brush it on the fish as it cooks. Do the same with any remaining oil. This stops the fish from drying out.

8 Cook on both sides, turning the steaks with a fish slice. See the chart on page 100 for cooking times. To tell whether the fish is done, try to remove the central bone using a fork. If it comes away easily, the fish is cooked. Once the bone is removed, you can also see into the middle of the steak: if the flesh is still slightly translucent, let the steak cook for a little longer.
9 Serve immediately with lemon wedges. You can also serve it with Garlic, Lemon and Parsley Butter (*see page 86*).

Opposite: Traditional Fresh Fruit Salad (page 120).

Salmon Steaks with Anchovy Butter

The combination of salmon and anchovy is an unexpected one. As salmon is expensive (though becoming less so), serve this on a special occasion. Don't feel obliged to buy wild salmon; farmed salmon is just as good (and costs less). Serve this with a Green Salad (*see page 46*), boiled new potatoes (*see page 58*) and a glass of white wine.

For 2

2 tablespoons butter
4 tinned anchovy fillets
2 teaspoons lemon juice
Pepper
Vegetable oil
2 × 125–175 g (4–6 oz) salmon steaks

1   Put the butter in a small bowl and let it soften to room temperature.
2   Drain the anchovy fillets of oil by patting them with kitchen paper. Put the anchovy fillets, lemon juice and pepper in the bowl with the butter and mash with a fork until all the ingredients are completely blended.
3   Pre-heat the grill to its highest setting. Grease the grill rack with a few drops of oil so that the fish steaks do not stick to it. Place a heatproof plate or a piece of aluminium foil under the grill rack to catch the butter.
4   Wash the salmon steaks and dry on kitchen paper.
5   Smear half the butter on the top of the steaks.
6   Put the steaks on the greased grill rack, buttered side up, place under the grill and cook until the top is browned. See grilling chart (*page 100*) for the correct cooking time.
7   Half-way through the grilling time, turn the steaks over with a fish slice, then smear the rest of the butter on them. Continue cooking until the fish is done.
8   Pour over the fish the juices and melted butter that have collected on the plate or foil under the grill rack and serve immediately.

Steamed Fish Steaks or Fillets

This is a good way of cooking fish as it treats the flesh delicately. Steamed fish is good to serve to invalids (as is most steamed food) because it's lighter and more digestible than food cooked in other ways, especially as it uses no fat.

If you have a steamer large enough to hold the fish, use it. (The little metal steamers which fit inside saucepans will do for one portion.) Otherwise you can use ordinary earthenware or glass plates – you can usually fit up to four fish steaks or two fillets on one dinner plate.

1 × 125–175 g (4–6 oz) fish steak or fillet per person
1 teaspoon butter
Salt and pepper
Few sprigs parsley (optional)
Squeeze lemon juice
Lemon wedges and chervil or parsley to garnish

Plate Method

1   Choose a saucepan with a width slightly smaller than the width of the plate you're going to use. Quarter-fill it with water and bring to the boil over the highest heat.
2   Meanwhile, wash the fish and dry it on kitchen paper.
3   Smear the butter very thinly over your chosen dinner plate and place the fish steaks or fillets on the plate.
4   Season them with salt and pepper and place a few parsley sprigs (if using) on top, plus a squeeze of lemon juice.

5   Place another dinner plate upside down on top, making sure that the fish is completely covered.
6   Sit the plates on the pan containing the boiling water.
7   Lower the heat to medium so that the water is boiling gently. Steam the fish until it feels firm to the touch and it's no longer translucent. This should take at least 15 minutes for a fillet and up to 20 minutes for a steak. If necessary, pierce it with a knife to make sure that it's cooked all the way through.
8   To serve, carefully remove the top plate and, using a fish slice, transfer the fish on to warmed plates. Add the juice from the cooking plate and then garnish with some wedges of lemon and a little chervil or parsley.

Steamer Method

For 1

1   Wash 1 × 125–175 g (4–6 oz) fish steak or fillet and dry it on kitchen paper.
2   Put 2.5 cm (1 in.) cold water in a saucepan and bring to the boil over the highest heat.
3   Meanwhile, sprinkle salt and pepper on the fish. Wrap it in a piece of aluminium foil with a parsley sprig (if using) and a small squeeze of lemon juice, making sure that it's completely sealed.
4   When the water boils, put the steamer in the saucepan and place the fish parcel inside. Cover the steamer tightly, turn down the heat to medium-high and cook for 15 minutes, or until the fish is done – you will need to check it after 10 minutes, following the instructions given in stage 7 above.
5   Serve garnished as described in stage 8 above.

Shallow-fried Fish Fillets

Photograph on page 52

The combination of browned butter, lemon juice and parsley with golden fish fillets is one of the greatest traditional fish dishes. This easy recipe is ideal for flat fish such as sole and plaice. Make sure that the fish has been filleted so that no bones remain. The fillets may still have skin on one side and you can leave this on while you cook the fish, and eat it if you wish. As there are no bones in fillets, they need to be treated gently before, during and after cooking so that they don't fall apart. A long fish slice is the best implement with which to handle fish.

It's easier if you try this dish for one or two people. Any more than that and a lot of cooking is involved as you usually cannot fit more than two fillets in a frying pan at once. Also, the cooked fish cool and dry out quickly if they are kept hanging about.

The only hazard in this recipe is that you might burn the butter, both while cooking the fish and while making the sauce. The heat should never be higher than medium-hot, never cooler than medium. Too low a heat will make the fish taste greasy and won't turn the butter sauce the right colour. If you can use unsalted butter, this will prevent the butter from burning at too low a temperature.

For 2

2 × 125–175 g (4–6 oz) fish fillets
1 lemon
2–3 sprigs parsley
2 tablespoons plain flour
3 tablespoons butter
Salt and pepper

1   Wash the fish and pat dry with kitchen paper.
2   Cut the lemon in half. Cut one of the halves into four thin slices. Using your hands or a lemon squeezer, squeeze the juice from the other half of the lemon into a small bowl, removing any pips. Set the juice aside. Then chop the parsley finely.
3   Put the flour on a dinner plate and dip both sides of the fish fillets in it. Carefully pat off any excess flour. Set the fish aside on a clean plate.
4   Pre-heat the oven to 140°C (275°F, gas mark 1).
5   Melt 2 tablespoons of the butter over a low heat in a large shallow frying pan.
6   Turn the heat up to medium. When the mixture is hot, slip the fillets carefully into the frying pan. Try to put the whiter side of the fish into the butter first: at this stage the butter will not have browned and will be relatively free of sediment, and this side of the fish will therefore look more attractive uppermost during serving.

7   Cook the fillets for about 3–4 minutes and then, using a
fish slice, turn them over. Cook the other side for 5–6
minutes, then lift the fillets on to a clean warmed serving
dish. Remove the pan from the stove without turning off
the heat. Do not wash the pan.
8   Put the fish fillets, whiter side uppermost, on a warmed
serving dish. Place this in the pre-heated oven.
9   Return the pan to the heat. Put the remaining butter in
the pan with a little salt and pepper. Stir the mixture until
it begins to foam. Pour in the lemon juice and the chopped
parsley. Stir again.
10 Remove the fish from the oven and pour the nut-brown
butter over the fish.
11 Serve immediately with the lemon slices on top.

Microwaved Fish Steaks and Fillets

Photograph on page 254

As fish has so much moisture, microwaving is one of the
best ways to cook it. It needs no extra liquid or fat, just
seasoning. Try to make sure that the fish pieces are about
the same size so that they cook evenly. The more pieces
there are, the longer they will take to cook.

Use the cooking time recommended below as a guide.
Towards the end of the cooking time, open the microwave
oven door (without pressing STOP) and check whether the
fish has cooked. If it has, it should have lost its
translucence and be firm to the touch. You may need to
pierce the fish to see the interior flesh. If it isn't quite
cooked, close the door and press START. You may need
extra time at the end.

To cook a single 125–175 g (4–6 oz) fish steak, place it
in a dish and season it with a little salt and pepper. Cover
and microwave on HIGH for 2–3 minutes. Half-way
through the cooking time, turn the steaks over. Serve
immediately with a squeeze of lemon.

If you are cooking more than one steak, arrange the
thick part of the steaks around the outside of the dish as
that is where the heat is concentrated. Add an extra
minute's cooking time, then see if the steaks are done.

The same method applies to fillets. Arrange thick
fillets, like cod and haddock, with the thickest part towards
the outside of the dish. With thin fillets, like plaice and
sole, you may need to fold the slimmer tail section
underneath the fillet so that it doesn't cook too quickly.
Season as above, cover and microwave on HIGH for 3–4
minutes for fillets weighing 125–175 g (4–6 oz). Half-way
through the cooking time, re-arrange the fillets on the dish
so that they cook evenly. Serve immediately with a squeeze
of lemon.

Smoked Fish

Britain must have more types of smoked fish than any other country in the world. Some of it we're used to eating as is, like smoked mackerel, trout or salmon. Other types need to be warmed through – the easiest ways are poaching, grilling and microwaving. The first two methods leave a fishy smell in the kitchen, the last is very clean. The methods given below (except for microwaving, of course) are the traditional ones for the most common smoked fish. Remember that no smoked fish needs any added salt!

Grilled Kippers

Kippers (smoked herrings) are very bony, though you can buy them filleted. Even with the bones in they are always popular, both for supper and breakfast. Serve with slices of buttered brown bread and cups of strong tea. As whole kippers are so big, you may have to cook them one at a time, and keep the cooked ones warm.

Kippers can be poached and microwaved as well as grilled – use the recipes following this one.

For 2

2 whole kippers
2 teaspoons butter

If you're grilling kipper fillets, smear the skinless side with butter and grill them for 4–5 minutes, skin side down. Make sure that you don't overcook them as they harden very quickly.

1   Pre-heat the grill to its highest setting.
2   Place the kippers, skin side up, under the grill and cook for 5 minutes watching them carefully to make sure that they do not burn as they begin to buckle.
3   Turn the kippers over and smear the skinless side of each one with 1 teaspoon butter. Cook for another minute.
4   Remove from the heat immediately and serve, or keep warm in a low oven until all the kippers are cooked.

Poached Smoked Haddock Fillets

When buying smoked haddock, try to choose the traditionally smoked, tawny, pale yellow fillets, *not* those that are a lurid yellow colour: they have been artificially dyed. Poaching smoked haddock (or kippers) gets rid of a lot of the salt in the fish. The poaching liquid can be given to your cat, if you've got one!

For 4

1 tablespoon butter or margarine
4 × 125–175 g (4–6 oz) smoked haddock fillets
Pepper
About 250 ml (8 fl oz) milk or water, or half and half

1   Smear the butter over the bottom of the inside of a wide shallow pan.
2   Lay the smoked fish in the pan. Season with pepper.
3   Pour the liquid over the fish so that it comes two thirds of the way up the fish. You may need extra liquid, depending on the size of the pan.
4   Put the pan on the stove and turn the heat up to medium-high. When the liquid bubbles a little, turn the heat down to medium-low so that it is barely simmering.
5   Cook for 3–4 minutes. If the fish overcooks, it will fall apart, so test after 3 minutes to see if it's done by flaking the flesh with a fork. If it flakes easily and the flesh has turned opaque, it's cooked.
6   Remove the fish from the cooking liquid, drain on kitchen paper if necessary and serve immediately.

Poached Kippers
Follow the recipe for Poached Smoked Haddock Fillets, using only water instead of half-water and half-milk.

Microwaved Smoked Fish

You can microwave whole smoked fish and fillets. Place the awkwardly shaped whole kippers in a loosely sealed plastic roasting bag (remember not to use metal ties). Fillets can be placed in a covered microwave dish. Cook 250 g (8 oz) smoked fish with 1 tablespoon water on HIGH for 2–3 minutes. Half-way through the cooking time, turn the whole fish over inside the bag, or re-arrange the fillets in the dish. Serve immediately.

Pasta and Rice

Pasta is the saviour of the reluctant cook. This must be true, judging by the number of people who can only cook spaghetti but who cook it all the time.

Pasta is available in all sorts of interesting shapes. It's usually eaten as a first or a main course with a savoury sauce and it's very, very filling. It has other virtues: it's fast, nutritious and extremely inexpensive. You could really eat it every day, with a variety of sauces, and never get tired of it – well, anyway, lots of Italians do.

Buying Pasta

You can buy either fresh pasta, limp and soft, which is found in the refrigerated section of your supermarket, or dry pasta. There is no shortage of fresh pasta shops in large cities, where they have sprung up recently. Fresh pasta tastes very nice (it has been enriched with egg) but it's quite a bit more expensive than the dried packet pasta. Until you master pasta, stick to the dried variety, which is actually equally good – it just tastes different.

The Italians have theories about what pasta shape should go with what sauce. For the time being, stick to spaghetti. Buy a brand whose label says it's made from durum wheat as it has the best flavour. The 2-foot-long packets of spaghetti look nice if you have a jar to keep it in, otherwise buy the shorter pasta; the long stuff usually gets broken in half when you cook it anyway.

Cooking Pasta

How much pasta should you serve per person? Of course, it depends on your hunger, but here's a guide: allow 75 g (3 oz) per person for a starter, 125–150 g (4–5 oz) per person when you serve it as a main course. When you are new to cooking, it's best actually to weigh it out, until you begin to judge by eye. Yet even the most experienced pasta cook can end up with half a pan of cooked pasta too much. Remember that pasta swells up enormously with water as it cooks. A small amount of dried pasta may look hardly enough to feed a child; once it's cooked you realise you haven't got enough sauce to go round! Don't try to brazen it out. If you've cooked too much pasta, don't put your sauce on all of it and hope that it works out, because it won't. The pasta will simply not be moistened enough and will be dry and boring to eat. It's more sensible to serve only the right amount and throw away the rest, or heat it up in the microwave later or turn it into a pasta salad.

This is the appropriate place to pontificate on Parmesan cheese. When you go to Italian restaurants and order pasta, the waiter usually comes round with the 3-foot-high pepper mill, plus a bowl of grated Parmesan. If the restaurant is half-decent, the Parmesan won't have come out of those cardboard tubs but will be freshly grated. And you can taste the difference. When you serve pasta, giving people fresh Parmesan makes a huge difference to the flavour of the dish. It's not pretentious and it's not more expensive. You can buy chunks of Parmesan in supermarkets very easily, and when it comes to unit price, it's a lot cheaper than the packaged stuff. Wrap up the chunk well in foil or clingfilm to prevent it from drying out, store it in the fridge and it will keep for months; a little goes a long way, too. As for effort, you don't really even have to grate the cheese beforehand. Put the chunk on a plate with a little grater (also widely available) and let people grate it themselves over their food. Please, give it a try!

When it comes to cooking pasta, there are two main pitfalls, both easily avoidable. The pasta can stick together in the pot, or you can overcook it so that it becomes waterlogged, soggy and disgusting to eat. If you use plenty of boiling water in which to cook the pasta, you will overcome the first problem. Even though a lot of water takes a long time to come to the boil, it's worth the wait to avoid having a mass of spaghetti stuck to the bottom of the pan. You can also add 1 teaspoon of vegetable oil to the water to act as lubrication.

You've probably tasted soggy pasta in canteens or restaurants where they try to keep it warm for long periods. In the first place, don't keep cooked pasta hanging about in warm water. Second, taste it at regular intervals while boiling to avoid cooking it for even a minute too long. (A timer is handy here.) This is where the magic term *al dente* comes in: the pasta should feel slightly firm when you bite it, not soft. It shouldn't taste raw, nor should there be a little centre pinpoint of white when you look at a piece of pasta in cross-section. If you want to try different shapes, bear in mind that the thicker ones – shells, twists or bows – usually take a longer time to cook than spaghetti, while tagliatelle or fettucine (noodles) take slightly less time.

Pasta is best served in large-lipped or deep bowls out of which it cannot slither on to the table and thence on to your lap. Whether you serve it on plates or in bowls, do try to warm the dishes beforehand as pasta loses its heat very quickly.

By the way, it's really worth buying a large colander or sieve for draining cooked pasta. There's nothing worse than using a strainer that is too small and watching your spaghetti flow out over the top and into the sink from where you have to retrieve it and wash the bits off.

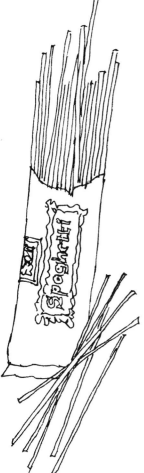

Spaghetti

For 4 as a main course

500 g (1 lb) spaghetti
1 teaspoon vegetable oil
Pinch salt

1   Fill up a large pan with lots of cold water – you need at least 1.5 litres (2½ pints) for 500 g (1 lb) pasta. Add the oil and a pinch of salt. Bring it to boil over the highest heat.
2   When the water is boiling vigorously, put the pasta in. You will have to bend it with your hands little by little so that it all curls round and fits into the pan. When it's completely submerged, stir the pasta so that the oil can get between the strands.
3   Bring the water up to the boil again. When it is boiling hard, turn the heat down to medium-high, so that there is a rolling (but not a fast) boil. Fork the strands apart.
4   Boil for 8 minutes, then taste a strand of the pasta. If it is cooked, it will be soft but not completely so – it will still have some resilience.
5   Take the pan off the heat and drain away the water over the sink using a large colander or sieve.
6   If you have to keep the pasta hot for a few minutes, put it back in the saucepan, pour over an extra teaspoon of oil and mix this in completely so that all the strands are coated. Cover the pan.
7   You can serve the pasta either into a big warmed bowl or into individual warmed plates. Spoon the sauce of your choice on top (see the following recipes for some suggestions) or mix it into the pasta.

Pasta with Sauces

The first two instant sauces given below are life savers when you have little inclination or time to cook. A green salad (*see page 46*), quickly thrown together while the pasta is cooking, is the best accompaniment to make a quick meal. If you have a little more time, try Spaghetti with Tomato Sauce (*see page 114*).

Spaghetti Carbonara

This was the dish Meryl Streep and Jack Nicholson ate in bed together in the film *Heartburn*. Think of it as eggs and bacon with pasta.

For 4

500 g (1 lb) spaghetti
1 teaspoon vegetable oil
Pinch salt

For the Carbonara:

4 rashers bacon
½ bunch parsley
3 eggs
Salt and pepper

1   Put the water on to boil for the spaghetti.
2   Meanwhile, cook the bacon (*see page 133*). When it's really crispy, drain it on kitchen paper until it's cool. Then crumble it up with your hands into little pieces.
3   Start cooking the spaghetti as described on page 111. Warm a bowl, large enough to hold the cooked pasta, in the oven at 110°C (225°F, gas mark ¼).
4   Meanwhile, wash and dry the parsley, if using. Chop it finely (*see page 9*).
5   While the pasta is cooking, beat the eggs together in a small bowl until the yolks and whites are almost completely mixed. Add salt and pepper, and the bacon pieces.
6   Decide whether you want dry or wet carbonara.

The trick is to end up with the texture of egg you like. Some people prefer their scrambled eggs runny, others like them dry. It's the same with carbonara.

7   To make dry carbonara, drain the pasta and return it to the pan. Pour the eggs over the pasta and place the pan over the lowest heat. Stir the mixture constantly so that the eggs cook and coat the spaghetti. When the eggs look cooked, but there is still a little wetness, pour the pasta into the warmed bowl, sprinkle the parsley over the top and serve immediately.
8   To make wet carbonara ensure that the serving bowl is really hot or you'll be left with a nasty puddle of uncooked egg at the bottom. Drain the pasta and put it into the bowl. Immediately pour over the eggs. Using two forks, lift the strands of spaghetti up into the air so that the egg mixture coats them. Keep lifting and separating until there are no slimy bits of uncooked egg left and the egg mixture has turned into a creamy sauce. Sprinkle the parsley on top and serve immediately.

Spaghetti with Oil and Garlic Sauce

This will sound weird if you've never tasted it, because there's not much to this sauce. But it's very popular in Italy, largely because it's so tasty and inexpensive. You have to take care not to burn the garlic: that's about the only thing that can go wrong. The red pepper is definitely optional, but you do have to use olive oil, preferably as green and fruity as possible, or it's not worth making.

For 4

500 g (1 lb) spaghetti
1 teaspoon vegetable oil
Pinch salt

For the Oil and Garlic Sauce:

2 (or more) cloves garlic
½ bunch parsley (optional but preferable)
6 tablespoons olive oil
1 dried red chilli pepper (optional)
Salt and pepper

1   Cook the spaghetti as described on page 111. Warm the serving bowl(s) in the oven at 110°C (225°F, gas mark ¼).
2   Meanwhile, peel the garlic cloves and chop them finely (*see page 9*).
3   Wash and dry the parsley, if using. Chop it finely (*see page 9*).
4   About half-way through the pasta's cooking time, heat the olive oil for the sauce over a medium-low heat in a small frying pan.
5   Add the garlic and the chilli pepper, if using.
6   Cook the garlic over a medium-low heat for 3–4 minutes or until it is soft but not coloured. Don't let it go brown or it will taste bitter.
7   When the spaghetti has cooked, drain it and return it to the pan in which it was boiled.
8   Remove the chilli pepper from the frying pan and discard, and immediately pour the garlicky olive oil over the pasta. Mix thoroughly with two forks (or whatever you find easiest) to make sure that each strand is coated with the oil.
9   Add the chopped parsley and salt and pepper. Mix again.
10 Serve immediately in the warmed bowls.

Spaghetti with Tomato Sauce

Photograph on page 101

There are many ways to make tomato sauce; the Italians leave theirs to simmer for hours. This is a quick one, using tinned tomatoes, and it tastes extremely delicious. Two good things about simple tomato sauces are that you can freeze them easily and you can add extra ingredients to dress them up. The variations follow the main recipe. Try to use Italian tinned tomatoes for this, as they usually have the best flavour.

For 4

500 g (1 lb) spaghetti
1 teaspoon vegetable oil
Pinch salt
Grated Parmesan cheese to serve

For the Tomato Sauce:

1 medium onion
1 carrot (optional but preferable)
1 stalk celery (optional but preferable)
2 cloves garlic
2 tablespoons vegetable or olive oil
2 × 397 g (14 oz) tins tomatoes
1 bayleaf
1 teaspoon dried oregano
Salt and pepper

1   First make the sauce. Peel the onion, discarding the root and stem ends, and chop it finely (*see page 9*).
2   Peel, trim and wash the carrot and wash the celery stalk, if using, and dice them finely.
3   Peel the garlic cloves and chop them finely (*see page 9*).
4   Put the oil in a medium saucepan over medium-high heat. Add the onion, carrot and celery immediately.
5   Cook the vegetables over medium-high heat, so that they are sizzling softly, for 2 minutes.
6   Add the chopped garlic and stir. Cook for 3 minutes or until the onion is soft but not coloured. Add the bayleaf and oregano.
7   Open the tins of tomatoes. With a sharp knife, cut the tomatoes into smaller chunks while they are still in the tin.
8   Add the tomatoes to the pan. If the chunks are still a bit big, mash them with a fork against the side of the pan. Bring the vegetables to the boil, turn the heat to low and cover.
9   Cook, covered, for 15–20 minutes, stirring occasionally so that the tomatoes don't burn. They will eventually break down into a sauce. If they look as though they are drying out, stir in 50 ml (2 fl oz) water.
10 While the sauce is simmering, cook the spaghetti as

This is just a quick way of making the tomatoes smaller so that they'll cook faster. It saves putting them in a bowl to cut them up!

described on page 111. If you allow about 8 minutes for the water to come to the boil, and 8 minutes to cook the spaghetti, the sauce will have finished cooking at about the same time as the pasta.

11 While the pasta is cooking, season the sauce with salt and pepper to taste. You can cook the sauce more quickly by raising the heat, but make sure that you check constantly that it's not burning.

12 Warm the serving bowls in the oven at 110°C (225°F, gas mark ¼).

13 When the pasta is cooked, drain it thoroughly and place in the warmed bowls. Serve with the sauce ladled over or mixed into the pasta. Sprinkle with grated Parmesan cheese.

Variations

Any number of additions will enliven this sauce. Add them after you've started to cook the tomatoes. Try the following:

1 × 200 g (7 oz) tin tuna, drained of oil or brine.

1–2 tablespoons capers, drained and rinsed.

10 black olives, stoned and halved.

1 chilli pepper (take it out before you serve the pasta).

3 bacon rashers, grilled and crumbled into pieces.

Rice

More controversy surrounds the cooking of rice than any other food, it seems. And when it fails, it fails spectacularly – burned to the bottom of the pan, either crunchy or sloppy, or clumped in claggy lumps. That's why, when people find a foolproof method, they stick to it and extol its virtues to the exclusion of all other methods.

As in all cooking, there is no scientific, failsafe way of guaranteeing fluffy rice on every occasion. But the following are three ways of cooking it successfully most of the time. It's a question of finding what's best for the type of rice you buy. If you want rice whose grains remain separate, use a long-grain variety – patna is the most common.

Rice is usually measured by volume, unlike other dry ingredients which tend to be measured by weight. That's because the ratio of liquid to rice is important – too much and the rice becomes mushy, too little and it's hard. We recommend a ratio of 1 volume rice to 2 volumes liquid. However, you can cut down on the amount of water needed if you soak the rice, both white and brown, in several changes of cold water for about 30 minutes before cooking. This washes off the starch that makes the grains stick together as the water is absorbed during the cooking process. If you're in a hurry, you can simply rinse the rice in a sieve. You may eventually be able to reduce the ratio to 1 volume rice to 1⅓ volumes liquid. Replacing the water with chicken stock results in a lovely savoury rice.

The methods given work equally well for brown long-grain rice as for white. However, you have to cook brown rice for a longer time.

Boiled Rice

Use as shallow a saucepan as possible for the rice. The pan must have a lid: if it does not fit properly, place a piece of aluminium foil tightly over the top of the pan, then place the lid on top and press it down.

For 4

300 ml (10 fl oz) white long-grain rice
600 ml (1 pint) water
½ teaspoon salt (optional)

1   Measure the rice in a measuring cup. Place in a medium, lidded saucepan.
2   Measure the water and pour it into the saucepan. Add the salt, if using. Cover the pan tightly with its lid.
3   Place the saucepan over a high heat until the water boils, then turn the heat down as low as possible.

Brown rice takes at least 40 minutes to cook using this method.

4   Simmer the rice for 20 minutes undisturbed.
5   The rice is cooked when the liquid has been completely absorbed, there are small indentations on the top of the rice and it is soft but still has a little 'bite' when tasted.
6   Serve immediately.

Baked Rice

As the rice is cooked in the oven in this method, you have to use a completely ovenproof casserole dish with a lid. The water is boiled before being added to the rice. Depending on the reliability of your oven, you may need

Brown rice will take at least 45 minutes to cook using this method.

less or more time to cook the rice than indicated below. Test it after 20 minutes and keep testing at 5-minute intervals until it is cooked.

For 4

600 ml (1 pint) water
300 ml (10 fl oz) white long-grain rice
½ teaspoon salt (optional)

1   Pre-heat the oven to 170°C (325°F, gas mark 3).
2   Measure the water and boil it in a kettle.
3   Meanwhile, measure the rice in a measuring cup and place it in the casserole dish. Add the salt, if using.

The rice is cooked when the liquid has been completely absorbed, there are small indentations on the top of the rice and it is soft but still has a little 'bite' when tasted.

4   When the kettle boils, pour the water into the casserole, put the lid on and place the casserole immediately in the oven.
5   Cook undisturbed for 20–25 minutes. Serve immediately.

Microwaved Rice

This is a highly successful and tidy way of cooking rice. However, timings depend on your own microwave and the shape of container you cook the rice in (a shallow round container results in the shortest cooking time). If the rice is still a little undercooked after the standing time, re-cover it and give it an extra minute on microwave HIGH.

For 4

450 ml (15 fl oz) water
300 ml (10 fl oz) white long-grain rice
½ teaspoon salt (optional)

The same quantity – 300 ml (10 fl oz) – of brown rice needs 600 ml (1 pint) water and will take 14–16 minutes' cooking on microwave HIGH, plus 4 minutes' standing time.

1 Measure the water and boil it in a kettle.
2 Meanwhile, measure the rice and pour it into a microwave dish. Add the salt, if using.
3 When the kettle boils, pour the water into the dish.
4 Cover the dish loosely, either with a lid or with microwave-safe clingfilm.
5 Microwave on HIGH for 10–12 minutes.
6 Remove from the oven and let it stand for 5 minutes to cook further.
7 Serve immediately.

Reheating Rice in a Microwave

Any type of cooked rice can be reheated very easily in a microwave. Put the rice in a microwave dish and cover loosely with a lid or with microwave-safe clingfilm. Allow a minimum of 1 minute on microwave HIGH, more if there is a lot of rice. Stir before serving.

Fresh Fruit

If you've succeeded in making one or two savoury courses really well, you're likely to want to take a rest when it comes to the pudding. This is where fruit is invaluable.

Fresh fruit, at its best, tastes better than any pudding, so there's no shame in serving it, even to guests. And it's very easy to make fruit look good. Just think of all the 'still lifes' hanging in galleries. Artists know that fruit on its own in a bowl needs little adornment: they don't paint dishes of Peach Melba, do they?

Buying

When buying fruit, you'll find that nowadays there's a year-round abundance of almost everything. Supermarkets, particularly, stock a wide range of exotic fruits. Beware, however: if a fruit is not in season – in other words, if it's forced under glass – it's likely to be tasteless. You don't want to arrive home with punnets of expensive American strawberries in January only to find them all texture and no flavour. Do buy domestic fruit in the appropriate season, especially if you're going to serve it raw as a pudding.

Here are some guidelines to help you when buying fruit:

1   If you're going to eat fruit on the day of purchase, you can afford to buy it absolutely ripe. This is especially true of soft-fleshed fruit, like apricots, peaches and plums. Otherwise, buy the fruit a little hard and let it ripen at home.
2   Naturally crisp fruit should feel firm to the touch, naturally soft fruit should give slightly when you press it.
3   Good specimens should have smooth, unblemished skin and should smell fresh. They should, where applicable, have a vibrant colour.
4   Try to sample all the different varieties of each fruit to find the one you like best. Don't just stick to Golden Delicious apples, for example, when Cox's or Spartans are in the shops.
5   Buy fruit in small quantities so that you can be sure you will eat it before it goes bad or dries up.
6   Soft-fleshed fruit from the Mediterranean usually has a more intense flavour than the home-grown variety as it's had more sun to bring out the sugar.
7   If you find yourself at a pick-your-own farm, don't go overboard and buy vast quantities of fruit. Unless you want to make lots of jam, you will find that your fruit will rot long before you have a chance to eat it.

Storing

You've bought your fruit. How do you make sure that it will last until you want it?

1   Soft-fleshed fruit, like peaches, that are ripe when purchased need to be eaten within 24–48 hours. Don't store them in the fridge unless there's a heat wave. If the

fruit are very ripe, don't place them on top of each other as that hastens decay.
2   Berries should be separated out and put on a plate for storage. Don't let them sit on top of each other and don't wash them until you are ready to eat them. Keep them in a cool dark place.
3   Thick-skinned fruit survive perfectly well unrefrigerated. Oranges, lemons, pineapples and so on are fine left in bowl on the table, provided that it's not in the sun. Otherwise, you can put them in the vegetable drawer in the fridge.
4   Apples can last a few weeks at least if they're wrapped individually in newspaper and stored in a cool, dry place. You can keep them in a bowl if you're going to eat them within a week or so.

Preparing

Wash all fruit thoroughly and dry it on kitchen paper before eating or preparing it. The only exceptions to this rule are raspberries, blackberries and loganberries, which can become mushy and deteriorate in contact with water. Obviously, you don't need to wash fruit whose peel or skin you throw away.

Always use a stainless-steel knife to cut fruit. The acid in the fruit can discolour other metals which in turn can leave stains on the flesh. A lot of fruit – apples, pears, bananas (as well as avocados) – turns brown when it is cut open. To prevent discoloration, have ½ lemon ready to rub on the cut sides of the fruit as soon as you slice it. If you're going to cut fruit in advance of a meal, you can sprinkle lemon juice on the cut sides, then put the fruit on a plate and cover it with clingfilm. This will prevent oxygen from reaching the fruit and browning it further. Alternatively, slices of hard fruit like apples and pears can be put into a bowl of water which has been acidulated with 1 tablespoon lemon juice or vinegar. You obviously don't have to worry about fruit containing a lot of natural acid, such as citrus fruit or berries.

To prevent fruit from drying out once you've cut it, put it on a plate and cover it with a piece of kitchen paper soaked in water then squeezed dry. Put the fruit in the fridge until you need it. This will keep it moist for several hours.

Serving

There are various ways of serving fresh fruit, all equally easy. You can either put a selection of fruit in a bowl and let people choose for themselves; or you can serve one fruit by itself, sliced (pineapple, for instance) or whole (for example, a bunch of grapes immersed in a bowl of iced water).

Traditionally, the British like summer berries served with a sprinkling of sugar and single or double cream. Make sure that you allow the fruit to come up to room temperature if it has been stored in the fridge, and that the cream isn't cold either (unless you like it like that). Serve the berries either in a big bowl or in individual ones (if you fear the greed of your diners!) and hand round the cream separately. Of course, peaches, apricots and nectarines are equally nice served in this way; they just require that you cut them up beforehand.

Alternatives to fresh cream are commercial sour cream, yoghurt (the thick-set Greek type for preference) and *fromage blanc*. (See page 258 for another interesting accompaniment for berries.)

Traditional Fresh Fruit Salad

Photograph on page 102

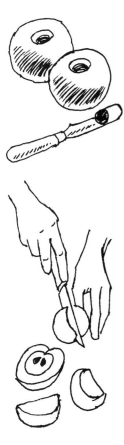

After a heavy meal, fruit salad should be a welcome pudding, both for its lightness and its refreshing taste. When it's good, it's fantastic. More often than not, unfortunately, it's served because people can't think of anything else. If you really don't like fruit salad, feel free to hand round a bowl of mixed fruit. However, with a variety of really ripe fruit, you can create a surprisingly lovely dish.

As the fruits in this salad don't give off their own juice, they are served in a light sugar syrup. You can substitute all sorts of other ripe fruit for the ones suggested below: there's no one recipe for fruit salad. Just bear in mind the importance of including several different colours and textures. You can serve this salad on its own or with single cream.

For 4

2 eating apples (ideally 1 red and 1 green)
2 pears
50 g (2 oz) grapes (ideally half green and half black)
2 oranges
1 banana
1 sprig fresh mint (optional)

For the syrup:

125 g (4 oz) white sugar
300 ml (10 fl oz) water
1 lemon
¼–½ teaspoon vanilla essence

1 First make the syrup, as it needs to cool before you add the fruit. Put the sugar and water into a saucepan and bring it to the boil over a high heat
2 When the water has come to the boil, turn down the heat so that the water is simmering gently. Cook, uncovered, for 8–10 minutes, stirring occasionally to make sure that the sugar has completely dissolved.
3 Take the sugar syrup off the heat and let it cool to room temperature.
4 Squeeze the juice from the lemon, discarding any pips, and add it to the cooled syrup, together with the vanilla essence.
5 Meanwhile, prepare the fruit. Wash the apples, pears and grapes.
6 Core but do not peel the apples and pears.
7 Cut the apples in half from top to bottom and then cut across the fruit into slices about 6 mm (¼ in.) thick. Place the slices in a bowl large enough to hold all the fruit.
8 Do the same with the pears.

9 Add enough of the sugar syrup to cover the fruit.
10 Peel the oranges and remove the pith completely, discarding the pips. You can either cut the oranges in horizontal slices or in segments. Add the orange pieces to the salad bowl.
11 Gently remove the grapes from the bunch. If they are not seedless, cut them in half and remove the pips. Add the grapes to the bowl.
12 Finally, peel the banana and slice into 6 mm (¼ in.) pieces. Add to the rest of the fruit. Using a spoon, thoroughly mix the fruit together.
13 Add more syrup to cover the salad.
14 Leave the salad to chill in the fridge for at least 1 hour so that the flavours can develop.
15 Just before serving, garnish with the sprig of mint (if using).

Yoghurt Fruit Salad

This is an aromatic salad to be made in strawberry season. You can use slightly over-ripe berries if necessary (cutting out any squashy bits), as they'll be sliced into the yoghurt. The crucial ingredients are bananas and strawberries, but you can use other types of soft-fleshed fruit as well, such as peaches and nectarines. The amount of honey you add depends on the sharpness of the yoghurt. Add it little by little and taste as you go along; the same applies to the spices and orange juice.

For 4

1 × 450 g (15.9 oz) carton plain yoghurt
2 oranges
4 tablespoons runny honey
2 eating apples
2 large bananas
1 × 250 g (8 oz) punnet strawberries
1½ teaspoons powdered cinnamon
½–1 teaspoon powdered cloves

1 Pour the yoghurt into a bowl large enough to hold all the fruit.
2 Squeeze the juice from the oranges into the bowl, discarding the pips.

If you use the Greek thick-set yoghurt, you may need to add extra orange juice to thin the mixture down. It should be like soup.

3 Add the honey and mix thoroughly to combine all the ingredients.
4 Wash the apples, core and slice them thinly or cut them into small chunks. Add these to the yoghurt mixture.
5 Peel the bananas, slice them into 6 mm (¼ in.) rounds and add them to the mixture.

121

6   Quickly wash the strawberries and drain them on kitchen paper. Remove the green stem and woody core with a small knife. (This is known as hulling.) Roughly quarter them and add to the bowl.

7   Add the cinnamon and cloves to the bowl and mix thoroughly so that the spices are spread evenly throughout and the fruit is completely coated with the mixture.

8   Taste the liquid. Add extra honey, orange juice or spices to your taste.

9   You can serve this salad immediately. However, it is better if you cover and refrigerate it so that the flavours can mingle and the strawberries can tint the yoghurt pink.

Baked Apples and Custard

This must be one of the easiest and most foolproof recipes imaginable. Make sure that you use cooking apples (Bramleys for preference) as they expand during cooking and the flesh achieves the right degree of fluffiness. Instead of using whole cloves you can, if you wish, add 1 teaspoon powdered cloves to the sugar/sultana mixture. Take care not to add too much as they have an overpowering flavour.

For 4

4 medium-sized cooking apples
50 g (2 oz) brown sugar
50 g (2 oz) sultanas or raisins
4 whole cloves
4 tablespoons water
2 tablespoons butter

1   Pre-heat the oven to 230°C (450°F, gas mark 8).

2   Cut four squares of aluminium foil large enough to fit round the bottom of each apple to form a cup that reaches one third of the way up the fruit.

3   Wash the apples and core them to create space for the filling ingredients.

4   Make a shallow horizontal cut around the outside of each apple about half-way between the base and the top. If you don't do this, the apple may burst out of its skin as it cooks. Place each apple on a square of foil, wrap the foil around the bottom of the fruit to form a cup and place on a baking tray.

5   In a small bowl mix the sugar and sultanas together.

6   Divide this mixture into four and stuff each apple with it.

7   Bury a clove in the centre of the sugar/sultana mixture in each apple.

8   Pour 1 tablespoon water into each of the apples.

9   Top each apple with ½ tablespoon butter.

Foil is used to catch the aromatic juices that come out of the bottom of the apples. If you don't use foil, cook the apples in an ovenproof dish and simply drain the juices from this over the apples when serving.

10 Place the baking tray in the oven and cook for 30–40 minutes, or until the apples are done – they should be bulging out from the cut round the centre and be very soft to the touch.

11 Carefully lift the apples from the foil and place on warmed individual serving plates, taking care not to spill any of the juices in the foil. Pour the juices over the apples.

12 Serve immediately on their own or with cream, ice-cream or custard (see following recipe).

To microwave: Although it doesn't produce quite the same flavour, microwaving baked apples takes a much shorter time than conventional cooking. Prepare the apples up to stage 9 of the above recipe but omit the foil – just place the apples in a buttered microwave dish. Microwave on HIGH for 9 minutes.

Custard from a Powder

Tins of custard powder are readily available across the country. The cooking instructions are on the back, but here are extra tips to make sure you get it right.

1 Use whole (full-fat) milk, not semi-skimmed or skimmed. The latter two do not contain enough fat to thicken the custard. (You can stir until you're blue in the face and nothing will happen!)

2 600 ml (1 pint) milk makes enough custard for four people.

3 Mix the initial powder/milk paste in a big jug as you'll eventually be pouring the heated milk from the saucepan into it.

4 When you make the starter paste using 1–2 tablespoons of the milk and 1 tablespoon custard powder, you'll find that it's very stiff as the starch in the powder quickly absorbs the liquid. Add a little more cold milk to thin it out. You have to get rid of the lumps *now* – you can't get them out later. You should end up with a few tablespoons of smooth liquid.

5 Heat the rest of the milk until it comes to a slight rolling boil. It shouldn't boil violently or become frothy. Now add 1 tablespoon sugar (caster dissolves more quickly), then taste the mixture. Add extra sugar if you want it.

6 Pour the milk into the jug containing the paste. Stir well so that there are no lumps.

7 Pour the milk back into the saucepan and cook it over medium heat, stirring constantly with a wooden spoon. The custard should thicken as it cooks. It's ready when its thick enough to coat the back of a spoon, but thin enough to pour easily. Serve immediately.

Bread

Of all the countries in Europe we eat the least bread. There's none of this fresh three-times-a-day stuff, as enjoyed by the French. Yet we actually have a better variety of bread in Britain: not just the traditional cobs and twists and farmhouse loaves, but all the Greek, German, Polish, Arab and Jewish breads as well. We are spoiled for choice, and we largely ignore it.

Bread is good for you. It fills you up at little cost and it tastes fantastic – at least, a lot of it does. It is also the essential ingredient of bread sauce and bread and butter pudding. Bought bread is, of course, effortless to serve.

Bread keeps best if it's sealed loosely in a plastic bag and left at room temperature, not in the fridge. If you see any specks of mould, throw the bread away immediately. Pre-sliced bread does keep better than whole loaves because it usually contains preservatives. You may wish to buy small whole loaves which you can eat quickly, and keep a sliced loaf ready for emergencies.

Here are some guidelines for serving bread:

1   Try not to serve pre-sliced bread to guests. It's fine for sandwiches but it's normally very bland and does nothing to enhance the taste of a dish.
2   Warm bread speaks volumes. Wrap a loaf in foil to stop it from drying out and place it in a pre-heated oven at 200°C (400°F, gas mark 6) for 10–15 minutes. Slice it at the table. Alternatively, warm crusty rolls in the same way. Bring them to the table wrapped in a clean teatowel to conserve their heat.
3   You can buy part-baked rolls and loaves and use them immediately or freeze them until you need them. They taste more freshly baked than ordinary fresh bread. Bake them for 8–10 minutes in an oven pre-heated to 220°C (425°C, gas mark 7). They can be baked straight from the freezer.
4   If your bread is slightly stale, you can serve it as warm toast instead. Cut the bread into triangles after toasting. Alternatively, you can pop stale bread in the microwave to revive it: microwave on HIGH for 20 seconds. Toast can also be reheated in the microwave – use the same method as for stale bread.

Real French baguettes (as opposed to long French sticks) are now found in a major nationwide food and clothing chain. They're made with real French flour and are worth buying for a treat. They're good eaten at any stage of a meal, especially at the beginning with unsalted butter. If you're a real francophile, you can even dip a baguette in your café au lait! The only drawback is that they stale within a day.

Pitta bread (Arab) can double for the Indian bread (or nan) if you want to serve it with Curried Lentil Soup (*see page 39*), or as part of an Indian meal (*see page 218*). It's also good with dips and salads and can be used as another implement to help shovel the food in!

Light or dark rye bread is good for making sandwiches with strong-tasting fillings and garnishes. It's also good with spicy (not Indian) dishes. It has a strong flavour, so it shouldn't be eaten with mild cheese as it will mask the taste.

Warm crusty wholemeal or brown rolls, available in most supermarkets, are excellent for serving with soups or cheese. There's little waste involved as you are not left with sliced bread drying out.

Garlic and Herb Bread

It takes very little time to make this snack, and it's a lot less expensive than buying a prepared loaf. Choose either a French stick (not a real French baguette) or a Vienna twist. The loaf should be white, long and with a good crust to keep the inside moist. Remember that the garlic doesn't really cook, so it stays at its most pungent. It takes days for the smell to disappear from the breath! The loaf should be finished in one sitting (which shouldn't be too much of a problem) as it tastes unpleasant when cold.

For 1 loaf

125 g (4 oz) butter or margarine
1 long white loaf
2–3 cloves garlic (according to taste)
3 sprigs parsley
Few sprigs of any other fresh green herb, like tarragon or basil (optional)
Salt and pepper

1   Remove the butter from the fridge in time for it to soften before you start to prepare the bread.
2   Pre-heat the oven to 220°C (425°F, gas mark 7).
3   Cut the loaf in slices almost all the way (but not completely) through.
4   Peel the garlic and chop it finely, or crush it in a garlic press. Add the garlic to the butter.
5   Finely chop the parsley and the other herb, if using, and add them to the butter.
6   Using a fork, mash the butter, garlic and herbs until they are completely blended. Season with a little salt and pepper.
7   Spread the garlic butter on one side of each bread slice, taking care not to break the bread open. Make sure that the end pieces are also buttered. You'll undoubtedly find that you are too generous at the beginning with the result that you run out of butter before you have finished the loaf, so you will have to go back and scrape the excess butter off the first few slices!
8   Wrap up the loaf completely in aluminium foil and place it in the oven.
9   Warm it through for 15–20 minutes, then serve immediately, straight from the foil.

Tea

Considering that tea is supposed to be our national beverage, it's surprising how rarely one tastes a really good cup. There are two factors which influence this: the method of preparation and the type of tea.

The first decision you have to make is whether to use teabags or loose leaves. Bags are undoubtedly easier, but try both to see which you prefer. Most teabags contain a blend of tea varieties and some are better than others. However, you should try out the different varieties on their own – Earl Grey, Darjeeling, English Breakfast and so on – to find one that you like. If you want to play safe, Assam is a good all-purpose tea. Earl Grey has a delicate flavour, while Lapsang Souchong is tarry, an acquired taste.

If you don't want vast amounts of caffeine after dinner, try a Chinese or a herbal tea. There's a good selection in health food stores, and quite a number, like peppermint, chamomile and rose hip, in supermarkets. They're usually drunk without milk or sugar.

How to Make a Good Cup

1 Start with good-quality tea and use the correct amount. One teaspoonful or bag per person and one for the pot is an excellent guideline when you are making small quantities.
2 An earthenware pot makes the best tea. Don't use an aluminium or a cracked enamel one. The pot should be clean and free from the tannin deposits that can build up.
3 Fill the kettle with cold water from the tap. Don't use water that's already in the kettle and don't use water from the hot tap. Good tea must be made with cold oxygenated water – that is, straight from the mains (usually the kitchen tap).
4 It is absolutely essential to warm the pot. It's not a myth: the tea *will* taste better. When the water boils, pour a little in the pot to warm it. Swill it around to make sure that the heat reaches all parts of the pot.
5 Only boiling water brings out the flavour of tea, so bring the water back up to the boil. Empty the water out of the pot and put in the tea.
6 Bring the teapot to the water, not the other way around, to make sure that the water is still boiling when it's poured over the tea.
7 All tea, especially teabags, should be given time to brew (or mash, or infuse). For a 4–5 cup teapot the brewing time should be around 5 minutes.

8 Stir the tea once while it's brewing to get an even flavour and colour.

9 If the leaves are loose in the pot, pour the tea into the cups through a tea strainer.

10 Don't cover the pot with a cosy as a bitter tannin flavour will develop.

What to Add

Milk and lemon are the most popular additions to tea. Don't use UHT milk, except in an absolute emergency, and don't ever add cream. You can use semi-skimmed or skimmed milk perfectly happily – you do not need whole milk. The usual rule is: 'MIF' – milk in first, though of course it's up to you. If you do put milk in first, you will find that it blends so well you don't need to stir the tea with a spoon afterwards. Add sugar or not, as you please.

Many people drink tea clear to taste the true flavour. If you serve it with lemon, give people thin lemon slices that they can float on top of the tea and retrieve when they want to. Don't add bottled lemon juice.

Coffee

Many people drink instant coffee throughout the day and save 'real' ground coffee for visitors or special occasions as it's more expensive and takes more trouble to make, depending on what method you use.

Instant Coffee

This is liquid coffee which has the water removed to form either a fine powder (spray-dried) or granules (freeze-dried). It is made quickly and easily and is much less expensive than ground coffee. Freeze-dried coffee is generally considered to taste more real but, again, it all comes down to what you like.

To make instant coffee, read the instructions on the label to discover the proportion of coffee to water that the manufacturer recommends. It's generally 1 teaspoon per cup. (You can vary the proportions according to what strength you prefer.) Put the coffee in the bottom of the cup, add boiling water and stir. If the water isn't hot enough, it won't dissolve the granules or powder completely. That's about the only thing that can go wrong with instant coffee!

Ground Coffee

Ground coffee is made from beans which have simply been roasted and ground and brewed in an infusion, just like tea. People start to panic when they have to choose among hundreds of varieties, and a dozen or so different brewing methods, and then select the grind!

You can buy coffee ready-ground or buy whole beans. Some supermarkets even have a grinding machine in the coffee section so you can grind the beans on the spot. You do get much fresher-tasting coffee if you grind the beans just before you make it, but if you can't be bothered, or you don't have a grinder, go ahead and buy ready-ground. You will find that, ground or otherwise, coffee will lose less of its taste if you keep it in an airtight container in the fridge or freezer.

Coffee beans are roasted to bring out their flavour. The four main types of roast are light, medium, strong and Continental which, unsurprisingly, relate to how strong the coffee will taste. From here, it's a matter of taste and experimentation.

There are many varieties of bean from all around the world, broadly divided between *arabica* and *robusta*, the former grown at a high altitude, the latter grown lower down. As its name implies, *robusta* is the stronger and less subtle of the two types, and it's usually cheaper. So start with a medium-roast *robusta* (Kenyan, for example) and then try other types.

If you enjoy espresso-type coffee, either black or with milk, like the kind you are often served in France and Italy, you have to go for a dark roast, finely ground. It's labelled either as Italian roast or Continental roast. (Incidentally, the strength of a coffee bears no relation to how much caffeine it contains. It just tastes that way!) You need a special piece of equipment to obtain the special espresso or cappuccino flavour.

How to Make Ground Coffee

The drip method

This is the fastest. You need a jug, a filter and filter papers, all widely available. Make sure that you buy filter papers of the right size for your filter. Use finely ground coffee as the water goes through the coffee only once – it doesn't sit in the grounds.

Put the paper in the filter, and place the filter on the jug. Place in the filter paper 1 tablespoon coffee per cup you intend to make. Boil enough water for the number of cups you are making. Pour the water on to the grounds slowly. The coffee will drip through the filter and is then ready for drinking. The only drawback with this method is that the coffee goes cold quickly.

The cafetière method

This is definitely the easiest. You need medium-ground coffee for this as the coffee is brewed in the water before being filtered through a fairly wide mesh.

Take the plunger out of the jug. Put into the jug 1 tablespoon coffee per cup you intend to make. Boil enough water for the number of cups you are making (the water level may be marked on the side of the jug). Pour the water on to the grounds and let the coffee brew for 3–5 minutes. Then plunge the filter down to the bottom of the jug; a bit of effort is required to get it right to the bottom. Again, you have to serve the coffee at once because it doesn't stay hot.

Automatic Electric Coffee Machine

This is probably the most convenient way to make coffee in larger quantities. These machines can be very fancy, with built-in grinders, but you can buy simple models. Because they use the filter method you need a finely ground coffee.

Put the paper into the filter and add 1 tablespoon coffee per cup you intend to make. Slot the filter into the machine. Measure out the amount of water you need – the jug that comes with the machine will have the cup levels marked. Turn on the machine and leave it to do its work. After about 10 minutes you'll have a jug of coffee, keeping warm on its built-in hotplate. Don't let the coffee stew for too long over the heat, however, as it eventually gets a burnt bitter taste.

Moka Express

Continental roasted coffees need to be prepared in a special way to obtain their strong flavour. They're easiest made with those metal pots called Moka Express which unscrew in the middle. These use steam to force the water up through the grounds to achieve a good strong taste. They come in different sizes; choose the one you're likely to use most often.

The machines have three main parts. Unscrew the top from the bottom and fill the bottom part with cold water. Fit the little long-stemmed metal cup inside and fill it with finely ground coffee. Screw the top part on tightly and close the lid. Put it to boil on the stove over the highest heat. When you can hear the water start to boil, turn the heat down to low. The water is forced up through the grounds, up the metal cylinder in the middle and flows down into the top part. When the coffee makes a sputtering noise, that usually means it's ready.

Make sure that you wash all the parts of the Moka thoroughly. The rubber seal on the underneath of the top part will start to rot after a few years. You can easily buy replacements in specialist coffee shops.

To make café-au-lait pour equal amounts of hot milk and Continental roast coffee into a large cup. (The French traditionally use handleless bowls but never seem to burn their fingers!)

To make cappuccino, heat milk almost to boiling point, then froth it in a blender for 10 seconds. Pour it into the coffee (again, use Continental roast) and sprinkle a little cocoa powder or cinnamon on top.

Whatever method you use to make ground coffee, the following points all apply:

1 Never reheat or boil coffee. The resulting taste is revolting.
2 Try serving ground coffee with hot milk; be sure not to let the milk boil.
3 Always use fresh cold water to make coffee.
4 Don't try to re-use grounds or filter papers!
5 For extra flavour you can add a small pinch of powdered cinnamon or a cardamom pod to the grounds.

129

Cocoa

Cocoa is a comforting drink, though too rich to enjoy more than occasionally. It can be made easily in two ways: with unsweetened cocoa powder and with drinking chocolate. The former tastes better because you control what's in it, especially the amount of sugar; the latter has the sugar pre-blended with the powder. Make sure that you know which one you're using *before* you start. You can use whole, semi-skimmed or skimmed milk. Obviously the less butterfat in the milk, the less rich the cocoa will taste (and the less fattening it will be). Here are the two methods of making it.

How to Make Cocoa

Cocoa Made with Unsweetened Powder

Measure the milk in the cups you will use to serve the cocoa – that way you will not end up with too much or too little milk. Measure out as many cups of milk as you want cocoa and pour it into a saucepan.

Place 1 tablespoon cocoa powder and 1–2 teaspoons sugar per person in a large jug big enough to hold all the milk. Ladle a little milk from the saucepan into the jug and mix with the powder and sugar to form a smooth, lump-free paste.

Heat the milk over medium heat until it is bubbling slightly. Do not let it come to a full boil. Pour it immediately into the jug and stir well.

Taste the cocoa for sweetness and strength of chocolate. If it lacks sugar, just add more. If it lacks chocolate, you'll have to make up a little extra powder/milk paste in a small bowl, omitting the sugar. Pour a little of the hot cocoa on to the paste and blend well, then add to the main quantity of cocoa and reheat until bubbling slightly. If the cocoa is too sweet, again make some more powder/milk paste and use as above. If it's too rich, add extra plain milk.

Pour the milk back into the saucepan and turn up the heat to medium-high so that it boils gently. Let it cook for another 1–2 minutes, whisking vigorously with a balloon whisk so that the cocoa froths. Serve immediately.

Cocoa Made with Drinking Chocolate

Follow the instructions on the tin: the recommended amount is generally 1 tablespoon powder per person. Measure out the milk as described above and heat it over a medium heat until it's hot but not boiling. Sprinkle the powder into the hot milk and stir until the powder has dissolved. Serve immediately.

The Great British Breakfast

As all bed-and-breakfast landladies know, a cooked breakfast is one of the most difficult meals to achieve with success. The problem is not the constituent parts, it's the combining of the elements so that everything arrives on the table at the right temperature, without being overcooked or undercooked, or dried up and cold.

The most difficult thing is to co-ordinate the meal for two or more people. As encouragement, remember that the only real cooking skill comes in frying the eggs; the rest is actually very easy. Read the cooking instructions below for the individual items before starting to cook breakfast. You may wish to practise each item separately before trying to serve them all for one meal.

The guidelines below are for the most typical breakfast you might want to serve. We've opted for grilling as it's less fattening than frying.

The menu is as follows:

> Half grapefruit or glass of orange juice
> Cereal
> Fried Eggs, Grilled Bacon and Sausages
> Grilled Tomatoes and Mushrooms
> Toast with Jam and Marmalade
> Tea or Coffee

Order of Preparation

1 Have the table already laid, including salt, pepper, mustards, butter, jams and marmalades, milk and sugar. Place out the cereal packet(s).
2 Prepare the grapefruit, if serving (*see page 132*).
3 Alternatively, pour out the orange juice.
4 Clear an area close to the cooker from where you can serve the food.
5 Your guests can be called to table as soon as you start to cook. While they eat their grapefruit and cereal, you'll be preparing the rest of the food. Unless they eat abnormally slowly or quickly, the cooked breakfast should arrive on the table at about the time they finish the cereal.
6 Pre-heat the plates in the oven, set at 170°C (325°F, gas mark 3).
7 The thickest items are cooked first. Grill the sausages on the grill rack with the tomato halves. (Instructions for grilling tomatoes are on page 69). This will take 5–8 minutes. Place the cooked sausages and tomatoes on a warmed plate in the bottom of the oven. They can sit there for 10 minutes keeping warm without drying out.
8 While the sausages and tomatoes are cooking, make the tea and/or coffee (*see pages 126–9*). Refill the kettle after you've made the tea, so that you can top up the pot with more boiling water or make a fresh pot when it's needed.
9 Grill the bacon rashers and the mushrooms together. Instructions for grilling mushrooms are on page 133. This will take about 5 minutes. Place them on a warmed plate and keep them warm in the oven.
10 While the bacon and mushrooms are grilling, heat the frying pan over a medium heat and add the oil.

131

11 As soon as everything is cooked and keeping warm in the oven, fry the eggs in the hot oil.

12 While the eggs are cooking, make the toast (*see page 134*).

13 Just before the eggs are done, place the bacon, sausages, tomatoes and mushrooms on individual warmed serving plates which you have positioned near the stove.

14 As soon as the eggs are cooked, place immediately on the plates and serve.

15 Be ready to jump up during the next 20 minutes for toast, tea and coffee.

Grapefruit

Cut the grapefruit in half horizontally. Using a curved grapefruit knife or a similar sharp serrated knife, cut along the lines of the individual segments from the centre of the fruit to the outside edge, slicing right down to the skin. Then cut round the perimeter of the grapefruit just inside the skin and pith. This makes it easier to eat the segments.

Sausages

Buy home-made sausages from a good butcher or buy a reliable brand name from a chain store. Remember that the cheaper the sausages are, the more unsavoury are the parts of the animal used to make them. Sausages with herbs and spices, whether they're made from pork or beef or a mixture, are more interesting than the mass-produced plain ones.

Allow 2–3 sausages per person. Separate the sausages, if necessary by cutting through the little piece of connecting skin with scissors or a sharp knife.

To grill sausages, place them close together on the rack to prevent them from rolling around. Turn the heat to its highest setting if you can put the sausages at least 7.5 cm (3 in.) from the heat. Otherwise, set the heat to medium. If the heat is too high, the skin will burn without cooking the interior.

Turn all the sausages over at the same time at frequent intervals, so that they cook uniformly. This will take about 5 minutes for chipolatas and about 8 minutes for bangers. You may need to cook them on all sides more than once. Check that they're completely cooked by slicing one through the middle. If it's at all pink inside, continue to cook.

To fry sausages, place ½ teaspoon vegetable oil in a frying pan over a medium heat. Put the sausages in the pan and fry on all sides, turning frequently, until they are golden brown. Test to make sure that they are cooked all the way through as above. Drain on kitchen paper to remove excess fat.

Bacon

Allow 2–3 rashers per person. Either remove the rind or leave it on but snip it with scissors in several places so that the rasher doesn't curl up during cooking. Streaky bacon will go quite crunchy as it cooks; the leaner bacon, such as back bacon, tends to dry out.

To grill bacon, lay the rashers flat on the grill rack. Heat the grill to its highest setting and place the rack 5–7.5 cm (2–3 in.) from the heat source. Grill for 2–3 minutes on each side or until the bacon is golden brown. Don't overcook it as it will dry out further while it keeps warm in the oven.

To fry bacon, place ½ teaspoon vegetable oil per person in a large frying pan. Heat the oil over a medium heat, then add the bacon rashers and cook on each side for 2–3 minutes or until golden brown; longer if you like your bacon crisp. Remove from the pan and drain the bacon on kitchen paper before putting it in the oven to keep warm.

If you are frying the bacon, you can use the fat left in the pan to cook the eggs. This makes the eggs taste better, but it's less healthy.

You can cook bacon in the microwave very successfully. Remove the fat and rind. Place the bacon on a piece of kitchen paper and cover with another piece of kitchen paper. Cook on microwave HIGH for 4 minutes.

Mushrooms

Try to buy the largest mushrooms possible for grilling. The large flat ones are ideal: allow 1 per person. Place them on the grill tray, smooth side down. Place ½ teaspoon vegetable oil on top, season with salt and pepper and grill for 2 minutes. Turn them over, smear with a little butter on the uncooked side and grill until they're brown and soft when pierced with a knife.

Fried Eggs

There are two main difficulties in frying eggs properly. First, you should be careful not to break the yolks as you crack the eggs. To lessen the likelihood of this, crack the eggs, one at a time, gently on to a saucer and carefully slide them into the pan. (See also page 25 for more tips.) Second, you should not overcook the yolks (unless you like them hard), or undercook the whites. Again, this is down to timing and experience. It is much easier to remove the eggs if you use a non-stick pan.

Heat ½ teaspoon vegetable oil per egg, or a mixture of vegetable oil and butter (for a better flavour) in a large frying pan over medium heat. When the fat is hot but not sizzling, slide the eggs gently into the pan. If you're cooking more than one or two, the eggs whites may flow into each other. This doesn't matter: you just have to cut the eggs apart gently with a kitchen knife before removing them.

Spoon the hot fat in the pan over the whites so that they set more quickly. Fry for about 3 minutes or until the whites are firm but the yolks are still soft. Lift the cooked eggs carefully out of the pan with a fish slice on to the waiting warmed plates.

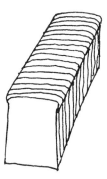

Toast

The better the bread (*see page 30*), the better the toast – and it will be better still if it's brought to the table piping hot. Pre-heat the grill to its highest setting. Place the slices of bread on the grill rack and toast them on both sides until golden brown. Watch them like a hawk as they can burn (and catch fire!) very easily. Alternatively, use a toaster. Serve the toast immediately, wrapped in a clean cloth placed on a warmed plate. Avoid toast racks, which result in cold unappetising toast.

Breakfast Variations

Scrambled or boiled eggs may be preferred to fried eggs. See pages 24 and 25 for how to prepare these. Real poached eggs are put directly into boiling water to cook; as they are rather tricky, we have omitted them from this book. You can buy an item called an egg 'poacher' which steams the eggs over simmering water – in fact, coddling them. If you choose this method, follow the instructions supplied with the poacher, making sure that you don't overcook the yolks.

Lamb's kidneys and slices of black pudding are also popular for breakfast. They can be either grilled or fried. See page 182 for how to fry kidneys. To grill kidneys, prepare them as described on page 182. Smear them with ½ teaspoon vegetable oil, season with salt and pepper, and place them under a medium grill. Cook for 2–3 minutes on each side or until there is no sign of red. Black pudding is already cooked so needs only to be warmed up.

Real porridge has to be cooked for a long time with much stirring. Reluctant cooks prefer the equally good but much faster instant porridge oats. Follow the failsafe instructions on the packet.

Opposite: Indian Feast (page 218), including Tandoori Thighs (page 83), Potato Curry (page 158), Boiled Basmati Rice and Tomato Raita (both page 218).

Sunday Roast Lunch

Co-ordinating a cooked breakfast is a dress rehearsal for Sunday roast lunch. However, cooking the latter meal has a potentially far greater stress level because there can be more individual items which need to be cooked and ready at the same time.

The easiest way to master the technique is to proceed step by step. Start by serving simple meat with two vegetables. Then you can add the extras as you build up your confidence. The most complicated meals are a roast beef and a roast chicken or turkey dinner. The former needs to have the Yorkshire Pudding and gravy ready at the same time, the latter the Bread Sauce (the recipe for which is given on page 139), stuffing and gravy – not to mention the roast potatoes and other vegetable(s).

The principles for preparing a Sunday lunch are the same as for a cooked breakfast – deciding what the cooking order of dishes is, what can be kept warm in the oven and what has to be served hot from the oven. The easiest way of approaching these problems is actually to make a list, then back-time from when you want to serve the meal. Read pages 22–3 on organising before you proceed any further!

Roast meals are usually very filling, so don't feel obliged to serve three courses. The starter is most often the course that's dispensed with. However, if you do want a starter, choose one that can be made in advance like a salad or the more interesting Locket's Savoury (*see page 229*). People do tend to like a pudding, no matter how full they feel. A fruit pudding, like Traditional Fresh Fruit Salad (*see page 120*) or a Tropical Fruit Platter (*see page 252*), can be made in advance and it won't be too heavy. See pages 262–3 for wine recommendations.

Timings for only one roast meal are given here as an example: you can easily apply the theory to other roasts of meat. As the meat carves most easily after it has rested, this resting time can be used to finish cooking the vegetables and make the gravy (*see page 138*). Any time you can use to prepare the vegetables or other accompaniments before the last hectic half-hour will be time well spent.

Here is the menu:

Roast Beef
with
Creamed Horseradish, Gravy and Yorkshire Pudding
Roast Potatoes
Glazed Carrots

Opposite: Guacamole (page 142), Crudités with blue cheese dip (page 144) and Spanish Tortilla (page 154).

Order of Preparation

Previous day Decide on the menu, read all the relevant recipes, do all the shopping.

11.00 Read all the recipes again.

11.15 Pre-heat oven to 220°C (425°F, gas mark 7).
Peel the potatoes and cut them up.
Prepare the beef.

11.30 Put the beef in the oven.
Boil some water for the potatoes.
Make the batter for the Yorkshire Pudding (*see page 91*) and chill in the fridge until needed.

11.45 Turn the oven temperature down to 200°C (400°F, gas mark 6).
Heat some fat in a small roasting tin in the oven. This is for the potatoes. You can, if you prefer and if there is room, roast them in the same tin as the meat, but they are less likely to turn out crisp.
Peel and slice the carrots.

12.00 Put the potatoes in the roasting tin in the oven.
Boil some water for the carrots.

12.15 Boil the carrots until cooked but firm, drain and set aside.
Baste the potatoes.

12.30 Lay the table and open the wine.
Heat some fat in a Yorkshire pudding tin in the oven.
Boil some water in a kettle to make gravy.
Put the serving dishes and plates to warm under the grill.
Baste the potatoes.

12.45 Take the beef out of the oven and put it on a large warmed serving dish, reserving the juices in the roasting tin to add to the gravy.
Pour the Yorkshire pudding mixture into the prepared pudding tin and bake in the oven for 15 minutes.
Make the gravy, pour into a saucepan and keep warm over the lowest heat.
Glaze the carrots (*see page 62*)
Check the potatoes to see if they are done.

1.00 Carve the meat (*see page 140*).
Take the Yorkshire puddings out of the oven and serve.
Serve the vegetables and creamed horseradish.
Eat. Congratulate yourself!

Gravy

Depending on your taste, you can make either a thin or a thick gravy. Thin gravy is simply the meat sediment mixed with stock, then strained. Thick gravy is the same but uses flour as a thickener. If you don't have any stock, make some up from a cube (*see page 35*) – use a chicken cube for roast chicken, turkey and pork, a lamb cube for roast lamb and a beef cube for beef.

After the meat or bird has been taken out of the oven and is resting, spoon off the fat in the roasting tin. (The fat is the lighter-coloured liquid which lies on top of the meat juices.) If you want thin gravy, get rid of all the fat. If you want thick gravy, leave 1–2 tablespoons of the fat in the bottom of the tin. Discard the fat or save it for later use.

To make thin gravy, pour the hot stock into the roasting tin and place over a medium-high heat. Stir and scrape all the little bits of meat sediment up from the bottom so that they dissolve in the hot liquid. Season with salt and pepper and bring to the boil. Taste the gravy, adjust the seasoning if necessary and continue to boil, stirring, until the liquid reduces in volume and it reaches the desired strength. Pour the gravy through a sieve into a clean saucepan. Put the lid on and keep the gravy warm over the lowest heat until you're ready to serve the meal. Add to the gravy any juices exuded by the resting joint.

To make thick gravy, sprinkle 1 tablespoon plain flour over the fat left in the roasting tin. Place the tin over a medium-low heat and stir the flour and fat together to make a roux (see page 144). It doesn't matter if the bits of meat sediment are mixed into the paste as well. Cook, stirring, for 3–4 minutes. Then slowly pour in the hot stock, stirring all the time so that no lumps form. Scrape as much as possible of the meat sediment stuck to the bottom of the tin into the gravy. Season with salt and pepper and continue to cook until you have a thick smooth gravy of the desired consistency. Taste it and adjust the seasoning if necessary. Pour the gravy through a sieve into a clean saucepan, cover and keep warm over the lowest heat until you're ready to serve the meal. Add to the gravy any juices exuded by the resting joint.

Bread Sauce

Bread Sauce, traditionally served with roast chicken or turkey, will take about 1 hour to make, including preparation.

Makes about 600 ml (1 pint)

1 medium onion, peeled and left whole
4 cloves
450 ml (15 fl oz) milk
1 bayleaf
Salt and pepper
3 thick or 4 thin slices white bread
1 tablespoon butter
3–4 tablespoons cream or milk

1 Stick the pointed ends of the cloves into the onion.
2 Put the onion in a saucepan with the 450 ml (15 fl oz) milk, bay leaf, salt and pepper. Bring the milk to the boil over a medium-high heat. As soon as it starts to boil, take it off the heat immediately, cover it and leave it for 20 minutes so that the flavours can develop.
3 Remove the crusts from the bread and cut it into 1 cm (½ in.) dice.
4 Stir the bread into the milk, cover and leave for another 20 minutes.
5 Remove the bayleaf and the onion from the milk and discard. Whisk the milk with a fork to break down the bread and add the butter. Stir over a low heat until the butter has melted.
6 Stir in 3–4 tablespoons cream or milk to enrich the sauce.
7 Set aside and reheat over a medium heat when needed.

Carving Meat

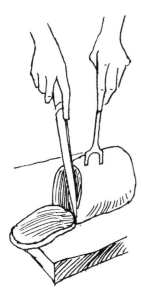

There are no hard-and-fast rules which apply to carving; some people prefer thick slices, others thin. The thing to avoid is tearing the meat, but even this is inevitable around bones or underneath poultry. If you have some knowledge of biology, you might be a natural carver. Otherwise, you'll simply improve with practice. However, there are some guidelines to start you off.

First, it's important to use a large sharp carving knife. One with serrated edges is easiest for the beginner to manage. A fork, whether a kitchen fork or the large carving type, will help hold down the meat while you carve. Second, the meat will be much easier to carve if it rests for 15–20 minutes after it comes out of the oven. Place it on a warm lipped dish to rest, then transfer it to a dry wooden board to carve.

To avoid stringy slices of meat, you have to identify which way the meat fibres run and then slice across (not along) them. This applies to poultry breasts as well as to joints of meat (*see pages 82–3*).

Cut slices of meat dry out quickly, so it's a good idea to slice off only as much as you need at one go. Keep the joint warm in the oven at 170°C (325°F, gas mark 3) covered with aluminium foil.

SECTION TWO

Advanced Recipes

You could cook for the rest of your life using only the basic dishes you've just mastered, but you might grow tired of the lack of variety in your diet. This section uses the principles you've learned and applies them to slightly more difficult dishes. New cooking methods will also be introduced, such as casseroling and sauce making.

You'll notice that preparation instructions are not spelled out here as they are in Section One. In the ingredients list a description of the way an ingredient is to be dealt with is shown next to the ingredient itself. In the method we simply remind you that the task needs to be done. At first you will probably often find yourself referring back to the recipes in Section One.

The dishes in this section are a selection of well-known British ones, with some from other countries. The latter recipes simply reflect how our cuisine has become much more cosmopolitan over the past few decades. If you are not familiar with a recipe title, don't let this put you off trying it. Most of the ingredients in this section are not terribly expensive, so you won't have wasted too much money if you find that you don't like the dish.

Easy baking – including the dreaded bread making – is also included in this section. You won't always have the opportunity to nip round the corner at the last moment to buy a packet of biscuits.

If you start to feel uneasy, you can always go back to Section One for a few more weeks until you've regained your confidence.

Dips, Spreads and Sauces

'Dip' and 'spread' are rather unattractive terms used to describe foods which, when home-made with good ingredients, are perfectly respectable. It is the unsavoury overpriced concoctions of emulsified fat, chemicals and food colourings (often 'bacon-flavoured', 'beef-dripping-flavoured' or 'prawn-cocktail-flavoured') that the unwary stumble upon in supermarkets which have given dips and spreads a bad name.

Dips and spreads are often useful when you – or your family or guests – want to nibble on something. They can be a starter to a meal, when accompanied by good bread or crackers, or served with cut-up vegetables as part of a buffet.

For an idea of how to serve dips and vegetables in an attractive way, have a look at the colour photograph on page 136.

Guacamole

Photograph on page 136

Mexican food has hit Britain, mostly in the form of packaged taco shells, tortilla chips and nachos (all forms of cornmeal crackers). Guacamole is the avocado dip, flavoured with lemon and a hint of chilli, with which these crackers are often served. Fresh coriander is available in supermarkets and Asian and Cypriot groceries. Don't mistake it for flat-leaved Continental parsley, which it resembles. Coriander has a distinctive fresh taste, and is sold with the roots still attached. To use guacamole as a starter to a meal, present it on a bed of lettuce leaves, decorated with chopped tomatoes and black olives.

The consistency of Guacamole should be slightly chunky, not smooth. However, if you want it as a smooth dip for vegetables, you can blend or process it. Avocado flesh goes brown when it's exposed to air, so mix in the lemon juice as soon as possible to prevent this from happening.

For 4

2 large ripe avocados
Juice 1 lemon
1–2 cloves garlic, peeled and crushed
Small pinch salt
Large pinch cayenne pepper
Few lettuce leaves, washed (optional)
1 tablespoon chopped fresh coriander (optional)

1   Cut the avocados in half lengthways, remove the stones and scoop the flesh out of the rind into a bowl.
2   Add the lemon juice, garlic and salt. Mash with a fork until the ingredients are well blended.
3   Add a pinch of cayenne pepper and mix in. Taste the mixture and add extra salt or cayenne pepper if necessary.
4   Put the lettuce leaves, if using, around the edge of a serving dish.
5   Spoon the Guacamole in and sprinkle on the fresh coriander, if using.

Variations

Add one of the following:
1 tomato, finely diced
5–6 black olives, stoned and chopped
1 small onion, finely chopped
1 green or red pepper, finely diced

Smoked Fish Pâté

This is where you can really see the price difference between packaged and home-made. You can use smoked salmon (buy the trimmings from a fishmonger), or fillets of smoked trout, smoked mackerel or kipper.

Smoked salmon shouldn't have any bones in it but you may need to pull the stray bones out of the other fish fillets with a pair of tweezers. The pâté will taste better if you allow time for the flavours to develop before you eat it – at least 2 hours. Serve it in neat mounds on a bed of lettuce with a lemon wedge as a starter, or with toast as a dip.

For 4–6

125 g (4 oz) cream cheese
1 tablespoon lemon juice
125 g (4 oz) smoked fish, skinned and boned
50–75 ml (2–3 fl oz) Greek-style thick plain yoghurt
Black pepper
1 tablespoon finely chopped parsley

1   Put all the ingredients into the bowl of a blender or food processor and blend until smooth. If the pâté is too thick, add extra yoghurt.
2   Taste the pâté and add more pepper if necessary. You may prefer a touch more lemon juice too.
3   Put in a serving dish and chill in the fridge until needed.

Garlic and Cheese Dip

This is more liquid than the Guacamole and the Smoked Fish Pâté. It's not for people who don't like garlic!

For 4

250 g (8 oz) cottage cheese
2–3 cloves garlic, peeled and crushed
2–3 spring onions, finely diced
2–3 tablespoons plain yoghurt
Salt and pepper

1   Place the cottage cheese in a sieve and let the liquid drain off. To speed up the process, place a plate directly on the cheese, weighted down with something heavy.
2   Prepare the garlic and onions.
3   Place the drained cottage cheese in a bowl with the garlic, onions, yoghurt and salt and pepper to taste and combine thoroughly.
4   Cover and chill in the fridge until needed.

Crudités with Dips

Photograph on page 136

One of the best types of party food is a colourful variety of fresh, firm-textured vegetables served with various dips – but the vegetables must be really good-quality with tight skins and no bruises. The familiar standbys are carrots, mushrooms, peppers, celery and cucumber; however, do try raw broccoli, cauliflower or fennel.

The most attractive way of presenting crudités is on a large platter (or you can even use a shallow basket – there's no formality about this kind of food). Don't be tempted to cut up the vegetables too small – it just looks silly. They should all be washed, of course, and peeled if you prefer. Small vegetables like radishes, cherry tomatoes and mushrooms should be left whole; cauliflower and broccoli cut into florets no smaller than about 5 cm (2 in.) long. If you cut up the vegetables in advance, keep them moist by covering them with kitchen paper soaked in cold water then squeezed out.

As well as the preceding recipes, try the following thin dips for crudités:

Blue cheese and single cream, blended until smooth.

Soured cream or yoghurt, to which have been added freshly chopped herbs, salt, pepper and paprika.

Mayonnaise (not salad cream), to which has been added crushed garlic and paprika.

Basic White Sauce

Sauces strike fear into people. Made badly, they can look and taste like wallpaper paste, thick with indigestible lumps. That's why packet sauces sell well; they seem foolproof and easy. Well, they are, but you pay a high price for success. They're expensive and full of a wide variety of artificial colourings and flavourings. Once you've produced a home-made sauce successfully – and it's not hard – you'll never go wrong again.

The best sauce, and the most useful, to start with has the uninspiring name of 'White Sauce' (*Béchamel* in French, which sounds better). Since the arrival of Nouvelle Cuisine, White Sauce has developed a bad reputation. But it's far healthier and cheaper than the little puddles of new-style rich cream sauces on the plates of expensive restaurants.

You may have heard the word 'roux' bandied about. It's simply a mixture of flour and fat (usually butter) that acts as a thickening agent in many sauces and soups. Once you master this, you'll be able to make a variety of dishes.

Cheese Sauce
Add 75 g (3 oz) grated mature Cheddar cheese to the sauce just before serving and stir until melted and blended. This is very good with cooked vegetables.

Mustard Sauce
Add 2 teaspoons mustard powder diluted with a little water or wine. This is great with grilled herrings.

Parsley Sauce
Add 3 tablespoons chopped parsley and the juice of ½ lemon. Nice with fish or gammon.

It should be a light sandy colour, no darker. If it burns, throw it away, wash the pan and start again. You will have wasted only a little butter and flour, so it's no disaster!

If you wish to keep the sauce warm for a short while before serving it, spread 15 g (½ oz) butter over the top to prevent a skin forming.

To make a white sauce, you start with the roux and simply add the milk plus extra flavourings. The following recipe is for basic White Sauce, which can be used to pour over vegetables or fish, or to flavour macaroni cheese. Other recipes in this section of the book will use the roux with stock as the liquid.

The point at which the infamous lumps can appear is when you add the liquid to the cooked butter and flour mixture. You must add the liquid a little at a time, stirring thoroughly between each addition. There must be no lumps before you add each ladle of liquid.

You can keep white sauce in the fridge, covered, for a few days. When you come to reheat it, you'll notice that it has thickened, and you can add extra milk (or whatever liquid you have chosen) to thin it down.

Whole, semi-skimmed and skimmed milk are all suitable for white sauce, but the flour should be plain, not self-raising. If you're in a hurry or you don't have the ingredients, you can forget about the clove-studded onion – it just adds extra flavour. If you're really pressed for time, you don't have to warm the milk, but you risk lumps unless you stir really well.

Makes 600 ml (1 pint)

½ onion, peeled
3 cloves
600 ml (1 pint) milk
50 g (2 oz) butter
40 g (1½ oz) plain white flour
Salt and pepper

1   Push the pointed ends of the cloves into the onion.
2   Pour the milk into a pan and add the onion. Bring to the boil, then pour into a jug.
3   Meanwhile, melt 50 g (2 oz) of the butter in a thick-bottomed pan over a low heat.
4   When the butter has just melted, add the flour. Mix thoroughly with a wooden spoon so that the butter is completely absorbed by the flour. (This sturdy mixture is called a roux.)
5   To get rid of any floury taste, cook the roux over a low heat for 2–3 minutes, stirring constantly so that it doesn't stick or burn.
6   Remove the onion from the milk and discard it. Add the warmed milk little by little to the roux, mixing it in thoroughly with a wooden spoon.
7   Turn down the heat to its lowest setting and cook the sauce for 5–7 minutes, stirring from time to time.
8   When the sauce is cooked, add extra flavourings if you like, and salt and pepper to taste.

Stocks and Soups

Fresh Stock

There's no mystique about stock. It's just flavoured water: a mixture of bones or giblets, as available, some vegetables and a few herbs, all simmered together for enough time for the ingredients to give up their best. Make it when you have the ingredients to hand, usually after you've roasted a joint or when you have a few left-over bones. Then, when you do need it, it's there in the freezer.

Why make stock? Well, having said earlier that stock cubes will do just as well, we can't turn around and reject them. But real stock will make whatever dish you're cooking taste nicer. This is especially true of delicate soups in which there are no strong flavours to mask the artificial taste of the cube.

Once you get into the habit of bunging the bones from your Sunday roast into a pot with some vegetables and cooking it for a few hours while you read the papers, you'll find that you'll make stock without thinking. You also feel virtuous doing it!

Stock-making Guidelines

1   Always ensure that the bones you use to make stock are fresh, whether raw or recently cooked. They should not feel sticky or have a strong odour. To prepare bones or a carcass for stock making, simply remove any attached fat; scraps of cooked meat remaining on the bones will add flavour to the stock. Break up the carcass or bones into smaller pieces to get the greatest goodness from them.

2   You can use tired or old vegetables for stock, but it will undoubtedly taste better if you use fresh ones. The indispensable vegetables are onions, carrots and celery; leeks are another good addition. Don't use potatoes or any cooked vegetables. The vegetables will need to be peeled and washed (where applicable) and cut roughly into large chunks. Don't cut them into small pieces or they will turn to mush and make the stock cloudy.

3   Always cover the bones or carcass and vegetables with cold water, and bring the liquid to the boil. Then turn the heat down so that the liquid simmers. Don't use boiling water to speed up the process.

4   During the cooking process, and especially when you bring the stock to the boil at the beginning, the bones or carcass will produce a certain amount of nasty grey scum, or froth, which rises to the surface of the liquid. It is crucial that you remove it or it will boil back into the stock and spoil the flavour and appearance. To remove the scum simply skim it off using a large metal spoon.

5   A good stock must be simmered slowly and not boiled. This is very important!

6   Never season stock with salt and pepper. You can season it when you use it later, whether for a soup, a stew or a sauce.

7   Cook the stock for the time indicated in the recipe. There's no point in overcooking: vegetables and bones have a finite amount of flavour to give! Strain the stock while it's still hot and discard the bones and vegetables.

8   Whatever type of bones you use, they will give off a certain amount of fat which needs to be removed after cooking and straining. The two conventional methods of removing the fat are as follows:

(a) Leave the stock to cool, then chill it in the fridge. The fat will solidify on the top of the stock and can then be 'lifted' off.

(b) Simply soak up the fat by placing plenty of absorbent kitchen paper on the surface of the stock.

9   Any stock can be concentrated by reduction once it has been strained. Reboil the strained liquid, without a lid, and reduce it by evaporation. The excess liquid vanishes while the flavour of the stock intensifies. You could literally reduce 4 litres (1 gallon) of stock down to 150 ml (5 fl oz). You would end up with a sticky substance which would give an explosion of flavour when added to soups, sauces or stews. Reducing a stock also means that it's easier to store because there's less of it.

10 If you are going to use the stock in the next day or two, you can store it, covered, in the fridge once it's cooled to room temperature. You can also freeze it in plastic tubs (which allow for expansion) or in ice-cube trays or special plastic ice-cube bags. It's useful having small quantities of frozen stock to add to a sauce.

Chicken Stock

Chicken stock is the most useful stock you can make. It is suitable as a base for all kinds of soups – chicken, vegetable or pulse – and for many sauces. If you're only ever going to make one kind of stock, chicken's the best one to have.

You can use the remains of a cooked chicken, the carcass of a raw bird, or any mixture of bones from both raw and cooked chicken. The best chicken stock uses a raw carcass because it has more flavour to give. If you're cooking chicken pieces, cut off the wing tips or the bottoms of the legs beforehand and reserve them to make a chicken stock together with the left-over cooked bones. The giblets (the organs usually contained in a plastic bag inside a prepared raw chicken) can also be added for extra flavour.

Makes about 850 ml (1½ pints)

About 350 g (12 oz) chicken bones, giblets, wing tips, etc.
2–3 carrots, peeled and roughly sliced
1 onion, peeled and quartered
2 stalks celery, roughly sliced
1 medium leek, roughly sliced
4 black peppercorns
1 bouquet garni
1 litre (2 pints) water

1   If using a raw carcass, discard all the skin and excess blobs of fat from the inside. Break the carcass into two.
2   Prepare the vegetables.
3   Put all the ingredients in a large pan and add the water. Bring to the boil.
4   Skim the top of the liquid to remove any scum. Turn the heat down to low and cover loosely, allowing some steam to escape. Simmer gently for 1½–2 hours.
5   Strain the stock, reserving the liquid only.
6   Remove the fat, using either of the two methods described on page 147.
7   Use immediately or store in the fridge or freezer. You may wish to reduce the stock further for easy storage.

Beef Stock

Raw marrowbones make the best beef stock. You can buy them cheaply on their own from a butcher; even supermarkets are beginning to sell beef bones just for stock making. Otherwise, you can easily use the bone from a joint, although the resulting stock will not be as good.

You can make two different kinds of beef stock using the same ingredients. Beef stock will be pale in colour and less rich in flavour if you simply boil all the ingredients up together. However, if you roast the bones in the oven prior to simmering them, you'll get a nice rich brown beef stock.

Makes about 2 litres (4 pints)

1.5 kg (3 lb) marrowbones
3 carrots, peeled and cut into thirds
4 stalks celery, cut into thirds
2 onions, peeled and quartered
10 black peppercorns
1 bouquet garni
3 litres (5 pints) cold water

1   Prepare the vegetables.
2   Place all the ingredients in a large pan. Bring to the boil.

3   Skim the top of liquid to remove any scum. Turn the heat down to low and cover loosely, allowing some steam to escape. Simmer gently for about 4 hours.
4   Strain the stock, reserving the liquid only.
5   Remove the fat, using either of the two methods described on page 147.
6   Use immediately or store in the fridge or freezer. You may wish to reduce the stock further for easy storage.

Variation: Brown Beef Stock

Before making the stock, put the bones in a roasting tin. Place the tin in an oven pre-heated to 230°C (450°F, gas mark 8) and brown the bones for 30 minutes. Then proceed with the recipe as above.

Ham Stock

This isn't a real staple of the kitchen but it's the ideal stock for making pulse-based soups such as Haricot Bean (*see page 150*). You can save time and effort if you cook a boiling ham surrounded by roughly chopped stock vegetables. Then eat the ham and strain the cooking liquid to use for stock. Otherwise, follow the instructions below.

Because ham is very fatty the stock needs at least 24 hours in the fridge in order to allow the fat to solidify.

Makes about 850 ml (1½ pints)

350 g (12 oz) ham bones
2–3 carrots, peeled and roughly sliced
1 onion, peeled and quartered
2 stalks celery, roughly sliced
1 medium leek, roughly sliced (optional)
4 black peppercorns
1 bouquet garni
1 litre (2 pints) water

1   Prepare the vegetables.
2   Place all the ingredients in a large pan and pour over the water. Bring to the boil.
3   Skim the top of the liquid to remove any scum. Turn down the heat to low and cover loosely, allowing some steam to escape. Simmer very gently for 1½–2 hours.
4   Strain the stock, reserving the liquid only.
5   Remove the fat, using either of the two methods described on page 147.
6   Use immediately or store in the fridge or freezer. You may wish to reduce the stock further for easy storage.

Haricot Bean Soup

The French term for this soup is *purée soissonaise*, which sounds a little more impressive than bean soup. You have to use ham stock for this recipe or it won't have a good strong flavour, so don't bother making it until you've cooked your ham joint. Like all bean dishes it's very filling and very inexpensive. Haricot beans are small white dried beans sold in supermarkets and health food stores. You could substitute other dried beans, but just make sure that you cook them long enough. And remember to soak the beans overnight first or they'll take forever to cook.

If you are in a hurry, you can use tinned instead of dried beans – these don't need soaking, of course, and require only a short cooking time, though they are more expensive. Add them to the soup at stage 4 of the recipe, about 15 minutes before the end of the cooking time.

For 4–6

500 g (1 lb) dried haricot beans
2 large carrots, peeled and left whole
1 medium onion, peeled and chopped
1.75 litres (3 pints) Ham Stock (*see page 149*)
300 ml (10 fl oz) hot milk
Salt and pepper

1   Cover the beans with cold water and leave them to soak overnight, or for a minimum of 8 hours.
2   Prepare the vegetables. Drain the beans and rinse them under cold running water. Put the vegetables and beans into a large thick-bottomed pan and add the stock.
3   Bring to the boil and skim to remove any scum from the surface of the liquid.
4   Let the soup simmer, very gently, for about 40 minutes or until the beans are completely soft.
5   Using a slotted spoon, remove the cooked beans and vegetables (reserving the cooking liquid) and put them into the bowl of a blender or food processor. Purée them with a little of the cooking liquid to a smooth consistency. Alternatively, you can leave the beans in the soup and mash them using a potato masher, or push them through a strainer.
6   Pour the bean mixture back into the pan and stir it completely into the liquid.
7   Pour the milk into a saucepan and bring it to the boil over medium-high heat. When it feels hot to the touch, take it off the heat.
8   Bring the soup back to the boil and add the hot milk, ladleful by ladleful, mixing it in until you bring the soup to the consistency you like.
9   Season with salt and pepper to taste and serve.

Cream of Spinach Soup

Frozen spinach works just as well as fresh in this soup; if you don't have a microwave to defrost it and you're in a hurry, you can speed up the process by holding the plastic packet under hot water and, without tearing the packet, breaking the spinach into chunks with your hands. The frozen chunks can go straight into the hot stock!

The recipe is also suitable for other delicate green vegetables, like watercress or asparagus.

For 4–6

500 g (1 lb) spinach, washed and shredded, or 175 g (6 oz) frozen spinach
125 g (4 oz) butter
75 g (3 oz) flour
1 litre (2 pints) hot chicken stock (*see page 147*)
Salt and pepper
150 ml (5 fl oz) single cream

1   Prepare the spinach, put it into a pan, cover with boiling water and cook on medium heat for 2–3 minutes. If using frozen spinach, defrost it and remove as much water from it as you can.
2   Immerse the cooked spinach immediately in cold water so that it keeps its colour. Then, using your hands, squeeze as much of the water out of the spinach as possible. Set the spinach aside.
3   Melt the butter in a thick-bottomed pan over a medium-low heat. Add the flour and mix it in thoroughly with a wooden spoon. Stirring continuously, allow the butter and flour mixture (roux) to cook for 3–4 minutes.
4   Gradually add the hot stock, mixing it in as thoroughly as possible. (See page 144 for the rules on sauce making – they apply here.) When all stock is mixed in, add the spinach and stir.
5   Simmer the soup very gently for about 20–25 minutes.
6   To obtain a nice smooth soup you can strain it, liquidise it or put it through a food processor – it doesn't matter which you use. Pour the soup back into the pan (which you have meanwhile rinsed out to get rid of any grit that might be lurking at the bottom).
7   Bring the soup back to the boil, season with salt and pepper to taste and stir in the cream. Check the seasoning and adjust if necessary. Serve immediately.

Easy French Onion Soup

This is an easy version of the traditional recipe. It keeps all the rich flavour but it's less fiddly. It's so filling that you can serve it as a lunch or supper dish on its own. If you can't find Gruyère cheese, you could substitute Cheddar, but it's not so lovely and gooey when it melts into the soup. French bread is the best for this dish but any good crusty white loaf will do just as well.

For 6

1 kg (2 lb) onions, peeled and sliced
1 clove garlic, peeled and crushed
125 g (4 oz) butter
1 tablespoon flour
1.75 litres (3 pints) Brown Beef Stock (*see page 149*)
Salt and pepper
6 slices crusty white bread
75 g (3 oz) Gruyère cheese, grated

1   Prepare the onions and garlic.
2   Melt the butter in a large, deep pan over medium heat. When it begins to foam, add the onions and garlic.

Adding 1 teaspoon sugar will help to brown the onions faster.

3   Fry them, stirring frequently, for 20–25 minutes or until they turn a golden brown colour. The trick is to cook them long enough and at a sufficiently high temperature so that the butter doesn't burn but the onions take on a nice brown colour. The browner the onions, the sweeter and richer the flavour of the soup.
4   Add the flour and stir for 2–3 minutes so that all the butter is absorbed.
5   Gradually add the stock and simmer for 30 minutes or until the onions are cooked and taste soft and tender.
6   With a metal spoon skim off any excess fat that has risen to the surface of the soup. Season with salt and pepper to taste.
7   Toast the pieces of bread under the grill and then cover them with the grated cheese. Put back under the grill to melt and brown gently.
8   Pour the soup into individual soup bowls and place the 'cheese on toast' on top. Serve immediately. Any left-over grated cheese can be sprinkled on top and left to melt in the soup.

Eggs

Omelette

Whatever you think an omelette is, it's definitely not flat, brown or chewy. A traditional omelette is the French one, folded in two or three with a soft, moist interior. It's not easy to master, so don't expect to get it right the first time.

It's not worth making omelettes for a crowd of people unless you have a crate of eggs and nothing else in the house. This is because omelettes are best made for one person, and one at a time. They don't take long to cook, but if you were making them for more than about two people, you'd either have to keep the cooked omelettes warm (disastrous, as they would go dry and rubbery) or everyone would have finished before you even started.

Use a non-stick omelette pan. The non-stick coating absolutely guarantees that the omelette will slide easily out of the pan without needing a lot of butter as lubrication. If you don't have a non-stick frying pan, make sure that you use enough fat so that all the surface of the pan is coated.

An omelette pan is about 17.5 cm (7 in.) across (smaller than a normal frying pan), and it has rounded edges. It is the right size to make one omelette. If you have only a large pan, do not cook an omelette until you have two people to feed, then double the quantity of ingredients given below and just cut the omelette in half to serve it.

For 1

3 eggs
Salt and pepper
25 g (1 oz) butter

1   Warm the dry omelette pan over a medium heat.
2   Meanwhile, crack the eggs into a small bowl and whisk them slightly with a fork for about 10 seconds or until the white and yolk are only just blended. Season with a small pinch each of salt and pepper.
3   Add the butter to the pan when the pan is hot, so that the butter melts quickly and froths but doesn't have a chance to burn before the eggs go in. (If the butter turns dark brown, wipe out the pan and melt some more butter.) Turn the heat up to high and swirl the butter round so that the bottom and sides of the pan are completely coated.
4   Pour the eggs into the pan. Then shake the pan back and forth so that the mixture covers the bottom and begins to set.

5   Hold the pan in one hand and tilt it towards you so that the liquid egg runs down. Lift the edges of the setting egg with a fork or spatula so that the uncooked egg runs underneath and sets. Do this, tilting the pan in several different directions, until all the liquid egg has run underneath and set.

6   The omelette is ready when there is no runny liquid left but the top is still very moist. Don't let the top of the omelette dry out. It's better to undercook rather than overcook omelettes because they'll still continue to cook in their own heat even after they've left the pan.

7   Have a warmed plate ready beside the stove. Lift up the pan so that it is right next to the plate, with the side furthest from the plate tilted upwards. Using a fork or spatula, gently fold the third of the omelette furthest from the plate into the middle. Then fold over the middle third and slide the omelette on to the plate – it should land on the plate folded in three. Eat immediately.

Variations

Cheese. Grate 25 g (1 oz) Cheddar, Edam, Gruyère (or whatever type of cheese you prefer) and sprinkle it on top of the omelette just before you fold it over.

Herb. Sprinkle 25 g (1 oz) chopped fresh herbs over the top of the omelette just before you fold it over. Parsley, chives and chervil are the favourites.

Spanish Tortilla

Photograph on page 136

Superficially, this seems like a thick, rather boring potato omelette. But if it's made carefully, with olive oil, it's a lovely dish, and even better at room temperature than straight from the stove. It's also an interesting alternative to sandwiches for picnics.

The only trouble you might have in making a tortilla is in keeping the egg from sticking tenaciously to the pan. You can avoid this problem by using a non-stick frying pan; or, if you don't possess one, by wiping away any little bits of food remaining in the pan after frying the vegetables and before adding the egg, and again before turning the tortilla, and also by making sure that you always coat the pan with enough oil. The recipe below explains the procedure if you do not have a non-stick pan.

As for the size of the frying pan, the larger the pan, the thinner the tortilla and the shorter the time it will take to cook. We prefer a smaller pan – the kind you would make an omelette in. The resulting omelette is thicker, like a cake, and remains moist inside.

For 4

2 medium potatoes, peeled and thinly sliced
1 onion, peeled and thinly sliced
1 green pepper, deseeded and thinly sliced
4 eggs
Pinch each of salt and pepper
4 tablespoons or more olive oil

1   Prepare the vegetables.
2   Whisk the eggs in a bowl and season with the salt and pepper.
3   Heat 3 tablespoons of the olive oil in a frying pan over medium heat. When the oil is hot, add the potatoes and fry, stirring constantly and turning them over, for about 7–9 minutes or until they are cooked. They can cook quite gently and needn't go brown. Using a slotted spoon transfer the cooked potatoes to a plate and set aside.
4   Add the onion and pepper slices to the pan. If you need more oil, add an extra tablespoon at this point and increase the heat slightly.
5   Cook the vegetables, stirring constantly and turning them over, for another 5–7 minutes. They should be cooked but not mushy.
6   Remove the vegetables from the pan and lay them in a dish lined with kitchen paper to absorb any excess oil.
7   Wipe the pan with kitchen paper to clean away any small stray pieces of potato.
8   Put ½ tablespoon olive oil in the pan and heat it on medium-high. Swirl it around to cover the sides and bottom of the pan.

Feel free to add to the egg mixture chopped-up garlic sausage, sliced mushrooms, or anything else that needs little or no cooking.

9   Meanwhile, add the vegetables to the beaten egg and stir gently to combine them.
10 Pour the egg and vegetable mixture into the pan and turn the heat down to medium-low.
11 As the egg sets, run a thin spatula around the sides to prevent it from sticking.
12 Cook until the bottom of the tortilla is firm and golden brown in colour, and the top is just set.
13 Have a large plate waiting. Hold the plate over the top of the pan and turn the tortilla upside down on to it. (If you don't have a big enough plate, you may be able to use the lid of the frying pan, or even a small chopping board.)
14 Quickly wipe the empty frying pan clean of any remaining bits of egg.
15 Heat the remaining ½ tablespoon of oil in the pan and swirl it around to cover the sides and bottom.
16 Slip the omelette back into the pan, uncooked side down.
17 Cook for a further 3 minutes or until the bottom is golden brown and firm but not too dry.
18 Serve hot or at room temperature.

Vegetables

Braised Fennel

Photograph on page 185

Fennel is the bulbous vegetable that smells and tastes of aniseed. It can be used raw in salads but is excellent cooked and served to accompany roast meat. Buy fennel that feels heavy in the hand and has no discoloration. The bacon in this recipe adds extra flavour, but you could omit it.

For 4

4 bulbs fennel
4 rashers streaky bacon
4 tablespoons butter
2 carrots, peeled and sliced
1 medium onion, peeled and sliced
150 ml (5 fl oz) hot Chicken Stock (*see page 147*)
Salt and pepper

1   Bring a large pan of cold water to the boil.
2   Meanwhile, prepare the fennel. Remove the green shoots from the top of each bulb and carefully trim off the base. If any of the outer leaves looked discoloured, remove and discard them.
3   Cut the bulbs in half lengthways and place them in the boiling water. Bring the water back to the boil, then lower the heat to medium and simmer for 5 minutes. Drain.
4   Meanwhile, trim the bacon of excess fat and cut the rashers into thin strips. Prepare the vegetables.
5   Melt the butter in a deep thick-bottomed pan over medium heat. Before it starts to burn, add the bacon strips and cook for 2–3 minutes.
6   Add the carrots and onion and cook for a further 2–3 minutes. Place the fennel on top of the vegetables and cover with the hot chicken stock.
7   Season with salt and pepper. Cover with a tight-fitting lid, turn the heat down to low and simmer for 45 minutes or until the fennel halves are soft all the way through when pierced with a knife.
8   Remove the fennel halves and place on a serving dish. Spoon over them the sauce in which they have cooked and serve immediately.

Green Beans with Tomatoes, Bacon and Almonds

This is a great combination of ingredients – simple, colourful and really impressive. It is a nice vegetable dish to serve at dinner parties, one reason being that it can be prepared in advance up to stage 5 and then finished off at the last minute. The quick boiling of the beans followed by sautéeing is a method of cooking vegetables to ensure that they retain a little bite.

Instructions are given in this recipe for skinning tomatoes. This is a useful technique to learn as recipes often call for it. It consists of immersing the tomatoes in boiling water for a few seconds, then 'refreshing' them in cold water. The skins will peel off quite easily.

For 4

250 g (8 oz) green beans, topped and tailed
2 medium tomatoes
25 g (1 oz) butter
3 rashers bacon, derinded and cut into small pieces
25 g (1 oz) flaked almonds
Salt and pepper

1   Prepare the ingredients. Bring a pan of water to the boil.
2   Place the green beans in the water and boil for 5–8 minutes, or until they are just crisp, not soft.
3   To save boiling water twice, place a sieve over a large bowl. Drain the beans through the sieve, collecting the cooking water in the bowl. Then hold the sieve under cold running water to refresh the beans and stop them cooking. Set them aside.
4   Place the tomatoes in the bowl of hot water which you have just drained off the beans and leave them to soak for 10 seconds. Retrieve them with a large spoon and hold them under cold running water. Then, using a small knife, peel off the skin.
5   Cut the tomatoes in half. Scoop out the seeds with a teaspoon, leaving the flesh behind. Cut the tomato halves into quarters and set aside on a piece of kitchen paper.
6   Melt the butter in a frying pan over a medium heat. When it foams, add the bacon pieces and fry for 2–3 minutes. Then add the beans, tomato quarters and almonds. Season with a little salt and pepper.
7   Fry for 5 minutes. It is important to keep turning the mixture over, otherwise it will burn on one side and be cold on the other.
8   The dish is ready when the vegetables are hot all the way through and the almonds are golden brown. The tomatoes may have broken down a little, but that doesn't matter. Serve immediately in a warmed dish.

Potato Curry

Photograph on page 135

The best curries don't include curry powder, which shouldn't come as a great surprise. As so many supermarkets, not to mention corner shops, sell Indian spices, you can try your hand at the real thing, especially an easy curry like this one. If possible, serve it with Basmati rice, which has a lovely flavour and is cooked in the same way as plain Patna rice (*see page 116*). The rice can be cooked at the same time so you'll end up with a fast and filling supper dish. See page 218 for serving it as part of an Indian meal.

The important points to remember with this dish are to make sure that the oil is hot enough to cook the spices properly and that the water has almost completely boiled away before you add the yoghurt.

Feel free to add more or less of the spices than recommended below, especially the cayenne pepper. You can also add frozen peas half-way through cooking the potatoes if you like, making sure that you add slightly less water at the beginning as the peas will give off liquid as they thaw and cook.

For 4

2 teaspoons cumin seeds
2 teaspoons black mustard seeds
1 teaspoon powdered turmeric
1 teaspoon ground coriander
½ teaspoon cayenne or chilli pepper
½ teaspoon salt (or to taste)
4 medium potatoes
2 tablespoons vegetable oil
150 ml (5 fl oz) water
75 ml (3 fl oz) plain yoghurt
1 teaspoon garam masala

1 Measure out the cumin and mustard seeds and put them into a small bowl. Put the turmeric, coriander, cayenne pepper and salt into another small bowl.
2 Peel the potatoes and cut them into 1 cm (½ in.) cubes.
3 Heat the oil in a large frying pan over the highest heat.
4 Add the cumin and mustard seeds. When they start to pop, which will be almost immediately, add the other spices. The spices will start to darken straight away.
5 Add the cubed potatoes, spread them out in one layer and turn the heat down to medium-high. Stir for 4–5 minutes so that the potatoes are completely coated with the spices and oil; they should also start to brown and crispen.
6 Add the water, making sure that the potatoes are still in one layer, and turn the heat down to low, so that the liquid is gently bubbling. Do not cover.

If you intend to serve rice with the curry, start cooking it when you put the potatoes in the pan to fry. The rice can hang about but the curry can't.

7   Cook for 15–18 minutes or until the water has almost evaporated and the potatoes are tender but not mushy. Add more water if it evaporates before the potatoes are cooked.
8   Add the yoghurt and mix in. Taste the sauce and add more salt if necessary. Take the curry off the heat, sprinkle the garam masala over and stir in.
9   Serve immediately.

Potatoes Romanoff

The only recipe in the book which is an unashamed tribute, this is adapted from Anna Thomas' *The Vegetarian Epicure* (Penguin, 1973) and is a terrific combination of seemingly ordinary ingredients.

For 4

6 large potatoes
250 g (8 oz) cottage cheese
75 g (3 oz) plain yoghurt
1–2 cloves garlic, peeled and finely chopped
1 teaspoon salt
2–3 spring onions, finely chopped
¼ teaspoon cayenne pepper (optional)
125 g (4 oz) Cheddar cheese, grated
½ teaspoon paprika

1   Pre-heat the oven to 180°C (350°F, gas mark 4).
2   Bring a large pan of water to the boil over the highest heat.
3   Meanwhile, peel the potatoes and cut them into 1 cm (½ in.) cubes.
4   When the water boils, add the potatoes and simmer over a medium heat for 5–8 minutes or until they are barely cooked. If anything, they should be a little undercooked, firm in the middle. Drain the potatoes on kitchen paper to make sure that they are absolutely dry.
5   Meanwhile, prepare the remaining ingredients.
6   Put the potato cubes in an ovenproof casserole. Add the cottage cheese, yoghurt, garlic, salt, spring onions and cayenne pepper, if using. Mix thoroughly.
7   Spread the grated Cheddar cheese on top and sprinkle the paprika over.
8   Bake in the oven for 30 minutes or until the Cheddar cheese is melted and golden. Depending on your brand of yoghurt, you may find that some liquid remains at the bottom of the casserole. If so, drain off as much as you can and put the dish back in the oven for another 7–10 minutes to dry off before serving.

Ratatouille

There are many versions of this Provençal vegetable stew; this one requires less work than most. It's good either hot or cold and its flavour improves if it is kept overnight to be eaten the day after cooking. Serve it with good bread, or on a bed of plain rice. In fact, you can even thin it down and pour it over spaghetti. If you want to make it more Mediterranean, add a few stoned black olives or capers.

The best time to make Ratatouille is in late summer when all the vegetables are plentiful. If you see inexpensive over-ripe tomatoes on sale at this time of year, substitute them for the tinned ones.

For 4–6

3–4 cloves garlic, peeled and crushed
1 large onion, peeled and chopped
1 medium aubergine, cut into 1 cm (½ in.) cubes
2 medium courgettes, cut into 6 mm (¼ in.) slices
2 medium green peppers, deseeded and cut into strips
50 ml (2 fl oz) olive oil
1 × 397 g (14 oz) tin tomatoes
1 teaspoon marjoram
1 teaspoon oregano
Salt and pepper
1 small bunch parsley, finely chopped (optional)

1   Prepare all the fresh vegetables.
2   Heat the oil in a large saucepan over medium heat with the garlic.
3   When the garlic starts to sizzle but before it turns brown, add the onion. Cook until the onion becomes soft and transparent.
4   Add the aubergine and the tinned tomatoes. Mash the tomatoes with a fork to break them up. Season with the marjoram and oregano, salt and pepper. Stir to mix well.
5   Put the lid on the pan and cook for 10–15 minutes with the liquid bubbling.
6   Test the aubergine to see if it's tender enough for a fork to pierce it easily. If so, stir in the courgettes and peppers. Cover again and cook for another 10 minutes.
7   Test the aubergine a second time. If it's completely cooked, take the lid off the pan, turn the heat up to medium-high and cook, stirring, until the liquid has evaporated and you're left with a thick vegetable stew.
8   Taste and add extra salt and pepper if necessary. Transfer to a warmed serving dish, sprinkle on the parsley, if using, and serve immediately.

Spinach Pudding

Photograph on page 187

This is a sort of spinach rice pudding – filling but with a delicate flavour. It can be eaten either as a side dish or as a quick light supper. If you're a determined carnivore, you can add cooked bacon to it to make it more substantial, but it's perfectly nice as it is. Try to serve it with another moister dish or with a Tomato Sauce (*see page 114*) as it's slightly dry.

Don't substitute frozen spinach for fresh in this recipe as it's too watery.

For 4–6

750 g (1½ lb) spinach
125 ml (4 fl oz) rice
Salt and pepper
4 eggs
300 ml (10 fl oz) milk
15 g (½ oz) Parmesan cheese, grated

1   Pre-heat the oven to 190°C (375°F, gas mark 5).
2   Fill one medium and one large saucepan full of water and bring both to the boil over the highest heat.
3   Meanwhile, remove and discard the thick stems of the spinach and wash it in three changes of water, making sure that you get rid of all the grit.
4   When the water in the medium saucepan boils, add the rice and ½ teaspoon salt. Let it come to the boil again, turn the heat down to low and simmer, uncovered, for 15 minutes or until the rice is tender. Drain the rice in a sieve and set aside; it should end up sticky but not waterlogged.
5   Meanwhile, put the spinach in the large saucepan when the water boils. Cook it for 30 seconds. It should wilt almost immediately. Take the spinach out of the water using a slotted spoon.
6   Place the spinach on kitchen paper to drain. Then roll up the leaves and roughly chop them into small pieces with a sharp knife. The spinach doesn't have to be chopped very finely, just cut into small enough pieces so that it won't be stringy in the pudding.
7   Crack the eggs into a large bowl and whisk them until the yolks and whites are blended. Pour the milk into the eggs slowly, whisking all the time.

You could add 2–3 rashers of diced bacon, grilled or fried until crisp, at stage 8.

8   Add salt and pepper. Then add the drained rice and the chopped spinach and mix thoroughly.
9   Pour the mixture into a shallow ovenproof dish. Sprinkle the Parmesan cheese on top.
10 Bake in the oven for 30 minutes or until the top is firm and there is no trace of liquid when you tilt the dish slightly.
11 Serve immediately.

Cauliflower Cheese

This much-loved dish can accompany any simple main course, particularly plain cuts of meat. However, it's best-known as a light supper dish and a very substantial one at that.

The recipe uses the basic Cheese Sauce given on page 145 and the cauliflower is cooked as described on page 65, but the instructions are combined here for ease of reference. If you like, you can read the basic recipes for extra hints before you start. The sauce can be made while the cauliflower is boiling, which saves time. Otherwise, you can make it the day before and simply warm it up while the cauliflower is cooking.

Use the strongest Cheddar you can buy. You need a sauce with lots of flavour to counteract the blandness of the cauliflower. However, you can also add ¼ teaspoon mustard powder or a pinch of cayenne pepper to sharpen the taste.

For 4

1 large cauliflower
Salt and pepper
600 ml (1 pint) milk
½ onion, peeled
3 cloves
65 g (2½ oz) butter
50 g (2 oz) flour
125 g (4 oz) Cheddar cheese, grated

1   Put 5 cm (2 in.) cold water in a saucepan large enough to hold the cauliflower and bring it to the boil.
2   Meanwhile, remove the outer leaves of the cauliflower and hollow out the centre of the stem with a vegetable peeler or small sharp knife. Wash the cauliflower in salted water: this will flush out any insects hidden in the crevices. Rewash in plain cold water.
3   Place the cauliflower, stem down, in the pan and bring the water back up to the boil. Then turn down the heat to medium and cook, covered, for about 20 minutes, or until the cauliflower feels tender when pierced through the thickest part of the stalk.
4   Gently lift the cauliflower out of the pan with two large slotted spoons so that all the water drains off. Be careful not to damage the florets. Place the cauliflower, stem down, in a warmed ovenproof serving dish and cover it with a piece of aluminium foil to conserve the heat.
5   While the cauliflower is cooking, make the sauce. Pour the milk into a small pan. Push the pointed ends of the cloves into the onion and place it in the milk. Bring the milk to the boil and immediately pour it into a jug and set aside.

6   Melt 50 g (2 oz) of the butter in a thick-bottomed pan over a low heat. Add the flour and mix thoroughly with a wooden spoon so that the mixture resembles a sandy-coloured paste (or roux).

7   Cook the roux very gently for 2–3 minutes, stirring constantly so that it does not burn.

8   Remove the onion from the milk and discard it. Add the warmed milk little by little to the roux, mixing it in thoroughly with a wooden spoon until no lumps remain.

9   Turn down the heat to its lowest setting and simmer the sauce for 5–7 minutes.

10 Pre-heat the oven to 220°C (425°F, gas mark 7).

11 Gradually add 75 g (3 oz) of the grated cheese and the remaining butter to the sauce and stir well until it is melted and blended in. Season with salt and pepper. Taste the sauce, and add any extra flavouring at this point if you want.

12 Pour the sauce over the cauliflower and sprinkle the remaining grated cheese on top.

13 Place the dish in the oven for 10–15 minutes or until the cheese topping turns a golden brown.

Chicken

Casseroles

This prosaically named method of cooking chicken pieces is exceptionally easy. The chicken is first browned in fat on top of the stove, then cooked gently in liquid in a covered pan (on top of the stove) or lidded dish (in the oven). You end up with very moist chicken smothered in a tasty sauce. In fact, it is the same method used in braising meat (*see page 170*) except that the word 'braise' doesn't usually apply to poultry. Poultry nowadays never needs really long cooking because it's not tough. Even so-called 'boiling fowls' don't need much more cooking than their roasting cousins. You casserole chicken pieces if you want them to absorb lots of flavour from the sauce, whether the flavour comes from the cooking liquid, from spices or herbs, or from vegetables cooked with the meat. The chicken pieces in the following recipes can either have the bone in or be boneless.

Casseroling is easy because once you've done the intial preparation, you can go away and leave it: perfect for when you have other things on your mind. The top-of-the-stove method is the quicker of the two but you will need to check the pan from time to time to make sure that it doesn't burn on the bottom as the heat is more direct; the oven method takes longer but as the heat surrounds the casserole, the chicken has little chance of burning.

For the top-of-the-stove method you will need a large thick-bottomed saucepan (an enamelled cast-iron one is ideal) with its own well-fitting lid. You may wish either to cook the whole dish in this or to fry the chicken and make the sauce in a frying pan and then transfer both to the saucepan. To cook the dish in the oven you will need a large ovenproof casserole, again with a tight-fitting lid; if it is also flameproof, you can start the dish off in it on top of the stove.

If you want to try cooking a casserole entirely on top of the stove, proceed to the point where you pour the sauce over the chicken and cover it with a lid. Bring the sauce to the boil over medium heat, then turn the heat down to its lowest setting. Cook for 30 minutes, stirring from time to time to make sure that the chicken doesn't stick to the bottom of the pan and adding extra stock if the sauce looks too thick. The chicken will be done if there is no evidence of blood when the flesh is pierced at its thickest part with a knife. Remember that it is always safer to overcook rather than undercook chicken. And in a casserole you can cook the chicken for quite a bit longer than the recommended time without any risk of failure; the flesh will simply drop off the bones!

The first two recipes are very easy and straightforward because the sauce is just the cooking liquid which has thickened solely through evaporation. The last recipe has a sauce which uses flour as the thickener, and two cooking processes are called for. You first brown the chicken in some fat to give it colour and flavour. Then you remove the chicken and make the sauce. Fat and flour, the thickening mixture, start off the sauce and then a liquid is added – stock, wine or a mixture of the two. Use a cube if you do not have any home-made stock and don't have time to make any. You can re-acquaint yourself with flour-and-butter sauce making by turning to page 144. Different vegetables and flavourings can be added as you go along. Finally, you gently cook the chicken in the sauce so that it remains moist. There are literally thousands of casseroled chicken recipes using this method.

Lemon and Herb Chicken

This is the easiest of the chicken recipes in this section because you don't need to make a separate sauce. However, because the dish doesn't have a substantial sauce, it's better to serve it with potatoes rather than rice.

Lemon and chicken are a lovely combination, and you get the lemon flavour from both the juice and the peel.

For 4

4 large or 8 small chicken pieces
2 lemons
8 tablespoons butter
Salt and pepper
2 tablespoons water
3 spring onions, chopped
1 teaspoon oregano
250 g (8 oz) mushrooms, cleaned and thinly sliced
2 tablespoons finely chopped parsley

1   Wash the chicken pieces and pat dry with kitchen paper.
2   Pre-heat the oven to 180°C (350°F, gas mark 4).
3   Cut 4 thin strips of peel from the lemons and squeeze the juice from the fruit. Prepare the rest of the ingredients.
4   Melt 6 tablespoons of the butter in a thick-bottomed frying pan or heavy flameproof casserole over medium heat. When the butter starts to foam, add as many chicken pieces as will fit in a single layer without crowding. Season with salt and pepper and cook for 3–4 minutes or until the chicken turns golden brown.
5   Turn the pieces over, season with more salt and pepper and cook for the same length of time. You may need to fry the chicken pieces in several batches.
6   Transfer the chicken to a casserole dish, if necessary. The pieces don't have to be placed in one layer so long as you move them around during cooking.
7   Add the lemon peel and juice, the water, spring onions and oregano.
8   Cover tightly with a lid and cook in the oven for 40–50 minutes or until the juices run clear with no trace of blood when the chicken is pierced to the bone with a knife. The flesh should also come away easily from the bone.
9   Just before the end of the cooking time, melt the remaining butter in a small frying pan over medium heat. When it foams, add the mushrooms and cook gently for 1 minute.
10 Stir the mushrooms into the casserole.
11 Transfer the chicken to a warmed dish (or leave it in the casserole), scatter the parsley over the top and serve immediately.

Italian Chicken with Tomato

It's the combination of onion, garlic and tomato which makes this dish Italian. Add extra oregano and garlic if you want a stronger flavour. The sauce goes particularly well with boiled rice.

If you can find a tin or carton of *passata*, which is simply liquid tomato pulp, this is actually better than tinned tomatoes for this recipe, but it is more expensive.

For 4

4 large or 8 small chicken pieces
2 onions, peeled and thinly sliced
2 cloves garlic, peeled and finely chopped
4 stalks celery, finely chopped
50 ml (2 fl oz) olive oil
Salt and pepper
1 × 397 g (14 oz) tin tomatoes
250 ml (8 fl oz) water
2 teaspoons oregano

1   Wash the chicken pieces and pat them dry with kitchen paper.
2   Pre-heat the oven to 180°C (350°F, gas mark 4).
3   Prepare the fresh vegetables.
4   Heat the oil in a thick-bottomed frying pan or heavy flameproof casserole. When it shimmers on the surface, add as many chicken pieces as will fit in a single layer without crowding. Season with salt and pepper and cook for 3–4 minutes or until the chicken turns golden brown.
5   Turn the pieces over, season the browned side with salt and pepper and cook the other side for the same length of time. You may need to fry the chicken pieces in several batches.
6   Transfer the chicken to a casserole dish, if necessary. The pieces don't have to be placed in one layer, so long as you move them around during cooking.
7   Separate the onions into rings and scatter them, together with the garlic and celery, over the chicken.
8   Mash the tomatoes to a pulp with a fork or potato masher. Alternatively, put them in a blender or food processor and blend until smooth.
9   Combine the tomatoes, water and oregano and pour over the chicken.
10 Cover tightly and cook in the oven for 40–50 minutes or until the juices run clear with no trace of blood when the chicken is pierced to the bone with a knife. The flesh should also come away easily from the bone.
11 Serve immediately.

Chinese Stir-fried Chicken and Vegetables

Normally, it takes an experienced cook to make a real success of Chinese cooking. But we're suggesting a light supper dish, which can also be a way of using up stray vegetables in the fridge. Of course, it's not a 'real' Chinese dish – it just uses Chinese flavourings – but it does taste very nice. It is also a good way of making meat stretch.

Unless you intend to take up Chinese cuisine seriously, don't buy a wok. A non-stick pan is a good substitute. But you do have to pretend that your frying pan is a wok. The art of wok-cooking is to cook the food very quickly in a small amount of oil over high heat, stirring all the time. The food mustn't steam in its own juices; the pieces must be small enough to cook completely while still retaining moistness and, in the case of vegetables, crispness. You probably won't get it absolutely right the first time, but in fact it's easy to get the hang of.

The best types of vegetables for this dish are those with a relatively low water content (don't use tomatoes, for instance) and which can be eaten raw (don't use potatoes or aubergines). The list below is a guide; you can also use courgettes, cauliflowers, mange-tout, and so on. The basic rule is: cut the vegetables into small pieces of uniform size, and cook the denser food first, leaving light items till last. Make sure that you don't start cooking until all the vegetables are cut up and placed ready alongside the stove.

If you want to be fussy about soy sauce, get the type marked 'superior'. The term 'light' denotes a salty sauce without as much of the characteristic soy flavour. Serve the dish with plain boiled rice and extra soy sauce, or commercial oyster sauce, on the side. You should have the rice completely cooked and keeping warm in the oven before you start stir-frying the chicken and vegetables.

For 2–3

125–175 g (4–6 oz) chicken breast, boned and skinned
2 tablespoons soy sauce
1 tablespoon dry sherry
2 teaspoons cornflour
1 × 5 cm (1 × 2 in.) piece root ginger, peeled and finely chopped
2 cloves garlic, peeled and finely chopped
2–3 spring onions, finely chopped, including the green part
½ medium green pepper, chopped in 2.5 cm (1 in.) pieces
A few broccoli florets, no more than 2.5 cm (1 in.) long
50 g (2 oz) mushrooms, cleaned and cut into 2.5 cm (1 in.) pieces if large, left whole if small
3 tablespoons vegetable oil
Boiled rice to serve (*see page 116*)

1   Cut the chicken into 1 cm (½ in.) cubes.
2   Place the soy sauce, sherry and cornflour in a bowl and blend thoroughly until there are no lumps. Put the chicken in this mixture and stir so that it's completely coated.
3   Meanwhile, prepare all the vegetables and place them in separate bowls. Have ready a utensil with which you can scoop and stir the chicken and vegetables.
4   When you have all the ingredients close at hand, heat the empty frying pan over the highest heat for about 1 minute. Add 1 tablespoon of the oil and swirl it around.
5   Lift the chicken out of the soy sauce mixture with a slotted spoon and place it in the pan. Move the chicken around, turning it over constantly so that it cooks without burning over the high flame. Cook the chicken like this for about 1 minute.
6   Remove the chicken from the pan and set aside.
7   Add the remaining oil to the pan and swirl it around. Add the chopped ginger, garlic and spring onions. Cook, stirring for 30 seconds. Add the green pepper to the pan. Cook, stirring and turning over constantly for 30 seconds.
8   Add the broccoli florets and cook, stirring, for 30 seconds to 1 minute. Then add the mushrooms and cook for a further 30 seconds.
9   Pour ½ tablespoon water into the bowl with the remaining soy sauce mixture and stir.
10 Return the chicken to the pan, followed immediately by the soy sauce mixture. Cook for a further 30 seconds to 1 minute, then serve immediately on top of boiled rice.

Chicken in Brandy and Tarragon Sauce

Photograph on page 185

This dish has a sophisticated taste. Make sure that you don't overdo the brandy – even when you burn the alcohol off (which happens during the cooking), the strong flavour remains and it must not overshadow the tarragon.

For 4

4 large or 8 small chicken pieces
75 g (3 oz) onions, finely chopped
½ clove garlic, crushed
50 g (2 oz) mushrooms, cleaned and sliced
50 g (2 oz) butter
Salt and pepper
2–3 teaspoons tarragon

15 g (½ oz) flour
150 ml (5 fl oz) hot Chicken Stock (*see page 147*)
50 ml (2 fl oz) brandy
Juice ½ lemon
150 ml (5 fl oz) single cream

1   Wash the chicken pieces and dry them with kitchen paper. Prepare the vegetables.
2   Pre-heat the oven to 180°C (350°F, gas mark 4).
3   Melt the butter in a thick-bottomed frying pan or heavy flameproof casserole over medium heat and, when it starts to foam, add as many chicken pieces as will fit in a single layer without crowding. Season with salt, pepper and tarragon. Fry for 3–4 minutes or until the chicken turns golden brown.
4   Turn the pieces over, season with more salt, pepper and tarragon and cook for the same length of time. You may need to fry the chicken in several batches.
5   Take the pan off the stove but do not turn off the heat. With a slotted spoon transfer the chicken from the pan to an ovenproof casserole and set aside.
6   Add the onions and garlic to the butter in the pan and cook for 2 minutes, then add the mushrooms and cook, stirring frequently, for a further 2 minutes.
7   Stir in the flour and mix thoroughly until completely blended with the butter into a sandy paste (or roux). Cook gently for 2 minutes and then gradually add the hot stock, stirring constantly.
8   Add the brandy to the sauce and mix in well.

You may wish to add more tarragon at stage 9 if you particularly like its taste.

9   Season the sauce to taste with salt and pepper, and then pour it over the chicken.
10 Put a tight-fitting lid on the casserole and place it in the oven. Cook for 40–50 minutes or until the juices run clear with no trace of blood when the chicken is pierced to the bone with a knife. The flesh should also come away easily from the bone.
11 Just before serving, add the lemon juice and cream, mixing them in thoroughly.
12 Serve immediately, either from the casserole dish or from a warmed serving dish.

Braising and Stewing

Most of the meat recipes in this advanced section call for the use of cheaper meat, longer cooking or more than one cooking process – or all three. In fact, the three things are not unconnected. Cheaper meat will almost always be tougher than expensive meat; long cooking alone will break down the tough fibres, but the addition of another cooking process, like frying, helps retain the flavour. Most of the meat recipes in this section use either braising or stewing, two similar techniques. In both cases, the meat is usually browned in oil beforehand to colour it and to bring out the meaty taste, then simmered in a liquid, usually stock or broth, in a covered pan. You can make the stock with a cube if you don't have any home-made to hand. Flour may be added to the meat during browning to thicken the sauce. (See page 144 for a reminder of how a roux is used.) This technique – frying, then cooking gently in liquid – is also used for chicken. Make sure the meat or poultry is as dry as possible before frying, otherwise it will not brown properly.

Ideally, stews and braised meats are most easily made in a heavy flameproof casserole which can go both on top of the stove and in the oven. However, you can start the stew off in a thick-bottomed frying pan and then put the stew into a glass or earthenware casserole dish. Whatever type dish you choose, it must have a tight-fitting lid so that the cooking juices don't evaporate.

Braising and stewing often create extra liquid both from the meat and from the vegetables used. Don't serve a watery sauce; this is a common mistake! If you need to thicken the sauce after the final cooking by reducing it over the heat, you may need to transfer it to a pan that you can use on top of the stove. Don't try to boil away extra sauce from a non-flameproof casserole or it may crack.

Carbonnade of Beef

This is a traditional Flemish method of cooking beef whose main ingredients are onions and beer. Use the strongest brown ale you can find – Newcastle Brown is a good one. If you buy your meat from a butcher, ask him or her to cut it into steaks for you. You should end up with 3 small steaks per person, 12 in all.

For 4

4 × 175 g (6 oz) topside steaks
3 medium onions, peeled and thinly sliced
25 g (1 oz) butter
25 g (1 oz) flour
Salt and pepper
300 ml (10 fl oz) beer
300 ml (10 fl oz) Beef Stock (*see page 148*)

1 Wash the meat and dry it with kitchen paper. Prepare the onions.

2 Pre-heat the oven to 190°C (375°F, gas mark 5).

3 Melt the butter in a frying pan over medium heat.

4 Meanwhile, put the flour on a plate. Dip both sides of each steak into the flour, shaking off the excess.

5 When the butter is foaming, place as many of the steaks in the pan as it will hold in one layer. Fry the steaks on both sides until golden, then set aside. Do the same with the rest of the steaks.

6 Put the sliced onions in the pan with the butter and meat juices and cook gently for 5–6 minutes, or until the onions are translucent.

7 Place alternate layers of steak and onions in a casserole, seasoning each layer with salt and pepper.

8 Pour the beer and stock over the layered steak and onions. Cover with a tight-fitting lid and cook in the oven for approximately 1 hour or until the steaks are tender.

9 Before serving, remove any fat that has risen to the top of the liquid either by floating some kitchen paper on the surface to absorb it or by skimming it off with a spoon.

10 Check the seasoning, adjust it if necessary and serve immediately.

Ragoût de Boeuf

This is the classic beef stew with vegetables, whether its title is in English or French. As with all slow-cooked dishes, once you've done the initial preparation you bung all the ingredients into the casserole and come back later to a delicious steaming cooked dish. The flavouring vegetables and the meat can simply braise undisturbed in the hot liquid.

Ragoût de Boeuf is a very flexible dish. If you want to use it as a filling main course to a dinner party, serve the vegetable garnish with plain noodles (fettucine or tagliatelle) as a good accompaniment. For less trouble, omit the garnish (skipping stages 7–9) and serve as a family dish with thick bread. Also, if any of the garnish vegetables are unavailable, simply leave them out; the main-recipe vegetables are more crucial.

The stew tastes just as good, if not better, the next day. Store it, covered, in the fridge. Reheat with a little water (just enough to 'loosen' the stew and prevent it sticking to the bottom of the pan) over a medium heat, or microwave on HIGH for 3–5 minutes, depending on the amount you have. You may find it useful to freeze the stew and defrost it later.

For 4–6

750 g (1½ lb) topside, cut into 2.5 cm (1 in.) cubes
1 medium onion, roughly chopped
2 carrots, peeled and sliced into thin rounds
3 stalks celery, washed and sliced into 1 cm (½ in.) pieces
1 large leek, washed, halved lengthways and thinly sliced
3 tablespoons vegetable oil
½ tablespoon flour
2–3 tablespoons tomato purée
1 clove garlic, peeled and crushed
600 ml (1 pint) hot Beef Stock (*see page 148*)
125 ml (4 fl oz) red wine (optional)
1 bouquet garni
Salt and pepper

For the Garnish:

250 g (8 oz) button onions, peeled
250 g (8 oz) turnips, peeled and diced
250 g (8 oz) carrots, peeled and diced
250 g (8 oz) potatoes, peeled and diced
1 tablespoon butter

1   Prepare the meat and the vegetables itemised in the main list of ingredients (not the garnish vegetables).
2   Pre-heat the oven to 200°C (400°F, gas mark 6).
3   Heat the oil over medium-high heat in a heavy flameproof casserole and, when it is hot, add the meat. Fry the meat, stirring constantly, so that it turns a light brown colour on all sides.

To colour the flour slightly and give the stew a richer flavour, do not stir it in after sprinkling it over the vegetables but place the casserole, uncovered, in the oven for 10 minutes. Stir the browned flour into the vegetables after you have taken the casserole out of the oven to proceed with stage 5.

4   Add all the prepared vegetables (except the garlic) from the main ingredients list. Fry for 3–4 minutes, stirring, then sprinkle the flour over them and mix in well for 2–3 minutes.
5   Add the tomato purée and garlic and stir thoroughly. Ladle in the stock gradually, mixing between each addition, then pour in the red wine. Finally add the bouquet garni and season with salt and pepper.
6   Cover the casserole with a tight-fitting lid and cook in the oven for about 1½ hours.
7   Thirty minutes before the end of the cooking time, bring two pans of water to the boil. Meanwhile, prepare the garnish vegetables, making sure that they are all cut into pieces of the same size so that they take the same length of time to cook.
8   About 15 minutes before the end of the cooking time, start to cook the garnish vegetables. Put the onions, turnips and carrots into one of the pans and simmer until the turnips are cooked through but not soft, by which time the other vegetables should be cooked too. Put the potatoes in the other pan and boil until they are cooked but not falling apart.

If the potatoes do fall apart during the cooking however careful you are, you won't have a nasty mess if they're cooking separately from the other vegetables.

172

9   Drain all the cooked garnish vegetables together and put into one pan with the butter. Cover and set aside.

10 Remove the stew from the oven, discard the bouquet garni and check the consistency of the sauce. It should be fairly thick, so that it will coat the back of a spoon. If it's too thin, place the casserole, uncovered, over a medium heat and stir constantly so that the extra liquid evaporates. If the sauce is too thick, add extra stock or red wine and cook over medium heat for an extra 5 minutes. Check the seasoning and adjust if necessary.

11 You can either serve the stew straight from the casserole with the garnish vegetables on top, or pour it into a warmed serving dish and place the vegetables at the sides.

Lamb with Haricot Beans

Although this dish takes a long time to cook, it's hearty, filling and uses a very inexpensive cut of lamb. The dried haricot beans, also very cheap and healthy, need to be soaked overnight before you make the dish. You don't really need to serve potatoes or rice with this – just mash the beans as you eat them and they'll absorb the sauce!

Lamb oozes fat so the trick in cooking it is to remove all the surplus at the start. Two minutes with a sharp knife before cooking saves 20 minutes trying to remove the liquid fat after cooking. If you can't find bacon bones at the supermarket, ask a butcher for some: they are inexpensive.

Try to use a flameproof casserole dish with a tight-fitting lid. Otherwise, brown the meat and vegetables in a frying pan and then remove them to an oven casserole.

For 4

750 g (1½ lb) boneless stewing lamb, cut in 2.5 cm (1 in.) cubes
1 medium onion, peeled and chopped
2 carrots, peeled and chopped
3 tablespoons vegetable oil
25 g (1 oz) flour
2 tablespoons tomato purée
1 clove garlic, peeled and crushed
600 ml (1 pint) Beef Stock (*see page 148*)
Salt and pepper
1 bouquet garni

For the Beans:

125 g (4 oz) dried haricot beans
6 whole cloves
1 medium onion, peeled but left whole
125 g (4 oz) bacon bones (optional)
1 carrot

173

1   First, prepare the beans. Cover them with cold water and leave them to soak overnight, or for a minimum of 8 hours. Drain and rinse well under cold running water.

2   Place the beans in a large pan and cover with fresh cold water. Bring to the boil over the highest heat. When the water is boiling, skim off any scum that rises to the surface. Lower the heat so that the beans are simmering.

3   Stick the pointed ends of the cloves into the onion at regular intervals.

4   Add the bacon bones (if using), carrot and onion to the simmering beans. Continue to simmer for 30–40 minutes or until the beans are tender.

5   Meanwhile, trim excess fat from the lamb. Prepare the vegetables.

6   When the beans are cooked, strain off the cooking liquid and reserve it in a jug. Put the beans to one side.

7   Pre-heat the oven to 180°C (350°F, gas mark 4).

8   Heat the oil in a flameproof casserole. When it's hot, fry the meat and vegetables until golden brown. Remove the meat and vegetables using a slotted spoon. Discard all the fat remaining in the casserole.

9   Place the meat and vegetables back in the casserole. Sprinkle the flour over them but do not stir it in. Place the casserole into the oven for 10 minutes so that the flour browns.

10 Remove the casserole from the oven. Add the tomato purée and garlic and mix in well.

11 Gradually add both the beans' cooking liquid and the Beef Stock, mixing thoroughly as you pour them in. Season with salt and pepper.

12 Bring the stew to the boil. Skim the surface and add the bouquet garni.

13 Cover with a tight-fitting lid and cook in the oven for approximately 2 hours or until the meat is tender.

14 Remove the cooked meat from the sauce with a draining spoon and place in a warmed ovenproof serving dish. Add the cooked beans and mix together with the meat. Cover and place in the oven to heat the beans through while you finish the sauce.

15 Remove the bouquet garni from the sauce and discard. Taste the sauce and, if necessary, adjust the seasoning. If the sauce is very watery, place it over a high heat and boil it hard to reduce the volume.

16 Pour the sauce over the meat and beans and serve immediately.

You can save time by making this dish with tinned instead of dried beans. If you do, add 300 ml (10 fl oz) extra Beef Stock at stage 11 to replace the missing beans' cooking liquid, and simply add the tinned beans, drained of liquid, at stage 13, just 15 minutes before the end of the cooking time. At stage 14, remove both meat and beans from the sauce and keep warm in the oven while you finish the sauce.

Pork Cooked in Milk

Photograph on page 256

Try this method of cooking a whole joint of pork as a change from conventional roasting. It may sound slightly odd but it's actually surprisingly sweet and moist, and it creates its own sauce too.

Because the meat is cooked on top of the stove, you need a large lidded casserole dish that is flameproof. Otherwise, you can use a large saucepan, but make sure that it has a thick bottom. The pan should be just large enough to hold the meat, but not so large that it will need lots of milk to cook in. Be very careful not to overcook the pork as it dries out easily.

For 4–6

1 × 1 kg (2 lb) boneless loin of pork
2 cloves garlic (optional)
2 tablespoons vegetable oil
25 g butter (1 oz) butter
Salt and pepper
1 litre (2 pints) whole milk

1   Wash the meat and dry it with kitchen paper.
2   Peel the garlic cloves, if using, and cut them into slivers lengthways. Insert the slivers into the ends of the joint.
3   Heat the oil and butter together in a flameproof casserole or saucepan over a medium heat until the butter foams. Do not let the butter burn.
4   Fry the meat on all sides to brown it.
5   Season the joint with salt and pepper and pour over the milk. Turn up the heat to medium-high and let the milk come to the boil.
6   Cover the casserole or saucepan but leave the lid slightly askew and turn the heat down so that the milk is simmering, not boiling.
7   Cook gently for 1½ hours, adding more milk if it looks as though it's boiling away completely. This method should ensure that the pork cooks through.
8   At the end of the cooking time, the milk should be a nutty brown colour and there should be clusters of milk solids in the remains of the liquid.

If you find that the pork has been undercooked by accident, you can microwave it on HIGH for 4–5 minutes. Alternatively, place the slices in a large frying pan with about 1 cm (½ in.) water, cover and cook on a medium heat until the flesh is white.

9   Take the joint out and place it on a warmed serving dish.
10 The fat that the meat has exuded will be clear and lying on the surface of the milk. Spoon it off and discard as much of it as possible.
11 If the milk isn't a nutty colour, turn the heat up and boil the liquid until it becomes golden brown. If necessary, add a little more milk and stir up the residue from the bottom. Whisk in the milk-solid clusters to thicken the sauce. Taste it and add extra salt and pepper if needed.
12 Slice the meat and arrange the slices on a warmed serving dish. Pour over the sauce and serve immediately.

Garlic Sausage with Red Cabbage

This is a dish of German origin, warm and filling on a winter's evening. Although it cooks for a long time, it tastes even better if it's reheated a few hours later or even the next day. It is so substantial that you need serve nothing with it except perhaps boiled potatoes or some German rye bread.

The apples, though optional, do add a lovely rich flavour to the dish. Use cooking apples, like Bramleys, that turn fluffy and 'collapse' during cooking. The bacon must be smoked and the sausage bought from a delicatessen or supermarket that sells Continental smoked meats. In fact, strictly speaking, the sausage need not be garlic-flavoured. You could use an Italian or Greek sausage that is uncooked, or a German or Polish cooked sausage. There are so many varieties of Continental sausage that, to avoid confusion, you should try to get advice from the butcher or shopkeeper. Your aim should be to buy a sausage that has a good strong spicy taste and that won't exude too much fat.

It doesn't much matter if you cook the dish for longer than the recommended time, but be sure not to undercook it. If you are using a raw sausage, give it at least 40 minutes' cooking with the cabbage before serving. The dish will reheat successfully in a microwave (on HIGH for 5–7 minutes) as well as on top of the stove.

For 4–6

2 medium onions, peeled and sliced
50 g (2 oz) butter
1 × 750 g–1 kg (1½–2 lb) red cabbage
125 g (4 oz) rashers smoked bacon
2 cooking apples, sliced but not peeled (optional)
2 tablespoons brown sugar
½ teaspoon powdered cloves
½ teaspoon powdered cinnamon
Salt and pepper
125 ml (4 fl oz) water
3 tablespoons vinegar
500 g (1 lb) garlic sausage

1   Prepare the onions.
2   Melt the butter over medium heat in a large lidded flameproof casserole.
3   Add the onions and cook gently for 5–7 minutes until they are soft but not brown.
4   While they are cooking, cut the cabbage in half and remove the core. Shred the cabbage roughly. Cut the rind and fat off the bacon and cut the lean meat into 2.5 cm (1 in.) strips. Prepare the apples, if using.

5   Lay the shredded cabbage on top of the onions, followed by the bacon pieces and the sliced apples, if using. Sprinkle over the brown sugar, cloves and cinnamon, salt and pepper.

6   Pour over the water and vinegar.

7   Bring to the boil over a medium-high heat. When the liquid is boiling, cover with the lid and turn the heat down to its lowest setting.

8   Cook for 2½–3 hours or until the cabbage is tender, stirring thoroughly at least every 30 minutes so that everything is turned over. After 2 hours, if you are using the kind of sausage that needs cooking, add this, whole, to the casserole. If using ready-cooked sausage, slice it and add it to the cabbage 15 minutes before the end of the cooking time to warm through completely.

9   There should be hardly any liquid left when the cooking is completed. If there is too much, remove the lid from the casserole, turn up the heat and cook a little longer until the liquid has evaporated.

10 Taste the dish and adjust the seasoning if necessary. Serve immediately.

If you are using cooked sausage, add it at stage 8 and cook for about 30 minutes. Uncooked sausage should be added at least 40 minutes before you want to serve the dish. You can, if necessary, cook the sausage for 15 minutes in boiling water on top of the stove and add it to the casserole when the cabbage has finished cooking. However, the flavour of the sausage doesn't have a chance to permeate the cabbage this way.

If you don't have a large thick-bottomed casserole with a lid that can go on top of the stove, you can cook this dish in the oven, although it will take longer. Fry the onions in a frying pan, then transfer them to a large lidded ovenproof casserole. Cook the dish, covered, in the oven at 150°C (300°F, gas mark 2) for at least 3 hours. After 2½ hours, take off the lid to evaporate all the liquid that has collected.

Chilli con Carne

This is a really delicious, inexpensive dish to serve to large groups of people, reminiscent of student days. Of course, the memory does play tricks: students' versions of Chilli con Carne were probably more often than not rendered inedible with huge amounts of raw chilli powder and undercooked kidney beans!

In fact, Chilli con Carne is very easy to make once you've got the hang of it. It does take a long time to cook, and you have to remember to soak the beans overnight beforehand in cold water.

Kidney beans, once soaked, need at least 30 minutes' fast boiling to remove any toxins before they can go into the casserole dish. Don't forget this stage! You can substitute tinned beans, in which case they must be added at stage 8 of the recipe.

There's little worse than a watery chilli: the sauce should be thick, rich and spicy. The flour in this recipe will help thicken the sauce, but if you find that it is too thin after the beans are cooked, empty the whole lot into a saucepan and cook over a medium-high heat, stirring constantly, until it reaches a good thick consistency. You can simmer Chilli con Carne on top of the stove, but the food at the bottom of the pan tends to burn unless you stir the mixture frequently.

The amount of chilli pepper you use, of course, depends on your own taste. If you're sensitive, use less than the amount given below; if you've a cast-iron stomach and tongue, add more. Chilli powder is readily available, but you can use little dried red chilli peppers instead. Whatever the form of chilli – don't overdo it! The taste is very potent and a little goes a long way. If you do use the whole chilli pepper, warn your guests so that they don't bite into it.

For 4

250 g (8 oz) red kidney beans
2 medium onions, peeled and chopped
1 or more cloves garlic, peeled and crushed
1 tablespoon vegetable oil
500 g (1 lb) lean minced beef
1 tablespoon flour
25 g (1 oz) or more tomato purée
1 bayleaf (optional)
600 ml (1 pint) hot Beef Stock (*see page 148*)
½ teaspoon (or more!) chilli powder or crushed dried red chilli pepper
1 large green pepper, deseeded and chopped
Salt
Boiled rice to serve (*see page 116*)

1   Cover the beans with cold water and leave to soak overnight, or for a minimum of 8 hours.

2   Drain the beans and put them in a saucepan. Cover them with fresh cold water, bring them to the boil and cook fiercely for 30 minutes. Turn the heat off and leave them to stand in the water for 1 hour.

3   Fifteen minutes before the standing time is complete, pre-heat the oven to 150°C (300°F, gas mark 2). Prepare the onions and garlic.

4   Heat the oil over medium heat in a flameproof casserole large enough to hold the meat and beans. When the oil is hot, add the onions and garlic and cook gently for 5 minutes.

5   Turn up the heat and add the beef and cook, stirring frequently, for a further 5 minutes or until the meat has completely lost its pinkness.

6   Sprinkle the flour over the meat and mix it in well to absorb the fat and juices.

If you use ordinary minced beef, it may give off a lot of fat. If there's more than 1 tablespoon of fat in the pan, discard the excess.

7   Add the tomato purée and the bayleaf, if using. Gradually mix in the hot stock.

8   Drain the beans and add them to the meat. Finally, add the chilli. Mix everything thoroughly.

9   Bring the mixture to the boil. Cover with a tight-fitting lid and cook in the oven for about 1 hour or until the beans are completely soft. The sauce should be rich and thick.

10 Almost at the end of the cooking time prepare the green pepper. When the dish is cooked, remove the lid and add the chopped green pepper. Put the casserole back into the oven without the lid for 10 minutes.

11 Taste the dish and adjust the seasoning if necessary. Don't add extra chilli powder at this stage because it won't have enough time to cook to lose its harshness. An extra dollop of tomato purée will add extra richness, if needed.

12 Serve immediately on top of boiled rice.

Many people prefer a stronger tomato flavour in their chilli; if you are one of them, substitute 1 × 800 g (1 lb 12 oz) tin tomatoes for half of the Beef Stock. Chop the tomatoes up roughly in the tin before adding them to the casserole so that they break down into a sauce more easily.

Chilli con Carne is ideal for parties or any large gatherings because you can make a lot in one go. This recipe is heavier on the beans than the meat, making it very inexpensive per portion. You can happily double or triple the quantities given below, if you have a big enough pot! Alternatively, make up large batches and freeze them. Chilli reheats very easily and the taste improves too. It's usually served with plain boiled rice to soak up the sauce.

Liver

The main problem in cooking liver is that it will toughen and become very dry if even slightly overcooked. The art is to cook the liver quickly and make sure that everyone is gathered ready to eat it immediately. However, it's a good idea to find out before serving it to them whether your guests actually like liver. Don't impose liver on anyone you don't know really well. It tends to be one of those foods that is either loved or hated.

Liver is one of the cheapest sources of iron and vitamins. There are four kinds of animal livers in the shops. The nicest and easiest to cook is lamb's liver, which has a very delicate flavour, a tender texture and is perfect for grilling and frying. Ox liver tends to be coarser and have a stronger flavour: it's not really suitable for fast easy cooking methods like grilling or frying but it's good when braised.

Calf's liver has a wonderful flavour with a luscious melt-in-the-mouth texture, but it's not widely available and is expensive when you do find it. However, once you've come to grips with cooking liver, give it a try for a special occasion (see page 243). Pig's liver is very strong-tasting and best left for pâté making.

If you buy liver from a butcher, ask him or her to slice it thinly for you – liver for grilling or frying should be sliced as thinly as possible. Otherwise, you can usually buy liver in supermarkets ready-sliced. If you have to slice the liver yourself, use a very sharp knife with a thin blade.

Liver and Bacon

The trick in this dish is to make sure that the bacon and liver both arrive hot on the table at the same time, which is achieved fairly easily by grilling the first and frying the second.

The liver must cook in one layer – the slices should not overlap. If your frying pan isn't big enough to allow this, cook the liver in two batches. The flour coating on the liver helps protect the tender flesh from the heat and stop the fat penetrating it. You can serve the fried liver on its own without the bacon, or with fried onions (see page 78).

For 4

500 g (1 lb) lamb's liver, thinly sliced
50 g (2 oz) flour
4 rashers bacon, derinded
25 g (1 oz) butter
Salt and pepper

1   Wash the liver and dry it with kitchen paper.
2   Put the dinner plates to warm in the oven at 110°C (225°F, gas mark ¼).
3   Put the flour on a large plate and dip the slices of liver in it, coating both sides. Don't stack the floured slices on top of each other or they will stick together.
4   Pre-heat the grill to its highest setting.

5   Put the bacon on the grill rack, place under the grill and start to cook it. The bacon will need about 2–3 minutes' grilling on each side.

6   Meanwhile, melt the butter in a large frying pan. When the butter starts to foam slightly, put the slices of liver in the pan in one layer and season them with salt and pepper.

7   Check the bacon. If necessary, turn the rashers over.

8   Once the liver slices have cooked for 2 minutes on the first side, turn them over and season the other side. If they are very thin, they'll need even less time. It's better to undercook rather than overcook liver; you can turn the slices over more than once if necessary.

9   Check the bacon again. If it's golden brown, it's ready. Turn the grill down to its lowest setting to keep the bacon warm while the liver finishes cooking.

10 Using a fish slice, lift the liver slices on to the warmed plates and place the bacon on top of the liver. Serve immediately.

Alternatively, you can fry the bacon (*see page 133*) and grill the liver. Omit the flour and simply brush the liver slices with a little vegetable oil. Grilled liver needs slightly more cooking time than fried liver. Again, remember to season both sides of the liver as it cooks.

You can create a mixed grill by simultaneously grilling tomatoes (*see page 69*) and sausages (*see page 132*) with the bacon, and by frying a small piece of steak (*see page 87*) in a separate pan. Because of the extra co-ordination and timing needed, you really have to love meat to go to the trouble of making this!

Kidneys

When absolutely fresh, kidneys are fantastic. Unfortunately, they don't keep fresh for long. After storage they tend to take on a much stronger smell and taste, so try to cook them on the day you buy them. If you are squeamish about kidneys because of their function, you can get rid of any tell-tale taste (real or imagined) by soaking them in milk for 30 minutes before cooking.

As with liver, there are different types of kidney. Lamb's kidneys are small and plump. They are at their best from spring to the end of summer, when English lamb is available. They are far superior to imported frozen kidneys. If you buy fresh lamb's kidneys from the butcher, they might be encased in a hard layer of fat which can easily be peeled away just before cooking. Frozen lamb's kidneys are widely available. Defrost thoroughly before cooking.

Veal kidneys have a beautiful flavour and texture but they're very expensive and not widely available. Pig's kidneys, though not as delicate in flavour as lamb's or veal kidneys, are still very nice and good for grilling and frying.

Ox kidneys are cheap, but they are best braised, stewed or in steak and kidney pie or pudding. They are not suitable for frying or grilling.

Grilled kidneys are a traditional breakfast dish (*see page 134*).

Kidneys in a Mustard Sauce

This dish goes well with plain boiled potatoes and a green vegetable like beans or peas.

If you don't cut out the white core, the kidneys will curl up during the cooking and take all day to chew.

For 4

125 g (4 oz) onions, peeled and finely chopped
1 clove garlic, peeled and crushed
50 g (2 oz) mushrooms, cleaned and sliced
12 small lamb's kidneys
75 g (3 oz) butter
Salt and pepper
¼ teaspoon tarragon
½ teaspoon chopped parsley
1 tablespoon French mustard
25 g (1 oz) flour
1 glass red wine
300 ml (10 fl oz) hot Chicken Stock (*see page 147*)

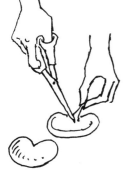

1   Prepare the vegetables.
2   Slice the kidneys in half lengthways. Carefully peel off the very fine outer skin which looks like a membrane and discard. Using a pair of scissors snip out the creamy-coloured core of each half-kidney.
3   Melt half the butter in a frying pan over a medium heat and, when it starts to foam, add the kidneys. Season with salt and pepper and cook for 3 minutes, turning the kidneys and moving them around the pan continuously.
4   Remove the kidneys from the pan and throw away the cooking liquor. Don't turn the heat off. Wipe out the pan and add the rest of the butter. Set the kidneys aside on a plate.
5   Once the butter is foaming, add the onions, garlic and mushrooms. Season with the tarragon and parsley and cook for 2–3 minutes, stirring occasionally. Add the French mustard and mix in well.
6   Sprinkle the flour over the mixture and mix in thoroughly. Cook for 1 minute, stirring frequently.
7   Pour in the wine and gradually add the hot stock, mixing well to form a sauce. Cook, stirring occasionally, for 2 minutes.
8   Put the kidneys, together with whatever juice they've exuded, into the sauce. Season with salt and pepper to taste. Cook, uncovered, over a low heat for 15 minutes. If the sauce starts to get too thick, add more stock to thin it down; it should be thin enough to pour, but only just.
9   Serve immediately.

Fish

Realising that fish present an aspect of cooking that most reluctant cooks would rather avoid, we dealt in the first section with fish (or, at least, bits of them) that didn't betray their origins; anonymous fillets and steaks with no heads, fins, tails or other obviously fishy characteristics. But one day you may come face to face with a whole fish *au naturel*. Don't panic – it can be cooked quite easily.

First of all, we'll presume that it's already gutted but is otherwise untouched. If it hasn't been gutted, get a fishmonger or a friend to do it. (A reluctant cook is allowed to be squeamish.) You needn't cut off its head or tail, or skin it. Make sure that it's fresh (*see page 99*) and then wash it and dry it with kitchen paper.

There are two easy ways to cook a whole fish: grilling and cooking in foil.

Grilling Whole Fish

Oily fish – mackerel, herring, fresh sardine and anchovy (not tinned) – are all good grilled whole, as are freshwater fish like trout and perch, and the red mullet and small sea bass common to the Mediterranean. However, less firm fish, like plaice and sole, tend to dry out and fall apart when grilled whole and they are usually too wide to fit whole more than one at a time on the grill rack anyway; see pages 100–106 for information on grilling and frying flat fish. Don't grill a fish that's too big and thick: the outside will scorch while the inside remains raw. A medium-sized mackerel is the largest you should try – anything over about 500 g (1 lb) you should bake in foil.

Remember that most of the fish mentioned above are quite bony, so serve them to people who don't mind picking over their food. It's funny how you don't notice the bones when you're sat in a Greek taverna with a glass of retsina, but suddenly find a mouthful of them back at home in the kitchen. Don't let this put you off. Really fresh fish, grilled or barbecued and served with a squeeze of lemon juice, can be the simplest and most wonderful of dishes. It goes well with brown bread and butter or boiled potatoes, a green salad or a simple steamed or boiled green vegetable.

As for portion sizes, allow about 250 g (8 oz) of whole unboned fish per person, bearing in mind that you need slightly less oily fish because they are more filling. However, you'll probably have to work out portion sizes simply by the size of the fish – 1 medium trout or mackerel per person, 2–3 large sardines, 4 anchovies, etc.

The cooking times are always variable and depend entirely on the thickness of the fish. Allow 6–7 minutes per side for a mackerel or a trout, 4–5 minutes per side for sardines, and 3–4 minutes per side for anchovies. They have to be brushed with oil frequently so that they don't dry out. If you don't have a little brush, dribble the oil or butter on in single drips and smear with the back of a spoon. You can tell if a fish is cooked by piercing the flesh near the bone. The flesh should shrink away from the bone and it should soft and opaque with no sign of blood. It's very easy to overcook fish, so keep a watchful eye on it.

To barbecue whole fish, follow the instructions below for the preparation. The general basics of cooking are also the same; see pages 219–23 for outdoor cooking.

Whole Grilled Fish

250 g (8 oz) whole fish per person, gutted
2 tablespoons olive oil or melted butter
Salt and pepper
Lemon wedges and/or melted butter to serve

1   Pre-heat the grill to its highest setting.
2   Wash the fish and dry it with kitchen paper.
3   Either cover the grill rack with foil, or lay foil underneath to catch the drips. If you're going to place the fish straight on the rack, oil it first so that the fish doesn't stick.
4   Wash and dry the fish. If it's large, make three diagonal slashes across the side you're going to cook first. Small fish do not need to be slashed.
5   Season with salt and pepper and place on the grill rack.
6   Brush the fish with the oil or butter.
7   If the fish is big, either turn the heat down to medium (if possible) or try to place the fish at least 10 cm (4 in.) away from the heat source. If the fish are small, they can be placed closer to the heat source.
8   Grill the fish according to the times given on page 183, keeping it moist by brushing with the oil or butter during cooking.
9   Once the fish is cooked on one side, turn it over with a fish slice to cook on the other side. Cut slashes on the other side if cooking a larger fish.
10 When the second side is done, serve immediately with wedges of lemon or more melted butter or both.

Opposite: Chicken in Brandy and Tarragon Sauce (page 168), Braised Fennel (page 156) and Sauté Potatoes (page 61).

Overleaf (left): Fish Baked in Foil (page 189), Monkfish with Oil and Garlic (page 190) and Kedgeree (page 191).

Overleaf (right): Spinach Pudding (page 161) and Stuffed Herbed Tomatoes (page 69).

Opposite page 189: Bran and Raisin Muffins (page 209), Scones (page 207) and Butterscotch Brownies (page 206).

Baking Whole Fish in Foil

This is an almost foolproof way of cooking whole fish. The principle is ridiculously easy: you seal the fish up completely so that it cooks in its own steam. There is no mess, no smell and no washing up. The authentic name of this methoid is *en papillote* (in a parcel) – the fish was traditionally wrapped in paper. Aluminium foil is more expensive but less likely to catch fire!

Not only can you cook whole fish in foil but the method also works well for fillets and steaks, though it's less good for soft fish like plaice and sole. You also need far less fat because the fish stays naturally moist so it's a healthier way of cooking, similar to microwaving fish. A 1.25–1.5 kg (2½–3 lb) fish will feed four people.

Only two things can go wrong when you bake fish in foil. First, if you don't completely grease the foil with oil or butter, the fish skin will stick to it and the fish will come apart. Second, you can undercook the fish and there's no way of judging until you unseal it. Because this is wet cookery, you can afford to be slightly generous with the cooking times if in doubt.

Suitable fish for cooking in foil are:

Whole fish – salmon trout, mackerel, trout, sea bass, bream, mullet.
Fish steaks – salmon, halibut, cod, turbot, haddock, tuna, swordfish.
Fillets – cod, haddock, sole, plaice.

The recommended cooking times are as follows:
175 g (6 oz) fish fillet, 1 cm (½ in.) thick – 10–15 minutes.
175–250 g (6–8 oz) fish steak, 2.5 cm (1 in.) thick – 15–20 minutes.
500 g (1 lb) whole fish – 20–25 minutes.
1 kg (2 lb) whole fish – 35–40 minutes.
1.25–1.5 kg (2½–3 lb) whole fish – 40–50 minutes.

Fish Baked in Foil

Photograph on page 186

250 g (8 oz) whole fish or 1 × 175 g (6 oz) fish steak or fillet per person
Butter or oil for greasing
Salt and pepper
1 bunch fresh mixed herbs (parsley, chervil, marjoram), finely chopped
25 g (1 oz) butter

You can certainly cook a whole salmon this way. However, we're not going to tell you how in case you spend a lot of money and something goes wrong. We don't want to take the blame. Wait until you feel entirely confident about this method of cooking. Then go out and buy a cookbook devoted entirely to fish.

1 Pre-heat the oven to 180°C (350°F, gas mark 4).
2 Measure out a piece of foil big enough to wrap the fish, allowing sufficient to make a baggy parcel and for the edges to be folded over twice to make a tight seal. If you are cooking several small whole fish, they must each be wrapped separately, as must fish steaks or fillets.
3 Smear the foil liberally on the shiny side with the butter or oil. Sprinkle salt and pepper on the foil.
4 Wash the fish and dry it with kitchen paper. Lay it on the foil.

189

5   Mash the butter and the chopped herbs together. Put the herb butter in the cavity of the whole fish or divide it up between the steaks or fillets and spread some on the top of each one.
6   Wrap the fish up loosely in the foil, and fold the edges over twice.
7   Place in the oven and cook according to the times given on page 189.
8   Transfer the individual small packets straight on to warmed plates and let your guests open them themselves. Place larger fish, still wrapped in the foil, on a warmed serving dish, and open at the table. Serve immediately.

Variations

Substitute 1 tablespoon white wine per person (or 4 tablespoons for a 1 kg (2 lb) fish) for the butter.
You can cook small pieces of vegetables in the foil with individual fish steaks or fillets for a more attractive presentation. Try finely shredded carrots, a wedge of tomato or chopped spring onions.

Monkfish with Oil and Garlic

Photograph on page 186

This is a slightly extravagant dish for those who love garlic – and it requires good olive oil to complete the real Mediterranean taste. You may balk at the amount of oil used; here it is not just a cooking medium but an essential flavouring ingredient, and the greener the oil you use, the better. Of course, olive oil is fattening in the way that all oil is, but there is strong evidence that it is positively beneficial to your health – and it does have a fantastic taste.
Monkfish has no bones except the spine, and it's sold headless and virtually skinless so it's easy both to prepare and to eat. You can substitute a large cod or haddock fillet.

For 4

2 × 125–175 g (4–6 oz) monkfish tails
150 ml (5 fl oz) olive oil
3–4 cloves garlic, peeled and roughly chopped
Salt and pepper
2 tablespoons finely chopped parsley
Lemon wedges to serve

If you chop the garlic roughly, there is a better chance that it won't suddenly burn. The garlic should flavour the oil and also cook itself, so that it has a lovely mellow taste.

1   Using a sharp knife, remove the translucent purplish membrane which covers the monkfish and trim off the fins, if they remain. Wash the fish and dry it with kitchen paper.
2   In a large frying pan, heat the oil over a medium heat. Add the garlic and fry it gently for 1–2 minutes, stirring all the time. It must not go brown or burn.

3   Place the monkfish tails in the pan and spoon some of the oil over them. Season with salt and pepper and cover the pan.
4   Cook over a medium heat for 15–20 minutes. Check whether the fish is done by piercing the thickest part with a knife. The flesh should be completely white and soft and should come away easily from the main bone.
5   Sprinkle the parsley over the fish and serve immediately with the lemon wedges.

Kedgeree

Photograph on page 186

Kedgeree is a lightly curried mixture of smoked fish and rice, usually served for breakfast or the now-trendy brunch. It also makes a good filling supper dish, accompanied by a green salad.

It can sometimes be difficult to make sure that Kedgeree is both hot and moist when you serve it. The different elements, when combined, quickly cool down, and when you reheat it in the oven the mixture dries out. That's why it's particularly important that the serving dish should be warmed beforehand. If the Kedgeree seems slightly dry, you can add a little cream or butter and stir it in well. (This does, of course, give the dish a wonderful luxurious taste!) Try to buy non-dyed smoked haddock.

For 4

750 g (1½ lb) smoked haddock fillets
600 ml (1 pint) cold water
2 eggs
125 g (4 oz) butter
1 medium onion, peeled and finely chopped
1 teaspoon curry powder
300 ml (10 fl oz) long-grain rice
Salt and pepper
Pinch cayenne
Juice ½ lemon
1 tablespoon finely chopped parsley

1   Put the haddock fillets into a wide shallow pan and add the cold water. Bring to the boil, turn down the heat and simmer for 3–4 minutes or until the fish flakes easily when tested.
2   Drain off the cooking liquor and reserve it. Place the haddock in a wide casserole dish and keep it warm. This is best done by covering the dish with a tight-fitting lid and placing it on the bottom shelf of the low oven at 110°C (225°F, gas mark ¼).

3   Meanwhile, hard-boil the eggs (*see page 25*) and plunge them immediately in cold water. When they're cool, shell them and chop roughly. Set them aside.

4   Melt half the butter in a pan over medium heat. When it starts to foam, add the onion and cook without colouring for 5–8 minutes.

5   Mix in the curry powder and then add the rice and cook, stirring, for 2–3 minutes.

6   Pour the reserved cooking liquid from the haddock into the rice, stir, bring to the boil and season with pepper and a little salt (remember that the fish liquor will already be quite salty). Turn down the heat and allow to simmer, covered, for 15–18 minutes or until the rice is tender and most of the cooking liquid has evaporated.

7   Meanwhile, take the haddock out of the oven. With a fork, separate the flesh from the skin and discard the skin. Then break up the flesh into large flakes, removing any remaining bones.

8   When the rice has cooked, add the chopped eggs, flaked fish, cayenne, the rest of the butter and the lemon juice. Gently mix everything together so that the flaked fish doesn't disintegrate. Adjust the seasoning if necessary. Put the empty casserole dish back in the oven to keep warm for serving.

9   Cover the pan, place it back on a low heat and warm the mixture through for 5 minutes, stirring occasionally to make sure that it doesn't stick.

10 Serve the Kedgeree in the warmed casserole dish with chopped parsley sprinkled on top.

Fish Kebabs

This is a really simple but impressive-looking dish. It can be a bit expensive, depending on the amount of fish you use, but you can easily eke out the fish by using more vegetables and nobody will notice, much less complain. Kebabs are best cooked outdoors on a barbecue (*see pages 219–22*), but they can be cooked very successfully under the grill. If you can manage to marinate the fish overnight, it will have a better flavour.

You can ask your fishmonger to cube the fish for you, but if you buy fish steaks you can easily do it yourself. You must choose a firm-fleshed fish or it will fall apart (and if you're barbecueing, the fish will fall into the coals and be impossible to retrieve!). Skewers for kebabs are widely available, in short and long sizes. Buy metal ones that are flat rather than round: the fish won't slide off them.

Swordfish, tuna, monkfish, kingfish, halibut, scallops and prawns (we said it was expensive), cod and haddock are all suitable for this dish. Avoid any soft fish like plaice or sole. Try to use two different kinds of fish, or fish plus scallops or prawns for variety.

You can use a variety of vegetables. Other than the ones suggested below, try sliced fennel and courgette, or firm cherry tomatoes. Onions are often threaded on to the skewers too, but they don't cook before the fish is ready, so don't use them unless you like the taste of charred raw onion. Avoid also vegetables that you wouldn't normally eat raw, like potatoes, or which are too hard, like carrots. The bayleaves you use must not be too dry and brittle as they may catch fire. Serve the kebabs with boiled rice.

For 4

4 × 175 g (6 oz) fish steaks, 1 cm (½ in.) thick, boned and cut into cubes
1 red or green pepper, cut into eighths
8 medium mushrooms, cleaned
8 bayleaves
Lemon wedges to serve

For the Marinade:

50 ml (2 fl oz) olive oil
Juice 1 lemon
1 teaspoon marjoram or oregano
½ small onion, peeled and grated
Salt and pepper

1   Marinate the fish for at least 1 hour before cooking or, if possible, the night before. Place the olive oil, lemon juice, marjoram or oregano, grated onion, salt and pepper in a deep glass or earthenware bowl. Mix thoroughly and add the cubed fish, turning it over so that it's completely coated. Cover with clingfilm or a plate and place in the fridge.
2   Shortly before you're ready to cook, prepare the kebab vegetables.
3   Pre-heat the grill to its highest setting.
4   Remove the fish from the marinade and thread alternately on to skewers with the vegetables, interspersing 2 bayleaves on each one. Brush the marinade all over the fish and vegetables.
5   Put the skewers on the grill to rack and place under the grill at least 5 cm (2 in.) from the heat source.
6   Grill on each side for 1 minute, brushing with marinade as you turn the kebabs over.

The initial cooking at a high temperature sears the outside of the fish, giving it a barbecued flavour, while the longer finishing time at the lower heat cooks the fish without drying it out.

7   Turn the heat down to medium and cook the kebabs on each side for 4–5 minutes more, keeping them moistened with the marinade. The fish is cooked when the flesh is completely opaque where the skewer pierces it.
8   Serve immediately with the lemon wedges.

Pasta and Rice

Spaghetti Bolognese

If you can't get lean minced beef, by all means buy the
ordinary type. However, be prepared to drain off the
excess fat before you pour in the tomatoes, or you'll end up
with grease slicks on top of the sauce. The red wine,
though optional, does improve the flavour out of all
proportion to its quantity. In fact, adding any more wine
than the recommended amount makes the sauce too dark.
If you're in a hurry, a carton of *passata* (puréed tomato
flesh) is a great timesaver.

Finally, like the Tomato Sauce (*page 114*) in Section
One of this book, this sauce freezes very successfully.
Because it's so useful, it's worth making in large quantities
so that you always have some on hand. As a change from
spaghetti, try serving the sauce with jacket potatoes.

For 4

500 g (1 lb) spaghetti
1 teaspoon vegetable oil
Salt
Grated Parmesan cheese to serve

For the Bolognese Sauce:

1 medium onion, peeled and finely chopped
2 cloves garlic, peeled and finely chopped
1 tablespoon vegetable or olive oil
250 g (8 oz) lean minced beef
2 × 397 g (14 oz) tins tomatoes
75 ml (3 fl oz) red wine (optional)
1 bayleaf
2 teaspoons dried oregano
Salt and pepper

1   Prepare the onions and garlic.
2   Put the oil in a saucepan over medium-high heat. Add
the minced beef and mash it into little pieces with a
wooden spoon.
3   When the meat has lost its red colour, add the onion
and the garlic. Cook, stirring, for 3 minutes.
4   Add the tinned tomatoes and mash them into smaller
chunks. Pour in the red wine, if using, and add the bayleaf
and the oregano.

5   Turn the heat up to medium-high. When the sauce boils, cover the pan and turn the heat down to low.

6   Cook for 20–25 minutes, stirring occasionally so that the tomatoes don't burn. They will eventually break down into a sauce.

7   While the sauce is simmering, cook the spaghetti as described on page 114. Allow about 8 minutes for the water to come to the boil and 8 minutes for the spaghetti to cook, then work backwards to calculate what time to put the spaghetti water on to boil so that the pasta and the sauce are ready at the same time.

8   While the pasta is cooking, taste the sauce and adjust the seasoning if necessary. If the sauce needs to be thickened, remove the lid from the pan 10 minutes before the end of the cooking time. You can also speed up the sauce by raising the heat, but be sure to check it constantly to see that it's not burning. Remove the bayleaf before serving.

9   Warm the serving bowls in the oven at 110°C (225°F, gas mark ¼).

10 Drain the pasta when it's cooked and place it in the warmed bowls. Serve with the sauce ladled over or mixed into the pasta. Sprinkle grated Parmesan on top.

Lasagne

Lasagne is the name of a dish consisting of layers of pasta, sauce and meat, as well as the term used to describe the type of pasta (in flat sheets) which characterise the dish. Lasagne pasta is widely available in supermarkets, both white and coloured green with dried spinach.

The trouble with lasagne (the dish), even the real authentic Italian variety, is that it's very heavy indeed, what with the pasta, the meat sauce and the even more stodgy white sauce. We propose here, quite unapologetically, a complete bastardisation of lasagne which doesn't take forever to cook and is considerably lighter. However, it still calls for at least three separate cooking processes, so it's not really worth making for any fewer than six people. That's why lasagne is so often served at buffet parties: you can double and treble the quantities quite easily.

As for ingredients, the colour of the lasagne – white or green – doesn't matter. If you can't find ricotta (a soft white cheese), cottage cheese is a good substitute, but try to drain some of the liquid off before you use it.

The dish can be prepared up to 24 hours in advance and left in the fridge, covered, until you are ready to bake it. Any lasagne left over after a meal can easily be reheated in a microwave. If it was originally cooked in a metal container, transfer it before reheating on to a plate.

For 6

1 quantity Bolognese Sauce (*see page 194*)
2 teaspoons vegetable oil
250 g (8 oz) dried lasagne sheets
300 g (10 oz) ricotta cheese, crumbled
250 g (8 oz) Mozzarella cheese, cut into 6 mm (¼ in.) slices

1   Make the Bolognese Sauce.
2   Meanwhile, bring a large pan of water to the boil. Add the oil to the water: this will prevent the sheets of lasagne from sticking together.
3   When the water boils, add the lasagne, one sheet at a time. Boil for 8 minutes or until the pasta is cooked *al dente* (*see page 114*). If you overcook them, they become waterlogged and soggy.
4   Drain the pasta and plunge it immediately into a bowl of cold water, one sheet at a time. This too helps keep the sheets from sticking together – a common problem.
5   Pre-heat the oven to 180°C (350°F, gas mark 4).
6   Oil a 18 × 24 cm (7 × 9½in.) roasting tin or shallow earthenware or glass dish. Prepare the cheeses.
7   Lay pasta over the bottom of the tin in one layer. Put 2–3 tablespoons of the sauce on top and spread it thinly over the pasta. Follow this with a handful of the ricotta cheese and finally a layer of the Mozzarella slices.
8   Repeat the process until all the ingredients are used up. The final layer of pasta should be topped only by the Mozzarella.
9   Place in the oven and bake for 30–35 minutes or until the cheese on top is melted and the lasagne is piping hot all the way through. Don't worry if the top pasta layer goes a bit hard – there's no way of avoiding it.
10 Serve immediately.

It's not easy to estimate how to divide up all the elements evenly so that you're left with exactly the right amount. If you run out of sauce and cheese and there's still a lot of lasagne left, it's best to leave the dish as it is and not try to use up all the pasta which, after all, is the least expensive element.

Rice Pilaf

This dish has its origins in the Middle East. You can serve it as a variation on plain boiled rice, or add lots of ingredients and turn it into a main course. Its virtue lies in the ease with which it is cooked – it's actually better if left alone. Use long-grain Patna rice or, better still, Basmati.

To make Rice Pilaf you need a casserole that can go on top of the stove as well as in the oven. If you don't have one, start off in a large saucepan and transfer the contents to an ovenproof casserole with a fitted lid. The dish can actually be cooked entirely on top of the stove, but unless you have a very thick pan (made, for instance, of enamelled cast iron) it's likely to burn on the bottom.

For 4

25 g (1 oz) butter
1 small onion, peeled and finely chopped
300 ml (10 fl oz) patna rice
600 ml (1 pint) hot Chicken Stock (*see page 147*)
Salt and pepper
1 tablespoon finely chopped parsley (optional)

1   Pre-heat the oven to 180°C (350°F, gas mark 4).
2   Melt half the butter in a flameproof casserole over a medium heat. Add the onion and cook for 2–3 minutes. Add the rice and stir so that the grains are completely coated with the butter.
3   Cook for a further 3 minutes, stirring frequently.
4   Pour the stock into the casserole and turn up the heat to high. When the rice boils, add salt and pepper, put the lid on the casserole and transfer it to the oven.
5   Cook for 18–20 minutes or until all the stock has been absorbed by the rice.
6   Remove the casserole from the oven and stir in the remaining butter. Taste and add extra salt and pepper if necessary.
7   Serve immediately with the parsley sprinkled on top, if using.

Variations

You can add all sorts of different ingredients at the same time, both meat and vegetable, to Rice Pilaf. In fact, this is a good way to use up left-over meat like chicken, turkey, ham or pork. Cooked meat should be stirred in at the end of cooking just to warm it through. If necessary, give the pilaf a few more minutes, covered, in the oven once you've added the cooked meat. Uncooked meat can be added with the onion at the beginning and fried until it's lost its pinkness. Chicken livers, lamb's liver, chicken meat and turkey meat are especially good additions. Cut them into small cubes before adding them. You can add as little or as much as you want. A little will go a long way if you add vegetables as well.

The vegetables should be sliced into fairly small pieces and cooked until soft with the onions right at the beginning. Particularly nice are mushrooms, green and red peppers, courgettes and tomatoes; all you need to do is to add them with the onion at the early stage of preparation.

If you want to make the pilaf more authentically Middle Eastern, add 2 teaspoons each of currants and pine kernels to the onion and fry until the pine nuts are golden before adding the stock.

Risotto

Risotto is an Italian rice dish which is cooked completely differently from plain boiled rice. It's actually meant to be sticky, not dry with separate grains. You achieve this by using Italian arborio rice, also known as risotto rice (available in large supermarkets and in Italian delicatessens), and by stirring it all the time so that the starch comes out and makes the grains stick together.

The recipe below is a less complicated version than the authentic one from Milan but it's still very good. Parmesan cheese adds a lovely flavour but you could try another cheese at a pinch. As the dish is so rich, it's served on its own, either as a starter or as a main course (halve the quantities for a starter).

For 4

25 g (1 oz) butter
½ onion, peeled and finely chopped
450 ml (15 fl oz) Italian arborio rice
Salt and pepper
1.4 litres (2½ pints) hot Chicken Stock (*see page 147*)
25 g (1 oz) grated Parmesan cheese

1   Melt the butter over a medium heat in a thick-bottomed pan.
2   Add the onion and cook for 2–3 minutes.
3   Add the rice, salt and pepper and cook, stirring, for a further 3 minutes.

If you have some white wine to hand, you can add a splash or two of that as well.

4   Pour in a ladleful of stock and stir with a wooden spoon until the rice has almost absorbed it. Continue adding the rest of the stock, a ladleful at a time, in the same way. The rice should be stirred continuously over a medium-low heat so that it is just simmering, not boiling too hard. This will take at least 20–30 minutes.
5   When the rice is creamy and the stock is used up, taste the risotto. You should be able to taste separate grains of rice but they should be soft with no hint of rawness. If the rice is still a little hard, add more stock (or boiling water, if necessary) until the rice is cooked.
6   Stir in the grated Parmesan cheese and add extra pepper, if necessary.
7   Serve immediately.

You can add extra ingredients (not more than one at a time) to the Risotto, like mushrooms, courgettes or chopped chicken livers. Add them at stage 2 when you are frying the onion and cook for 2–3 minutes.

Puddings

Summer Pudding

For those of you who have somehow missed the pleasure of this delightful pudding, it is nothing more than bread soaked in juicy summer berries. It may not sound particularly exciting but it actually ranks as one of the world's most sublime dishes, and it's quintessentially British.

The joy of this pudding is that it takes hardly any time to make, looks impressive and everybody loves it. So long as the fruit isn't mouldy, you can use fruit that's gone too soft to eat on its own. You can also use whatever proportion of fruit you want depending on what you like and what's available. Try to obtain a combination of both the soft sweet fruit (raspberries, strawberries, loganberries or blackberries) and the more acidic fruit (redcurrants and blackcurrants). The pudding is traditionally made with white bread.

If you're feeling energetic, you can actually serve individual puddings in little metal moulds, or ceramic pots (ramekins). Otherwise, you just need a pudding basin or a deep medium-sized glass or earthenware dish to make it in.

Double cream is the usual sinful accompaniment, plain yoghurt the healthy alternative of the 1980s.

For 4–6

8–10 thin slices bread
Butter for greasing
125 g (4 oz) blackcurrants or redcurrants
125 g (4 oz) strawberries
125 g (4 oz) blackberries or raspberries
Juice ½ lemon (or to taste)
150 ml (5 fl oz) water
50 g (2 oz) sugar

1   Cut the crusts off the bread. Grease a deep medium-sized dish with butter and line with the bread slices. You should fit the slices together so that there are no gaps between them. Reserve enough bread to cover the top of the dish.
2   Prepare the berries. Carefully pick them over, discarding any twigs, leaves and so on, and hull them. Rinse them briefly and place them in a non-corroding saucepan (not aluminium) with the lemon juice, water and sugar.

3   Bring the mixture to the boil over a medium-high heat. As soon as it boils, take it off the heat and let it cool to room temperature.

The only thing to watch is that you haven't got too little or too much fruit for the size of the dish. The fruit should come up to the top of the dish, with the bread lid fitting on neatly. If the bread is particularly thick, or stale, add some of the reserved juice so that the bread can soak it up.

4   Drain off the juice and reserve. Put the soft fruit in the dish.
5   Place the reserved slices of bread on top of the soft fruit so that it's completely enclosed. The juice will start to seep through the bread.
6   Put the dish in the fridge for at least 4 hours, or overnight if possible. It will help if you can put a heavy object on top of the bread.
7   Just before serving, turn the pudding out on to a large plate. It should come away easily from the dish. Serve with cream or yoghurt and hand the reserved juice separately.

Chocolate Mousse

Chocolate Mousse is sin in an edible form, and you don't even have to be a chocoholic to adore it. Surprisingly, it's not actually cooked – it's just chocolate combined with egg and cream and chilled in the fridge. However, it is a rich pudding, so serve it after something light, like fish. This is a good dish to serve for a formal supper, because it is such a classic and because you can make it up to a day in advance and just take it out of the fridge when you need it.

Not much can go wrong with Chocolate Mousse. Make sure that you've beaten both the eggs and cream so that they stand firm, without a trace of liquid left. The egg yolks must not cook – don't heat them by mistake or they'll curdle and you'll end up with chocolate scrambled eggs. If you want to make a larger quantity of mousse than that allowed for below, the formula is 1 egg and 50 g (2 oz) chocolate per person. Up to six people, the amount of cream can stay the same.

Chocolate Mousse is traditionally served in ramekins. If you don't have any, you can use wine glasses, which in fact make the pudding look more elegant.

For 4

4 eggs
250 g (8 oz) plain chocolate
50 ml (2 fl oz) brandy
125 ml (4 fl oz) double or whipping cream
4 whole walnuts, shelled, or grated chocolate to garnish (optional)

1   Bring some water to the boil in a small saucepan.
2   Separate the eggs (*see page 26*) and set aside so that they come to room temperature.

3 Break the chocolate into little pieces and place in a small mixing bowl which will fit over the top of the saucepan so that the bottom of the bowl is immersed in the water.

4 Turn the heat down to medium and stir the chocolate pieces until they melt with the gentle heat. Continue stirring until the chocolate has become a smooth paste, then mix in the brandy.

5 As soon as the chocolate has melted, remove the pan from the heat, but keep the melted chocolate suspended over the hot water. Whisk the egg yolks into the chocolate and mix thoroughly over the hot water for 1 minute. Set the bowl aside to cool.

6 Meanwhile, whip the cream. Pour it into a large bowl and beat with an electric mixer. Do not overbeat it or it will curdle. Stop as soon as the cream can hold its shape and there is no liquid left in the bottom of the bowl. Keep it in the fridge until you need it.

7 Now beat the egg whites in a large, clean grease-free bowl. Do this by hand with a large balloon whisk (*see page 16*), or with a rotary eggbeater or small electric mixer, moving the bowl round so that none of the white is missed. The egg whites should rise in large snowy peaks and there should be no unbeaten white left in the bottom of the bowl.

8 Transfer the chocolate mixture to a bowl big enough to hold both it and the whipped cream and egg whites.

9 Using a metal spoon, place 1 tablespoon of the whisked egg whites into the chocolate mixture and stir thoroughly to lighten the mixture. Then fold in the rest of the whites with the spoon, using a cutting motion. Fold in half the whipped cream in a similar way and mix in gently but thoroughly.

10 Spoon the mixture into serving dishes.

11 Carefully place 1 tablespoon of the remaining cream on each dish and top with a walnut or sprinkle with grated chocolate, if using. Chill in the fridge for at least 2 hours before serving.

Variation: Chocolate Orange Mousse

Substitute orange liqueur for the brandy in stage 4.

Bread and Butter Pudding with Whisky Cream

This is a good way of using up stale bread, and it's nicer if you use an unsliced loaf. Nothing can really go wrong with it unless you make it in a dish of the wrong size. You need a wide shallow dish which can hold three slices of bread in one layer. Otherwise, the egg custard mixture won't reach the top of the bread and the bread will dry up when it's cooking. However, if you don't possess a dish of this width, cover the pudding with aluminium foil before placing it in the oven and take off the foil 10 minutes before the end of the cooking time. This will keep the bread moist, yet allow enough time to brown the top slightly. Serve with the wicked Whisky Cream (opposite), or with Custard (see page 123).

For 4

50 g (2 oz) butter, plus a little extra for greasing
6 large slices white bread
25 g (1 oz) currants
50 g (2 oz) raisins
250 ml (8 fl oz) milk
125 ml (4 fl oz) double cream
3 eggs
50 g (2 oz) sugar
Grated nutmeg

1   Pre-heat the oven to 180°C (350°F, gas mark 4).
2   Butter the bread on one side only and cut each slice in half diagonally.
3   Grease a 1 litre (2 pint) ovenproof dish and cover the bottom with a layer of bread, buttered side up. Sprinkle half the currants and raisins on top.
4   In a saucepan heat the milk and cream together over medium-high heat.
5   Meanwhile, crack the eggs into a jug large enough to hold the milk/cream mixture. Whisk the eggs until the whites and yolks are well blended.
6   When the milk/cream mixture is warm and little bubbles appear around the edges, add the sugar and stir well. Take the liquid off the heat and pour it on to the eggs. Whisk thoroughly.
7   Pour half the liquid, through a sieve, over the bread in the bottom of the dish and leave to soak in for 3–5 minutes.
8   Meanwhile, bring a kettle of water to the boil.
9   Place the remaining bread in the dish, buttered side up, top with the remaining currants and sultanas and pour the rest of the liquid through a sieve over the top, making sure that all the bread is soaked through. Sprinkle with grated nutmeg.

10 Place the dish in a roasting tin and pour enough boiling water around the dish to come half-way up its side.
11 Place the roasting tin in the oven for 30–40 minutes, or until the top of the pudding is golden brown and the egg mixture has set and is no longer liquid.
12 Serve warm.

Whisky Cream

This recipe calls for clear, runny honey. If you find that your honey has thickened or crystallised in the jar, remove the lid and microwave on HIGH for 20 seconds to restore the honey to its original state.

For 4

150 ml (5 fl oz) double cream
35 ml (1½ fl oz) whisky
1 tablespoon clear, runny honey

1 Place all the ingredients in a large bowl and stir to blend them.
2 Using a rotary beater or small electric mixer, whip the mixture until it doubles in volume. Chill in the fridge until needed.

Microwave Treacle Pudding

We offer no apologies for including a recipe exclusively designed for microwave oven owners. As many traditional puddings are not suitable for microwaving, it's gratifying to be able to make one that cooks better in a microwave, and saves so much time.

No matter how it's cooked, Treacle Pudding is still a rich dish, good for cold winter nights. Serve it with Custard (*see page 123*), cream or plain yoghurt, or with extra syrup heated up and poured over.

The pudding-basin shape is the conventional one for this recipe, but you can make it in any shallow casserole dish (preferably round) suitable for use in a microwave. As all microwave ovens are different, you may need to cook the pudding for a shorter or longer time than recommended below.

For 4

4 tablespoons golden syrup
50 g (2 oz) softened butter or margarine
125 g (4 oz) soft brown sugar
2 eggs
125 g (4 oz) self-raising flour
2–3 tablespoons milk

1   Pour the syrup into a 1 litre (2 pint) pudding basin. Tilt the basin so that the syrup covers the sides as well as the bottom.

2   Put the butter in a mixing bowl. Add the sugar, a little at a time, and mix well with a wooden spoon. The mixture should become slightly fluffy.

3   Add the eggs, one at a time, beating the mixture after adding each one so it's blended in well.

4   Sift the flour on to a plate and add it to the mixture, a little at a time. Do not overbeat.

5   Add the milk, 1 tablespoon at a time, and mix in well. The batter should be soft and smooth and should easily drop from the spoon. Do not add too much milk.

6   Spoon the batter into the pudding basin and smooth it evenly.

7   Place the basin in the microwave and cook, uncovered, on HIGH for 4–4½ minutes or until the pudding has risen and is quite firm. The top may still look a little moist, but don't worry: the pudding continues to cook after it's been taken out of the oven.

8   To make sure that it's cooked all the way through, wait 2 minutes, then plunge a thin blade into the centre of the pudding. If it comes out clean and free from batter, it's ready to eat. If it has some batter sticking to it, put the pudding back in the oven and microwave for 1 minute longer.

9   Turn the pudding out on to a warmed plate and serve immediately.

Rhubarb Crumble

This has to be the ideal hot pudding for people who have no confidence in their pastry-making abilities – in other words, most of us. It doesn't matter if everyone knows it's easy – you're not trying to fool people into thinking you're a master *patissier*. However, it is popular and you can make it with all sorts of fruit; frozen fruit will work equally as well as fresh, but you must defrost it before cooking. (You can do this quickly in a microwave.) You probably won't need to add water when cooking it – or, at least, you won't need to add as much as with fresh rhubarb – because the frozen fruit will give off some liquid.

Serve the crumble with Custard (*see page 123*), cream or plain yoghurt.

For 4

750 g (1½ lb) rhubarb
75 g (3 oz) soft brown sugar

For the Crumble Mixture:

175 g (6 oz) plain white or wholewheat flour
1 teaspoon powdered cinnamon (optional)
75 g (3 oz) soft brown sugar
50 g (2 oz) butter

1   Pre-heat the oven to 180°C (350°F, gas mark 4).
2   First make the crumble mixture. Put the flour, cinnamon (if using) and sugar into a mixing bowl. Cut the butter into small pieces and add to the mixture.
3   Gently rub the butter into the flour, using the tips of your fingers. When the butter, sugar and flour are combined and you can see no separate bits of fat, put the mixture in the fridge to chill while you prepare the rhubarb.
4   Wash the rhubarb, cut it into 5 cm (2 in.) pieces and place in a saucepan (not aluminium) with the sugar and 2 tablespoons water. Cover with a lid and turn the heat up to medium. When the liquid starts to bubble, turn the heat down to medium-low and cook gently for 15 minutes.
5   Drain off half the juice and transfer the rhubarb and remaining juice into a shallow ovenproof glass or earthenware dish not wider than 15 cm (6 in.) in diameter.
6   Sprinkle the crumble mixture evenly over the fruit and smooth it with a knife. It must completely cover the rhubarb – hence the need to use a dish that is not too wide.
7   Place the dish in the oven and bake for 35–40 minutes. The top should be slightly browned in patches.
8   Serve hot or at room temperature.

If you don't drain off the excess juice, the fruit will be too wet and the crumble mixture will sink into it. However, do reserve the excess juice. If you've got rid of too much, and the crumble looks too dry after it's cooked, pour some juice over the top!

Variations

You can substitute apple, peach, apricot, plum or greengage for the rhubarb and you pre-cook it in the same way. Add less sugar, but taste the fruit as you go along to ensure that it is sweet enough. Berries like blackberries or raspberries need no pre-cooking. Spread them raw in the bottom of the dish, sprinkle over 1 tablespoon or more of sugar, depending on their sweetness, and then spread the crumble over them.

Cakes, Biscuits and Bread

Butterscotch Brownies

Photograph on page 188

The dentist's delight – soft, chewy, walnutty squares. It takes about 2 minutes to stir the ingredients together, and 30 minutes to cook the brownies. A larger tin makes thinner, chewier brownies; a smaller tin, softer and moister ones. Take your pick. If you're worried about the cost of the walnuts, reduce the recommended quantity by half.

Makes about 12

Butter for greasing
75 g (3 oz) plain flour
Pinch salt
¼ teaspoon bicarbonate of soda
1 egg
175 g (6 oz) soft brown sugar
1 teaspoon vanilla essence
125 g (4 oz) chopped walnuts

1   Pre-heat the oven to 180°C (350°F, gas mark 4).
2   Grease a shallow square or rectangular baking tin no bigger than 20 × 20 × 5 cm (8 × 8 × 2 in.) with butter.
3   Sift the flour, salt and bicarbonate of soda into a bowl.
4   In another larger bowl beat the egg thoroughly and mix in the sugar and vanilla until thoroughly combined.
5   Add the flour mixture to the sugar mixture and stir well so that the flour is completely blended in.
6   Stir in the walnuts.
7   Pour the batter into the greased tin and spread it out evenly with a knife. You may find that the batter is very thin in the tin: this doesn't matter at all.
8   Place the tin on the middle shelf of the oven and bake it for 30 minutes. It should be slightly soft to the touch in the middle, but the sides should be firm. Don't overcook it.
9   While it's warm, cut it into squares in the tin with a knife. Allow to cool before removing from the tin. Wrap the brownies in foil to keep them fresh.

Scones

Photograph on page 188

You have nothing in the house and your mother drops in for tea. Scones can be made in next to no time. A jar of good home-made jam – always sold at church fêtes and village fairs – is the best accompaniment, though you may want to gild the lily with thick cream (Devon clotted for preference, whipped double cream otherwise). Scones don't keep very well – not that they generally hang around for too long!

Don't be tempted to roll the dough out too thinly or hard thin scones will result. If you don't have a rolling pin, a clean empty milk bottle (the thin kind) will do at a pinch so long as you roll the dough evenly. You can also improvise if you don't have a pastry cutter by using a small glass or cup, or the lid of a jar – and it needn't necessarily be round.

Makes about 12

50 g (2 oz) cold butter, plus extra for greasing
250 g (8 oz) self-raising flour, plus extra for rolling out the dough
50 g (2 oz) caster sugar
Pinch salt
150 ml (5 fl oz) milk
50 g (2 oz) sultanas or raisins (optional)

1   Pre-heat the oven to 220°C (425°F, gas mark 7).
2   Lightly grease a baking tray.
3   Sift the flour into a large mixing bowl.
4   Cut the butter into small cubes and add it to the flour.
5   Rub the butter into the flour with the tips of your fingers until it is all incorporated and a crumbly, mixture has resulted. Try to do this as quickly and as gently as possible. The butter shouldn't melt from the heat of your fingers.
6   Add the sugar and salt and stir in by scooping up the mixture gently and letting it fall through your fingers.
7   Pour in the milk, a little at a time, and gently stir it in with a knife until it forms a soft sticky ball. If the dough feels very dry and crumbly, add a little more milk. However, if it's really soggy and wet, sprinkle on 1 extra tablespoon flour.
8   Knead the dough with the heels of your hands – not too hard: it's not a bread dough – for about 1 minute. It should be soft and smooth.
9   Sprinkle extra flour on a pastry board or clean work-surface. Flour the rolling pin.
10 Roll out the dough evenly to a thickness of 2–2.5 cm (¾–1 in.). If in doubt, use a ruler to check it: the dough must not be too thin.

11 Using a round pastry cutter 2.5–3.75 cm (1–1½ in.) in diameter, cut out the scones and place them on the prepared baking tray.

12 Gather the scraps together and gently form them into a ball. Roll the ball out and repeat the process. Don't handle the dough too much, however, or you'll end up with extremely heavy scones. When you're left with enough dough for one really big fat scone, or two smaller flat ones, make the big one.

13 Place the tray on the middle shelf of the oven and bake for about 15 minutes or until the scones have risen and the tops are golden brown.

14 Cool on a wire rack, if possible, for a few minutes before you devour them.

Flapjacks

The preparation takes a few minutes and there are only four ingredients, so there's little excuse not to make flapjacks. Of course, there is a lot of sugar in the recipe, but you can square that with your conscience by thinking about the healthy fibre in the oats! Use rolled oats (oat flakes), which are not the same as instant porridge oats.

Makes 16 small squares

75 g (3 oz) margarine, plus extra for greasing
2 tablespoons golden syrup
75 g (3 oz) soft brown sugar
150 g (5 oz) rolled oats

1   Pre-heat the oven to 170°C (325°F, gas mark 3).
2   Grease a 20 cm (8 in.) square shallow baking tin.
3   Put the margarine and syrup in a saucepan and set over a low heat until the margarine is melted, stirring all the time so that the two blend together.
4   Add the sugar and rolled oats and stir together until all the ingredients are thoroughly combined.
5   Transfer the mixture to the baking tin and smooth out evenly with a knife dipped in hot water.
6   Using the knife, divide the mixture into even squares, cutting down to the bottom of the tin.
7   Put the tin in the oven and bake for 15–20 minutes or until the top is golden brown and the mixture has set and is quite firm.
8   While the flapjacks are still warm but not too hot, remove them from the tin and break them into squares along the marked lines.
9   Store in an airtight container.

Bran and Raisin Muffins

Photograph on page 188

These are North American favourites which are making their way across the ocean. Their great virtue is that they're good for you but you don't notice because they taste so delicious.

A muffin tin is like a tartlet tin except that it's deeper. You can't really make muffins without the tin but it's not expensive and it can be used to make small Yorkshire Puddings in as well. Bran is widely available in supermarkets.

The muffin mixture differs from cake mixtures – it mustn't be stirred too much. Once the flour is blended in so you can't see it any more, stop stirring immediately.

Makes 12

125 g (4 oz) bran
175 ml (6 fl oz) milk
1 egg
125 g (4 oz) plain flour
2½ teaspoons baking powder
1 teaspoon salt
Butter for greasing
75 g (3 oz) brown sugar
2 tablespoons vegetable oil
125 g (4 oz) raisins

1   Pre-heat the oven to 200°C (400°F, gas mark 6).
2   Place the bran and milk in a large bowl and leave for 5 minutes so that the milk soaks into the bran.
3   Meanwhile, whisk the egg in a cup. Sift the flour, baking powder and salt together on to a plate. Grease the muffin tin.
4   Stir the sugar and the oil into the bran mixture. Add the beaten egg and mix well.
5   Add the flour mixture in one go. With a large spoon, stir until the flour has only just blended in.
6   Add the raisins and, again, stir them in with a few strokes.
7   Spoon the mixture evenly into the muffin tin, filling the indents only two thirds full.
8   Put the tin on the middle shelf of the oven and bake for 25 minutes or until a knife plunged through the centre of a muffin comes out cleanly.
9   Cool for a few minutes, then turn out on to a wire rack.
10 Eat warm, split in half and spread with butter. Allow any remaining muffins to cool before storing in an airtight container.

Parkin

This rich, spicy Parkin has two eating stages. First, it can be enjoyed straight from the oven with a cup of tea, or more adventurously topped with some lightly whipped cream. You can also eat it much later, but it has to be wrapped up and stored in an airtight container for at least 2 weeks, after which it is deliciously sticky and makes the most wonderful accompaniment to fine English cheese.

You can buy black treacle in most supermarkets but molasses is a good substitute. If you have a microwave, you can use it for stage 4 of the recipe. One minute at microwave HIGH will melt the butter and soften the treacle.

Don't worry too much about the size of the tin – better too small than too big. Using a smaller tin will simply result in a thicker Parkin that takes longer to cook.

Makes 16 squares

50 g (2 oz) butter, plus extra for greasing
125 g (4 oz) self-raising flour
125 g (4 oz) medium oatmeal
125 g (4 oz) soft brown sugar
2 teaspoons powdered ginger
125 g (4 oz) black treacle
5 tablespoons milk
1 egg

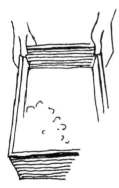

If you don't have any greaseproof paper, grease the tin, then tip 1 table-spoon flour into it and tilt it to and fro so that the bottom and sides are covered with a thin film of flour. Tip out the excess. The Parkin will be slightly more difficult to remove from the tin than if it were lined with greaseproof paper.

1   Pre-heat the oven to 180°C (350°F, gas mark 4).
2   Grease a 23 cm (9 in.) square tin and line it with greaseproof paper. To make the paper lining, place the tin on a piece of greaseproof paper and trace around the bottom. Cut the shape out and put it in the bottom of the tin. Cut strips of paper and stick them to the greased sides of the tin.
3   Place all the dry ingredients in a bowl and mix well.
4   Put the treacle, butter and milk into a pan and place over a low heat until the butter has melted and the treacle has softened.
5   Beat the egg and add it to the dry ingredients, stirring briefly. Pour in the warmed liquid mixture and mix thoroughly so that all the ingredients are completely combined.
6   Pour the mixture into the tin, making sure that it's spread evenly. Place the tin in the oven and cook for 45–50 minutes or until the top is springy to the touch and the edges of the Parkin have come away slightly from the sides of the tin.
7   Allow to cool in the tin. Eat when slightly cooled or, when it is completely cold, remove it from the tin and wrap it in greaseproof paper, then in clingfilm, and store it in an airtight container.

Easy Fruit Cake

Fruit cakes usually take a lot of time – and that's before they go into the oven! They will always need a long time to cook but in this recipe the preparation couldn't be easier. You just boil half the ingredients in a saucepan, chuck in the rest of the ingredients, stir and bake. Do be sure to allow about 2 hours from start to finish (though most of that time can be spent out of the kitchen). You can make this cake in a loaf tin if you don't have a deep, round cake tin.

Makes 1 cake

50 ml (2 fl oz) vegetable oil, plus extra for oiling
125 g (4 oz) raisins
125 g (4 oz) mixed peel
2 teaspoons mixed spice or 1 teaspoon powdered cinnamon, ½ teaspoon powdered cloves and ½ teaspoon powdered ginger
250 ml (8 fl oz) water
250 g (8 oz) sugar
275 g (9 oz) plain flour
¼ teaspoon salt
1 teaspoon bicarbonate of soda

1   Place the oil, fruit, mixed spice, water and sugar in a saucepan and bring to the boil over high heat.
2   When the mixture boils, turn it down to medium and cook for 3 minutes.
3   Take the pan off the heat and let the mixture cool to room temperature. This will take about 30 minutes.
4   Pre-heat the oven to 180°C (350°F, gas mark 4). Oil a 23 × 10 cm (9 × 4 in.) loaf tin or a 15 cm (6 in.) round cake tin.
5   Add the flour, salt and bicarbonate of soda to the cooled fruit mixture and stir well with a wooden spoon until the flour is completely blended in.
6   Pour the batter into the tin and smooth the top evenly.
7   Put the tin on the middle shelf of the oven and cook for 1–1¼ hours (depending on the size of your tin) or until a skewer comes out cleanly when the cake is pierced through the centre.

Fail-safe Sponge

The last thing a reluctant cook usually wants to try his or her hand at is baking a cake, especially when they can be bought so easily. Here's a challenge – we bet that you get this recipe right first time.

The reason why this is so effortless is that the ingredients (and there aren't very many of them) are all mixed in one bowl, so there's no complicated method and very little washing up. This particular cake does not keep well as it dries out very quickly, so plan to eat it at one sitting. Cake baking is a type of cooking where a timer really does come in handy, as one of the major reasons for failure is overcooking. You've got only yourself to blame for that!

Makes 1 × 400–500 g (14 oz–1 lb) cake

Butter for greasing
125 g (4 oz) self-raising flour
1 teaspoon baking powder
2 large eggs
125 g (4 oz) caster sugar
1 teaspoon vanilla essence
50 g (2 oz) apricot or raspberry jam
1 tablespoon caster or icing sugar

1   Pre-heat the oven to 180°C (350°F, gas mark 4).
2   Prepare two 17.5 cm (7 in.) sandwich tins. Grease them lightly with butter and line the bottom of each one with greaseproof paper (*see page 210*).
3   Sift the flour and baking powder into a large mixing bowl.
4   Add the eggs, sugar and vanilla essence. The best way to combine the ingredients is by using an electric hand mixer. Otherwise use a wooden spoon or a metal hand whisk. The ingredients must be completely mixed, resulting in a smooth batter with no lumps.
5   The consistency is right when the batter will fall from a spoon when persuaded by a gentle tap. If it won't, mix in 1–2 teaspoons hot water.
6   Divide the batter between the tins, making sure that you scrape all of it out of the bowl. Smooth the top of the batter evenly and tap the side of each tin to get rid of any air bubbles.
7   Place the tins on the middle shelf of the oven and bake for 25–30 minutes.
8   To test if the cakes are cooked, gently touch the top. They should feel springy and your fingerprint should leave no indentation on the surface.

9 Remove the cakes from the oven and let them stand in the tins to 'firm up' for about 1 minute. Then turn the tins upside down very carefully on to a wire rack. The cakes should slide out, but if they don't, carefully run a thin-bladed knife between the tin and the edge of each cake. Tap the bottom of the tins or, if necessary, hold each tightly upside down on a plate and shake hard. When the cakes are freed, transfer them to a wire rack. If the cakes still won't come out of the tins after all this, they may not be cooked, in which case you could try putting them back in the oven for a few minutes. This usually isn't very satisfactory, but it's better than nothing.

10 Peel the greaseproof paper off the cakes and leave them to cool for 10–15 minutes.

11 Spread the jam on one of the cakes. Place the other cake on top.

12 Rub the icing sugar through a fine sieve (if you don't have one, improvise with a tea strainer) over the top of the cake, sprinkling it evenly.

13 Store the cake in an airtight tin.

Variations

For a more luxurious cake, whip 150 ml (5 fl oz) double or whipping cream, mix in 2 teaspoons caster sugar and spread on top of the jam before placing the top sponge layer on. Keep this cake refrigerated or the cream will go sour.

To make a chocolate cake, add 3 tablespoons unsweetened cocoa powder with the flour and omit the vanilla essence.

For a moister, longer-lasting cake, add 125 g (4 oz) soft butter or margarine to the batter.

Bread

This is definitely the most difficult recipe in the book but we thought it was worth including because, when you make a few loaves successfully (as you will), you'll get a tremendous boost to your confidence. Also, there's nothing really comparable to home-baked bread.

As bread making is different from other kinds of baking we'll explain the procedure. Bread is basically flour, liquid and yeast. The yeast, through its fermentation, makes the bread dough rise. When the yeast has worked on the bread dough enough (this is called 'proving'), the dough is baked in the oven. The recipes below call for the dough to rise twice, which makes for lighter loaves. This does take quite a while, so once you've decided to make bread, allow yourself enough time – about 4 hours – to do so. Bread is best made on those days when you're engaged in a tiresome household task, like decorating, and you have to spend a lot of time at home anyway.

However, bread making has become much easier recently with the invention of 'easy-blend' yeast, which goes straight in with the dry ingredients and doesn't need pre-fermentation. Our recipes use only this yeast as it really has taken a lot of the heartache out of making bread. Just remember to combine it with the flour; don't sprinkle it on the water like conventional yeast. For interest's sake, 1 sachet easy-blend yeast weighs 7.5 g (¼ oz) and is equivalent to 15 g (½ oz) conventional dried yeast.

Finally, as the recipes make two loaves at a time, you'll need two bread tins. Don't think that you can cook one loaf after another, re-using the same tin!

You're ready to start. If we tell you the things that can go wrong, you should be able to avoid them. Your loaves can be a failure because:

1   The temperature of the water is too hot or cold. The water must be hand-hot, warm enough to dip your finger in for a few moments before it becomes uncomfortable.
2   You don't knead the dough for long enough. The dough won't rise if you don't knead it, resulting in a concrete-like loaf.
3   The dough isn't given enough time to rise properly, or you don't let it rise twice. Again, this results in a solid loaf.
4   The dough is not kept moist enough during rising so that the top dries out. This causes lumps in the dough.
5   The oven temperature is too low, or you cook the bread for too short a time, leaving it soggy and wet in the middle and impossible to resuscitate.

White Bread

White bread takes a shorter time to rise than brown, so you may want to try it first. Nevertheless, allow yourself plenty of time to make it.

You need strong white flour or white bread flour for this bread; you'll see the labelled packets in the shops. The cooking fat can be butter, margarine, white vegetable fat or lard. The milk powder is optional but it will give the bread a nice whiteness. You'll notice that the water is weighed and not measured by volume: this is to give you a more accurate measure. However, depending on the quality of your flour, you may need a little more as you mix the dough.

The general method for making bread is given below – the principles are the same for both white and brown bread, though the ingredients and timings are slightly different.

Makes 2 × 500 g (1 lb) loaves

750 g (1½ lb) strong white flour
15 g (½ oz) salt
15 g (½ oz) milk powder (optional)
15 g (½ oz) cooking fat, plus extra for greasing
1 sachet easy-blend yeast
425 g (15 oz) hand-hot water

1   Measure out all the ingredients except the water.
2   Warm a large mixing bowl in hot water, then dry it.
3   Put the flour, salt and milk powder, if using, into the bowl and stir with a fork so that all the ingredients are well combined, with no lumps.
4   Cut the fat into little pieces and drop them into the flour. Using your fingertips, rub the fat into the flour so that no discernible pieces of fat remain.
5   Sprinkle the yeast over the flour mixture and blend in with a fork. Make a well in the centre of the flour.
6   Measure out the water. It's easier if you start out with slightly warmer water than you want as it will cool down as you measure it out.
7   Pour the water slowly into the well, stirring all the time with a wooden spoon. You should end up with a sticky mess.
8   Abandon the spoon and start to work with your hands. Make sure that all the flour and water are mixed together and that a dough is starting to form. Scrape all the bits of dough and flour from the sides of the bowl and push them into the main lump of dough. You should end up with a relatively smooth dough that leaves the bowl clean. You may need to add extra flour or water at this stage if the dough seems too dry or too sticky.
9   Sprinkle flour on to a large board or clean work-surface. Place the ball of dough on the board and roll it around in the flour so that it's coated. You may also wish to sprinkle flour on your hands.
10 Knead for 10–15 minutes, preferably with the radio on so that the time goes more quickly. The purpose of kneading is to make the dough elastic. An elastic dough will rise well, and the resulting loaf will have a good texture. Kneading is energetic; you can't pat the dough timidly and you really do have to knead for a minimum of 10 minutes. Use a timer or you'll fool yourself into thinking that the time is up earlier!

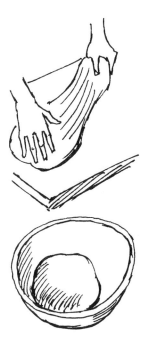

Start with the dough ball on a floured board or work-surface. First, stretch the dough by holding half down with one hand and pulling the other half away roughly. Fold the stretched part over the stationary part and punch it down. Then, using the heel of your hand, push half the dough away from you. Give the dough a quarter-turn and repeat the stretching, folding and punching until you achieve a rhythm. Continue this for at least 10 minutes or until the dough feels smooth and elastic, with no stickiness.

11 When the dough is smooth, wash out the mixing bowl, dry it and grease the inside. Put the dough in the bowl, cover with a damp teatowel (soaked in water and wrung out well), and place the bowl in a clean plastic carrier bag or bin liner. Loosely seal the bag, leaving enough room for the dough to rise. (Alternatively, you can simply cover the bowl with the damp cloth and put it in a warm airing cupboard.)

12 Leave the dough to rise in a warm place for 35–40 minutes or until it has doubled in bulk and feels slightly sticky to the touch. You can leave the dough at room temperature but it will take longer to rise.

13 Thoroughly grease two 500 g (1 lb) loaf tins.

14 When the dough has risen, take it out of the bowl and punch it down. You should be able to feel the air escaping. Place the dough on a floured board or work-surface and divide it into two equal pieces. Knead each piece for 2–3 minutes.

15 Shape the pieces of dough into loaf shapes. Tuck the ends underneath and pinch the seams closed with your fingers.

16 Grease the top of the loaves again and place in plastic bags, loosely sealed as before, for the second rising.

17 Leave for 30 minutes in a warm place (1 hour at room temperature) or until the loaves have risen to the top of the tin.

18 Fifteen minutes before the end of the rising period, pre-heat the oven to 230°C (450°F, gas mark 8).

19 Bake the bread in the oven for 30–40 minutes. It is done when the top is crisp, the loaf slips easily out of the tin and the bread feels and sounds hollow when you tap it on the bottom.

20 Leave the bread to cool, upside down, on a wire rack if possible. Leave a little time for the interior moisture to dry out before you eat it.

Brown Bread

This is made from wholewheat (also known as wholemeal) flour which results in a denser loaf, but one with more flavour than white bread. Try to buy flour which has 'stoneground' on the packet; flour simply labelled 'brown' may mean that it's white with extra colouring.

This loaf takes much longer to rise than white bread, so plan your time accordingly. The black treacle is an optional flavouring but it does add a rich taste.

The recipe method is the same as for White Bread (*see pages 215–16*) so it is not repeated here in full. Note the different timings, however.

Makes 2 × 500 g (1 lb) loaves

750 g (1½ lb) wholewheat flour
15 g (½ oz) salt
15 g (½ oz) cooking fat
1 sachet easy-blend yeast
425 g (15 oz) hand-hot water
15 g (½ oz) black treacle (optional)

1   Follow the instructions for White Bread to the end of stage 6, omitting the milk powder. This takes you up to the mixing of the dough.

2   Add the water as described in stage 7, putting in the treacle with the last of the water so that the treacle has some chance to dissolve in the heat.

3   Mix the dough, knead it and leave it to rise as described in stages 8–12. However, it will take at least 1 hour to double in bulk in a warm place, or about 1½ hours at room temperature.

4   When the dough has risen, punch it down, form it into loaves and place it into greased tins to rise again, as described in stages 13–18.

5   The second rise should take about 40 minutes in a warm room, or up to 1 hour at room temperature.

6   Fifteen minutes before the end of the rising period, pre-heat the oven to 230°C (450°F, gas mark 8).

7   When the dough has risen to the top of the tins, place them in the oven and cook for 30–40 minutes or until the top is crisp, the bread slips easily out of the tins and the bottom feels and sounds hollow when tapped.

8   Leave to cool upside down, on a wire rack if possible.

Indian Feast for Four

For some reason, it's generally considered that you can't make a real Indian meal at home. You certainly won't have the hot tandoor oven that dry-roasts meat and bread, but you can have a go at providing a good, and tasty, approximation of an Indian meal. Several Indian recipes have already been provided earlier in this book, so you're on your way. A recipe for raita is given below.

Start the meal off with poppadums, which just need to be heated up quickly under the grill or in hot oil in a frying pan, following instructions on the packet. Serve these with one or more of the wide range of Indian chutneys and pickles of varying levels of hotness which are now available in many supermarkets.

If you can use Basmati rice instead of ordinary long-grain rice, it will make a big difference to the meal. Add 1–2 cloves and 3–4 black peppercorns to the rice when you add the water for a delicate spiced flavour. Alternatively, add ½ teaspoon turmeric to the water to colour the rice light yellow.

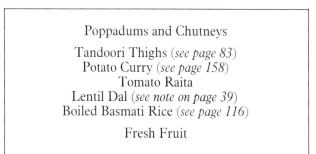

Poppadums and Chutneys

Tandoori Thighs (*see page 83*)
Potato Curry (*see page 158*)
Tomato Raita
Lentil Dal (*see note on page 39*)
Boiled Basmati Rice (*see page 116*)

Fresh Fruit

Tomato Raita

This can be served as a cooling accompaniment to many Indian meals. If you want it to be even more cooling, omit the chilli.

For 4

2 ripe medium tomatoes
300 ml (10 fl oz) plain yoghurt
½–1 teaspoon salt
125 g (4 oz) desiccated coconut
1 × 1 cm (½ in.) fresh green chilli (optional)

Be careful about how you handle chilli: if you get it anywhere near your mouth or eyes, it will sting for a good long time and it's very uncomfortable. You can either wear rubber gloves while you cut it up or make sure that you wash your hands well immediately afterwards.

1   Cut the tomatoes into small dice and place in a serving dish.
2   Add the yoghurt, salt and coconut and stir.
3   If using the chilli, chop it finely, discarding the seeds and the stem. Stir into the raita.
4   Chill in the fridge until needed.

Barbecues

This section is intended for people who have never tried barbecueing, or who aren't going to make a hobby of it but just want to cook outdoors on those two or three rare days during the summer when it's warm and sunny.

If you don't own a barbecue, we recommend spending as little as possible on an inexpensive one just to find out whether you take to both the method of cooking and the food. The most straightforward are the brazier-type, of which the best value are the Japanese-style hibachis. They come in different sizes but all have adjustable grill racks and draught control.

You don't need much by way of equipment. Tongs, skewers, a fish slice and a brush for basting are the basics. Special barbecue equipment, like bellows, pokers, long forks or double-handled fish grills, are useful but unnecessary unless you are really enthusiastic.

As fuel use charcoal lumps or briquettes sold in bags, widely available from garages. You will find firelighters absolutely invaluable for getting the charcoal lit, though they initially have an unpleasant smell. Alternatively, use crumpled newspaper or small pieces of kindling wood.

When you want to light the fire, take the grill racks out of the barbecue. Place some charcoal in the barbecue in a pile and stick pieces of firelighter, balls of crumpled newspaper or kindling into the pile. Light the fire, and when the charcoal looks as though it has caught, spread it evenly over the bottom of the barbecue and place another layer of fuel on top.

When the upper layer of charcoal is glowing and the flames have died down, there will be a thin layer of ash on top. It is only when the charcoal has turned grey-white that the fire is ready for cooking and not before.

The main reason for failure when barbecueing is not giving the fuel enough time to burn up and settle down to an even heat. If you put the food on the grill too early, it will scorch on the outside, taste of firelighter and remain absolutely raw on the inside. You have be patient and wait until the barbecue is ready; don't pretend to yourself that it will turn out all right if you start the food too early. Allow at least 1 hour from the time you make the fire to the time you want to start cooking. It may be ready more quickly than this but it's better to be overcautious, especially if you're expecting guests.

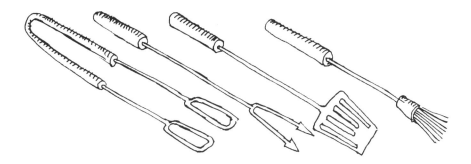

To prevent the outside of the food from cooking too quickly, you have to get the knack of judging how close to the heat to place the food and how long to cook it. A lot of meat (sausages, chicken, pork chops) has to cook all the way through for health reasons. Beef and lamb are cooked according to people's taste, and fish with its delicate flesh needs the shortest time of all.

Chicken pieces. The breast will dry out very quickly if it is cooked at too fierce a heat. Divide the leg into thigh and drumstick. Chicken wings are inexpensive and excellent for barbecues. Cook all chicken pieces 10 cm (4 in.) from the fire. Allow 12–15 minutes for breasts, 20–25 minutes for legs and 10–15 minutes for wings, turning occasionally.

Quail. Don't quail at the thought! These birds are grilled whole, after being flattened out evenly. Allow 6 minutes for a small quail and up to 10 for a medium one, with the bird 10 cm (4 in.) from the grill. Turn over once, half-way through.

Pork. Choose chops and spare ribs (cut into pieces by the butcher). The latter usually need a rich barbecue sauce to counter the fattiness. Cook pork 10 cm (4 in.) from the fire. Allow 15–20 minutes for chops, turning over once, and 30 minutes for spare ribs.

Lamb. Small chops and kebabs. Cook lamb 10 cm (4 in.) from the fire. Allow 7–15 minutes, depending on how you like your meat. Chops need turning only once; kebabs need to be turned frequently.

Beef. Good-quality topside or sirloin steak (not fillet!), cut to an even thickness of 2.5 cm (1 in.). Cook beef 7.5 cm (3 in.) from the fire. For rare steaks allow at least 6 minutes, 10 minutes for medium and 15 or longer for well done. Turn at least once.

Hamburgers. Cook 7.5 cm (3 in.) from the fire, allowing 6–10 minutes, turning once.

Sausages. Cook 10 cm (4 in.) from the fire. Allow 8–12 minutes, turning frequently.

Fish. Steaks of fish like tuna, cod, halibut and swordfish are excellent, either cut into kebabs (*see page 192*) or grilled whole. The oily fish – mackerel, herring, sardines, anchovies and sprats – are also very tasty, though they leave a bit of a mess on the grill. Barbecue them whole.

Larger whole fish and thick fish steaks need to be cooked 12.5 cm (5 in.) from the fire, thinner steaks and kebabs 10 cm (4 in.) away and small whole fish 7.5 cm (3 in.) away. Allow 10 minutes per 2.5 cm (1 in.) thickness for whole fish and thick fish steaks. Kebabs will take 5–8 minutes, 2.5 cm (1 in.) steaks 12–20 minutes and small fish 8–12 minutes.

Vegetables. These are often unjustly neglected as barbecue material. The following vegetables are very successfully grilled: large mushrooms, peppers cut into large chunks, small onions, whole tomatoes and small courgettes. Brush vegetables with oil frequently, season with salt and pepper and turn occasionally. Aubergine slices need, and absorb, vast amounts of oil while they cook.

Poultry, game-meat and fish for barbecueing should be bought fresh, then washed and dried with kitchen paper before marinating or cooking. If you are using whole fish, these should be gutted by the fishmonger.

As the heat of a barbecue is fierce, whatever food you grill needs to be kept as moist as possible. Food dries out very quickly indeed on the grill, so it's advisable to turn some items frequently, basting as you do so.

Identify the hottest and coolest areas of the barbecue. Generally, the centre is hottest and the edges cooler. If food is cooking too quickly, move it farther from the heat, and vice versa. Watch the food and move it around the grill as necessary.

The food is less likely dry out if you can marinate it beforehand in flavoured oil (see the following recipes) or brush it with oil while it cooks, or both. The marinade also adds extra flavour. Olive oil on its own is excellent for basting, if expensive. Marinated food can be brushed with the left-over marinade; otherwise, use a good vegetable oil. Unmarinated food will definitely need to be seasoned on both sides with salt and black pepper while it's cooking. The best accompaniment to barbecued food is freshly squeezed lemon juice.

Important: *Always brush the grill with oil otherwise food will stick to it.*

Eastern Lamb Kebabs

The lamb in this recipe is marinated in Middle Eastern spices. One kg (2 lb) meat is enough for five or six long skewers. You can cook the lamb on its own, or with vegetables as in the recipe for Fish Kebabs (*see page 192*).

For 4 as part of a large barbecue

1 kg (2 lbs) leg or shoulder of lamb, trimmed of fat and cut into 2.5 cm (1 in.) cubes
Salt and pepper

For the Marinade:

1 small onion, peeled and grated
Juice 1 lemon
125 ml (4 fl oz) vegetable oil, plus extra for greasing
2 teaspoons ground coriander
2 teaspoons ground cumin
¼ teaspoon chilli powder or cayenne

1   Prepare the meat. Wash and pat dry with kitchen paper.
2   Place all the marinade ingredients in a glass or earthenware bowl large enough to contain them and the pieces of meat.
3   Mix the marinade thoroughly and add the cubed meat, making sure that it is well coated.
4   Cover with clingfilm and refrigerate for at least 4 hours. Turn the cubes over in the liquid from time to time.
5   Just before cooking, thread the pieces of lamb on to long flat skewers. Season with salt and pepper.
6   Brush the grill with oil and place the skewers on top. Cook the lamb for 7–15 minutes depending on how well done you like it, turning frequently and brushing with the left-over marinade.

Marinade for Meat

This is suitable for all meat except sausages and hamburgers. It should not be re-used.

Makes enough for 1 kg (2 lb) meat

1 small onion, peeled and roughly chopped
1 small bunch parsley, roughly chopped
2 bayleaves
2 sprigs fresh tarragon or 1 teaspoon dried
2 sprigs fresh rosemary or 1 teaspoon dried
350 ml (12 fl oz) red wine
50 ml (2 fl oz) red wine vinegar
125 ml (4 fl oz) sunflower oil, plus extra for greasing
Salt and pepper

1 Prepare the onion and parsley.
2 Place all the marinade ingredients in a glass or earthenware bowl big enough to contain them plus the meat.
3 Mix thoroughly and add the washed and dried pieces of meat, making sure that it is well coated.
4 Cover with clingfilm and place in the fridge overnight, if possible, or for at least 4 hours. Turn the pieces of meat in the bowl from time to time so that they can completely absorb the flavours of the marinade.
5 Brush the grill with oil. Place the meat on the grill, season with salt and pepper and cook, brushing with the left-over marinade. See page 220 for cooking times.

Variation for Poultry and Fish

Use the above marinade, substituting white wine for the red, and white wine vinegar for red wine vinegar. Chicken can be left in the fridge overnight in the marinade but fish needs only 30 minutes.

Mustard Barbecue Sauce

If you don't have time to marinate your meat, you can brush it with spicy barbecue sauce as it cooks. The food is messy to eat, but delicious. The Chinese Hoi Sin sauce is excellent as an all-purpose barbecue sauce for meat and poultry (don't use it on fish). Otherwise, try this sauce.

Once you've tried the sauce, you may wish to alter the proportions to suit your own taste. Barbecue sauce is extremely personal! Allow enough time to make the sauce before you want to use it. It's especially good on pork spare ribs.

Makes 250 ml (8 fl oz)

125 ml (4 fl oz) Dijon mustard
2 teaspoons mustard powder
50 ml (2 fl oz) white wine vinegar
50 g (2 oz) brown sugar
75 ml (3 fl oz) clear honey
1 tablespoon vegetable oil
1 tablespoon dark soy sauce

1   Put all the ingredients into a saucepan and whisk until completely blended.
2   Set the pan over a medium heat and cook the sauce, stirring frequently, for 5 minutes.
3   Cool the sauce to room temperature. Cover and refrigerate until needed. It will keep for 3 weeks in the fridge.
4   Dip the meat into the sauce on both sides just before cooking. As the meat cooks, brush with extra sauce.

Recipes for Entertaining

You're ready for the big time now! But don't panic when you see the recipes that follow. They are a lot easier than their titles might indicate. This section contains what we call 'assembly' dishes – they require no great amount of cooking but are combinations of great ingredients which both look and taste good together. You simply prepare the constituent parts and bring the lot together just before serving. It may seem like cheating in some cases, but as long as it tastes good and looks fantastic, no one will care. Do read the section on Menu Planning (*see pages 264–7*) before you launch headlong into an important meal.

You'll notice that the ingredients used are generally more expensive than in the two preceding recipe sections. If you're entertaining, you may not mind spending a few more pounds on food than usual. In any case, the result will certainly be less expensive than either taking people to a restaurant for dinner or even buying ready-made meals and passing them off as your own.

Unlike in the preceding two sections, here we do not indicate in the method when the ingredients should be prepared. That description will be shown only beside the ingredients where they are first listed. This is to get you used to other cookery books where such instructions may be brief or non-existent. However, we do indicate timings throughout the recipe so that you can pace yourself.

Starters

Antipasto

This may be stating the obvious, but there is a lot of nice food about that neither you, nor the most accomplished cook, could possibly make at home. But there's no reason why you cannot *serve* it at home. After all, restaurants charge the earth for a plateful of delicacies they simply buy in and arrange nicely on a plate.

Italian delicatessens, or even the speciality counters of your supermarket, offer a wider range of preserved and cured food that can make lovely starters – and no one will ever accuse you of being lazy because the food tastes so good.

Antipasto simply means 'before the pasta' – in other words, a starter. What makes it so appealing is that there is no cooking involved, allowing you to concentrate on other parts of the meal. The secret of its success lies in the presentation, as the Italians know. Portuguese, French, Spanish and Greek delicatessens, as well as Italian ones, are found throughout Britain and they sell all sorts of delicious preserved food. If you feel friendly, ask the proprietors what they would serve.

The basic elements of Antipasto are:

Prosciutto crudo (cured raw ham). The most famous Italian varieties of this are Parma and San Daniele. Don't end up with cooked ham by mistake, easily done in an Italian delicatessen because *prosciutto cotto* is ordinary cooked ham.

You can buy raw cured ham pre-cut in supermarkets or get the grocer to slice it for you. It can be served by itself (it seems to be universally popular), or combined with other preserved meats or with melon, a common restaurant starter. If you want to serve *prosciutto con melone*, buy a really ripe melon – not honeydew – and give everyone 1 slice of melon plus 3–4 slices of ham, laid overlapping on individual plates.

A real stunner of a dish is Parma ham with figs. Again, buy ripe figs (which 'give' slightly when gently squeezed), allowing ½–1 per person, plus 3–4 slices of ham. Cut the fruit in half and place on individual plates with the ham slices.

Bresaola. This is beef which has been cured raw, like Parma ham. It's slightly drier than the ham so it needs a dribble of olive oil on the slices and some black pepper ground over it. It's much less common than Parma ham, so if you see it, give it a try.

Salame (cured sausage). There are many varieties of *salame*, not all of them from Italy. France, Spain, Germany and Hungary are also known for their cured sausages. They come in all sorts of flavours – fennel, garlic, peppercorn, chilli – and in different sizes. The harder they are, the thinner they should be sliced (if you're doing it at home). Don't buy the type with the neon-pink-coloured flesh studded with fat – it's disgusting. The skin should be dark red or pink and not greasy to the touch. Don't worry about taking off the skin before you serve it: let your guests do this themselves.

Olives. Try to keep some olives in the cupboard at all times. If you go to delicatessens or Greek grocers, they'll let you taste the different varieties of olives before you buy.

They really do all have different flavours, so it's worth buying a selection. Black olives, or a combination of black and green, look lovely in small bowls. But do avoid the mass-produced green olives stuffed with red pimento.

Preserved vegetables. If you have the money, or you are visiting the Continent, buy bottles of vegetables preserved in oil (not brine or vinegar). The best are artichoke hearts, peppers and sun-dried tomatoes. Drain them thoroughly of oil before serving them.

Presentation

Simple is best, a maxim known instinctively to good cooks. Take a large plate, overlap slices of Parma ham on it and place a few black olives here and there. Result? A dish any restaurateur would be happy to serve. It does sound ridiculously easy, but it works.

There are a few guidelines, though it comes down to what pleases you. For example, don't crowd too much on a plate. Think of contrasting colours, like the pink of the ham and the black of the olives. If possible, serve Antipasto on dishes that are plain, not patterned (unless they look Mediterranean). Often, one type of food arranged nicely on a plate looks better than a combination. And, of course, a loaf of good bread will complement anything you serve with it.

If you are serving a bowl of olives, enliven them with a teaspoon of olive oil, some black pepper and a sprinkling of fresh or dried herbs mixed through.

Cream of Celery and Apple Soup with Cheddar and Horseradish

This is basically an easy puréed vegetable soup, with a raw apple garnish. Its virtue lies in its subtle combination of ingredients: you get a mouthful with four different tastes at once. Use the strongest, most mature Cheddar you can find or the flavour of the cheese will be swamped. The same holds true for the apples: choose a tart eating variety with a lot of crunch like Cox's Orange Pippin. Although the parsley could be optional, the soup is a bit drab in colour without it and really does need a touch of green.

The soup can be made in advance and warmed up gently just before you serve it. However, don't let it boil when you reheat it or the cheese will become rubbery.

For 4

50 g (2 oz) butter
1 large leek, washed and thinly sliced
1 medium onion, peeled and chopped
6–8 stalks celery, washed and sliced
1.5 litres (2¾ pints) hot Chicken Stock (*see page 147*)
Salt and pepper
125 g (4 oz) strong Cheddar cheese, grated
50 ml (2 fl oz) single cream
1 medium eating apple, peeled and finely diced
4 teaspoons horseradish cream
1 tablespoon finely chopped parsley

1   Melt the butter over medium heat in a thick-bottomed pan until it foams. Add the leek, onion and celery and cook, covered, for about 5 minutes. The vegetables should not brown.
2   Pour in the hot stock, cover the pan and turn the heat up to high. When the soup boils, turn the heat down to low and simmer, covered, for 45 minutes. Using a spoon, skim the top of the soup to remove any floating scum or fat.
3   Pass the soup through a sieve, blender or food processor and place in a clean pan. Return to the boil and season with salt and pepper.
4   Add the grated cheese and stir through. The cheese need not melt completely.
5   Add the cream and mix in well.
6   Place a spoonful of diced apple in the bottom of four individual bowls. Pour in the soup and drop 1 teaspoon horseradish cream into the centre. Depending on the heaviness of your horseradish, you could try using the tip of a knife to draw it out in lines from the middle of the soup to create a classy effect.
7   Sprinkle on the parsley and serve immediately.

New England Chowder

Photograph on page 255

A chowder is more of a stew than a soup, very hearty and filling. This one is made from smoked haddock with the traditional smoked bacon as an extra flavouring. It's something of a strange choice for this section because it makes a light supper or lunch dish on its own. However, it has proved so popular with even the most cynical and world-weary of foodies that it has to be included here. As it is so substantial, follow it with something light; alternatively, treat the chowder as the main course and precede it with one of the light salad starters in this section.

   As mentioned earlier, the best type of smoked haddock fillet to buy is undyed, without chemical colouring.

For 4

1 teaspoon vegetable oil
125 g (4 oz) smoked bacon, rind and fat removed, cut into small dice
1 large onion, peeled and finely chopped
3 medium potatoes, peeled and cut into small dice
600 ml (1 pint) water
600 ml (1 pint) milk
1 kg (2 lb) smoked haddock fillets
Salt and pepper
1 small bunch parsley, finely chopped

1   Put the vegetable oil in a large thick-bottomed saucepan over medium heat. When the oil is hot, add the bacon pieces. Stir and cook until the bacon is crisp and brown. Remove it from the pan with a slotted spoon and drain on kitchen paper.
2   Add the chopped onion to the pan and fry, stirring so that the small bits of bacon stuck on the bottom of the pan are loosened. Cook until the onion is translucent and golden.
3   Drain away any excess fat, leaving the onion in the pan. Add the diced potatoes and the water and turn the heat up to high.
4   When the water boils, turn the heat down to medium and cook the potatoes for 7 minutes. The potato cubes should be cooked but still firm, not mushy.
5   Meanwhile, heat the milk in another large pan over medium heat. When bubbles appear at the edge of the milk, add the haddock fillets. Simmer for 5–7 minutes or until the haddock is no longer translucent and its flesh flakes easily.
6   Remove the haddock from the milk and place it on a plate. Reserve the milk.
7   Flake the haddock (though not too finely), discarding the skin and any stray bones.
8   When the potatoes are cooked, pour in the milk in which the haddock was cooked and then add the fish itself. Stir gently to combine. Taste the soup, then season with pepper, and salt if necessary.
9   The chowder should be quite thick. If it isn't, mash a few of the potato cubes and stir in well.
10 At this point, let the chowder stand at room temperature for 1–2 hours, if possible, so that the flavours can mature.
11 When you're ready to serve the soup, reheat it very gently over low heat. It must not boil.
12 Serve it in individual bowls with the chopped parsley sprinkled on top.

Mozzarella and Tomato Salad

This particular combination of tastes and colours is a real delight in summer when you can get sun-ripened beef tomatoes (even if they are imported from the Mediterranean) and fresh basil. It is a good standby dish which can happily accompany a green salad and some fresh bread for a light lunch. Rock salt, or sea salt, comes in big crystals and you need less of it than you need of the ordinary variety to flavour food. If you can't find it, use ordinary table salt instead. Prepared this way, the tomatoes on their own (without the Mozzarella) also make a terrific salad accompaniment to pasta and other light main course dishes.

For 4

3 large or 4 small tomatoes
250 g (8 oz) Mozzarella cheese
2 tablespoons olive oil
1 teaspoon rock salt or ½ teaspoon table salt
Pepper
6–12 fresh basil leaves or 1–2 teaspoons dried basil or oregano
6–8 black olives (optional)

1   Wash the tomatoes and dry them on kitchen paper. Cut them into 6 mm (¼ in.) slices. Set aside.
2   Slice the Mozzarella into 6 mm (¼ in.) slices.
3   On a large platter, lay alternate overlapping slices of tomato and Mozzarella in rows or in circles.
4   Sprinkle the oil in drops over the salad, followed by the salt and pepper.

If you want to make the salad in advance, don't sprinkle the oil over or season with salt and pepper until just before you are ready to serve. Otherwise, the tomatoes will become soggy.

5   Finally, tear the basil leaves into small pieces if they are large or leave them whole if they are small. Arrange the basil evenly over the salad. Alternatively, sprinkle the dried herb evenly over the salad.
6   Place the olives randomly on the salad.
7   Serve immediately.

Variation

For a more filling and colourful dish, peel an avocado and cut it into 6 mm (¼ in.) slices. Alternate the avocado slices with the tomato and cheese when arranging the salad.

Locket's Savoury

The combination of pears and blue cheese is unusual, but surprisingly the dish is traditionally British. Stilton is naturally the cheese to favour, but any hard blue-veined cheese will do just as well. The pears should be ripe but definitely not too soft.

229

For 4

1 bunch or packet watercress
2 large or 4 small pears
Juice ½ lemon
75 g (3 oz) Stilton or other hard blue-veined cheese
50 ml (2 fl oz) single cream
Salt and pepper
Buttered toast to serve

1   Wash and dry the watercress, discarding any bruised leaves and thick stems. Set aside.
2   Peel the pears. Cut them in half lengthways and core them. Cut each half lengthways into thin slices. Rub the slices with lemon juice all over to prevent them from turning brown. Cover with clingfilm.
3   Put the cheese in a bowl and add the cream, salt and pepper. Mash with a fork until you have a smooth paste, thin enough only just to pour. If it's too thick, add more cream. Taste to make sure that the seasoning is right and add more salt and pepper if necessary.
4   Divide the pear slices equally between four small plates, arranging them in a fan shape. Pour the sauce evenly over the slices. Place a small bunch of watercress on each plate to the side of the fruit.
5   Serve immediately with buttered toast.

Glazed Goat's Cheese with a Chive and Yoghurt Dressing

This is one of the easiest dishes in the whole book, even with its three elements of cheese, salad and sauce. But when you serve it to your friends, you can pretend that you have been busy in the kitchen all day.

Grilled goat's cheese seems to be on the menu of every trendy restaurant these days, but the taste is often overpoweringly strong because of the accompanying vinegary salad dressing. This dish is slightly different because it comes with a mild sauce to cut the sharpness of the cheese. Try to serve it with slices of crusty French baguette.

Goat's cheese is becoming more easily available, both imported from France and produced here by small suppliers, and it comes in a wide variety of shapes, textures and strengths. The best kind for this dish is small and round, about 1 cm (½ in.) deep and 5 cm (2 in.) across, light in texture and not dense like the pyramid-shaped ones. However, if you can find only dense thick slices of goat's cheese, they will also do, but they don't absorb the marinade so successfully.

Don't discard the oil from the marinade. You can use it later to make a cheese-flavoured vinaigrette!

The olive oil marinade – which adds extra flavour and moistness – should ideally cover the cheese. However, if it doesn't, you can spoon the olive oil over the exposed areas of cheese from time to time during the marinating period.

For 4

4 small individual goat's cheeses
75 ml (3 fl oz) olive oil
2 bayleaves
10 black peppercorns
A selection of salad leaves, preferably including one with red leaves (*see page 42*)

For the Chive and Yoghurt Dressing:

125 ml (4 fl oz) plain yoghurt
25 ml (1 fl oz) dry white wine (optional)
1 small bunch chives, chopped
½ teaspoon paprika
Salt and pepper

1   Place the cheeses side by side in a deep casserole dish. Pour over the olive oil and add the bayleaves and peppercorns. Leave the cheeses to marinate for at least 30 minutes. (If the oil doesn't cover the cheeses, put them in a narrower, deeper bowl, or add more olive oil, or spoon the oil over the uncovered areas of cheese from time to time during the marinating.)
2   Make the dressing. Combine the yoghurt, wine (if using), chopped chives, paprika, salt and pepper and mix thoroughly. Chill in the fridge.
3   Wash and dry the salad leaves.
4   When you are ready to serve the dish, pour a quarter of the dressing into the centre of each of four plates. Depending on its consistency, you can either tip the plate so that the liquid floods the bottom of the plate, or you can use the back of a fork to spread it in a neat circle in the middle of the plate.
5   Pre-heat the grill to its highest setting.
6   Place two small mounds of salad leaves at the 9 o'clock and 3 o'clock positions on the outer edges of each pool of dressing.
7   Just before serving, remove the cheeses from the marinade and place them on the grill rack. Spoon a little of the marinade oil on top. (You may also wish to put a peppercorn from the marinade on top of each cheese as decoration.) Place the rack under the grill for 4–5 minutes or until the tops of the cheeses have melted slightly. The cheeses may give off some liquid; try to drain away as much of it as possible.
8   Quickly place a cheese in the middle of each plate on top of the dressing.
9   Serve immediately.

Here are three recipes for the price of one, all using this most luxurious of fish. Look through them and then decide how adventurous you feel. The first two recipes can be served very simply on their own as starters. They require no cooking, and no real work. The third is one you should save for a special occasion.

Smoked Salmon

Smoked salmon, strawberries and champagne – nosh for the Wimbledon smart set. There's no denying that really good smoked salmon is a classically elegant starter, and one you can serve at almost any big occasion. Of course, you do pay for elegance but it's worth not skimping on quality.

Look for the lightly smoked salmon that's pale pink in colour and thinly sliced. The darker the colour, the coarser the taste. (The plebs among us often buy smoked salmon trimmings from the fishmonger at a fraction of the price of the prime part. These can be served with cream cheese on a bagel or added to scrambled eggs for a lovely brunch dish.)

If you serve smoked salmon as a starter, allow 25–50 g (1–2 oz) per person, depending on how much you can afford. Don't unwrap it until just before you serve it as it dries up very quickly. Overlap the slices on individual plates and place a lemon wedge artistically on the side of the plate. A professional-looking wedge is made by cutting a thin slice off the top and bottom of the lemon, cutting it in half lengthways and then cutting those halves lengthways into neat thirds. The traditional accompaniment is buttered triangles of brown bread (sliced very thinly from a whole loaf, not packet pre-sliced) with the crusts cut off.

Instead of lemon wedges you can serve this more unusual sauce.

For 4

125–150 g (4–8 oz) smoked salmon

For the Horseradish Sauce:

4 tablespoons creamed horseradish
2 tablespoons whipped cream
1 teaspoon paprika

1   Mix all the sauce ingredients together and chill until needed.
2   Arrange the smoked salmon slices on four individual plates and place 1 tablespoon of the sauce on the edge of each plate.

Gravadlax

This is an absolutely delicious form of salmon, Scandinavian in origin. If you want to serve a salmon starter but feel that smoked salmon is a bit too predictable (perish the thought), try gravadlax, or gravlax as it's also known.

It's not cooked but cured, with dill, sugar, salt, pepper and often lemon juice. You can buy it in many supermarkets, already prepared and sliced, in sealed packets. However, it's often sold with a rather cloying sauce which is best chucked out – the manufacturers won't thank us for that!

Allow 25–50 g (1–2 oz) per person as a starter, depending on how much you can afford. Some of us find it addictive and would happily gorge ourselves on it. You can adjust the amount to suit yourself. Serve it as you would smoked salmon (above) with buttered brown bread. Alternatively, try the sauce below.

For 4

125–150 g (4–8 oz) gravadlax

For the Yoghurt Sauce:

75 ml (3 fl oz) plain yoghurt
½ clove garlic, peeled and crushed
Juice ½ lemon
1 teaspoon chopped chervil

1   Mix all the sauce ingredients together and chill.
2   Lay the gravadlax on four individual plates in overlapping slices and place 1 tablespoon of the sauce on the side of each plate.

Trilogy of Salmon

This is a stunningly simple combination of cured, smoked and fresh poached salmon, all on one plate: same fish, three distinct and different tastes. As for garnishes, forget them – no parsley, no vulgar tomato roses – just subtle shades of pink and white. It involves a little more work than most of the starters in this book, but it's worth making for the gasps of admiration!

Presentation plays a large part in this dish. Use dinner plates, even though it's a starter – a trick picked up from expensive restaurants. As the gravadlax and the smoked salmon are already prepared, you needn't worry about them. The fresh salmon is served warm and barely cooked, with no sauce. The other two are served with the sauces described above and opposite.

For 4

1 quantity Yoghurt Sauce (*see page 233*)
1 quantity Horseradish Sauce (*see page 232*)
50 g (2 oz) gravadlax
50 g (2 oz) smoked salmon
Fresh parsley or chervil leaves to garnish (optional)

For the Poached Salmon:

4 × 50 g (2 oz) fresh salmon fillets
1 leek, washed and sliced
1 small carrot, peeled and sliced
1 bayleaf
3 peppercorns
25 ml (1 fl oz) white wine vinegar
4 or 5 sprigs parsley
Salt

1   Make the two sauces and chill them until needed.
2   Put the fresh salmon into a large shallow pan big enough to hold the fish in one layer plus the rest of the ingredients.
3   Add all the other ingredients except the salt, placing them around the fish.
4   Cover with cold water and bring to the boil over the highest heat. When the water is bubbling, turn the heat down to its lowest setting.
5   Season with salt and simmer gently for 5 minutes or until you are sure that the fish is cooked. It should feel springy and your fingers should not leave indentations when you touch it.
6   While the fresh salmon is cooking, place a portion of gravadlax on each plate and arrange the Yoghurt Sauce around it. Do the same with the smoked salmon and the Horseradish Sauce.

7   When the fresh salmon is done lift it carefully from the poaching liquid. Drain it on a piece of kitchen paper and place one piece neatly on each plate.
8   Place some of the cooked vegetables on top of each poached fillet. Garnish with fresh parsley or chervil leaves if using.

Variation: Duet of Salmon

If you wish, you can serve just the smoked salmon or the gravadlax with the fresh poached salmon. Don't serve the gravadlax and the smoked salmon together as they are too similar in texture. You need the temperature and the taste of the fresh poached salmon for contrast. Don't try to double the recipe if you're leaving out one of the elements, just serve a filling main course!

Mange-tout and Scallop Salad

To the practised eye, this will seem more like artifice than culinary achievement – which it is, of course. You can't go wrong combining one beautiful vegetable with one beautiful seafood and arranging it Japanese-style. If it were a main course you could complain that it would hardly feed a kitten, but as it's a starter you can justifiably call it an appetite whetter.

Scallops are usually sold fresh in their shells. Make sure that they're firm and white. Frozen ones (completely defrosted and drained) can be substituted.

For 4

5 ml (2 fl oz) vinaigrette (*see page 48*)
125 g (4 oz) mange-tout peas
1 teaspoon salt
2 large or 3 small scallops per person
125 ml (4 fl oz) dry white wine (optional)
Fresh chervil or parsley to garnish

1   Make the vinaigrette. Set aside.
2   Cut the stem and the tip off each mange-tout.
3   Fill a medium saucepan with cold water, add the salt and bring to the boil over the highest heat. When it boils, add the mange-tout and boil for 2 minutes or until they are cooked but still firm (*al dente*) when tasted.
4   Drain the mange-tout in a sieve immediately and hold the sieve under cold running water until they are no longer hot. Set aside.
5   Detach the scallops from their shells, if necessary. Separate the corals (the orange part) from the scallops with a sharp knife, taking care not to cut into the corals. Wash away any grit or sand.
6   Fill a large frying pan with water to a depth of 5 cm (2 in.) and add the wine, if using. Bring to the boil over highest heat. When it boils, turn the heat to its lowest setting and add the scallops and the corals in one layer.
7   Simmer the scallops and the corals for 2 minutes, then take them out immediately, using a slotted spoon, and drain them on kitchen paper. They must not be poached for too long or they become very rubbery. In fact, they are better slightly underdone.
8   Slice the scallops horizontally; the large ones should yield three slices, the smaller ones two. Leave the corals whole, on kitchen paper, to cool.
9   To serve the dish, divide the mange-tout between four individual plates, arranging them in a fan shape.
10 Overlap the scallop discs at the point of each fan, placing a coral on the top of each scallop.
11 Pour the vinaigrette over the scallops and top with a chervil or parsley leaf. Serve immediately.

German Seafood Salad

Although crab, prawns and mussels are British seafood, it's the addition of dill which gives this salad its German flavour. The colour combination works especially well – white, orange and pink seafood on a salad dressed with dill-flavoured vinaigrette.

You can buy cooked white crabmeat on its own but don't buy a cooked crab and try to extract the white meat from it unless you have a good instruction book and a lot of patience. Boiled prawns are sold either with their shells on or shelled – at a higher price. If you don't know how to shell a prawn, get the fishmonger to show you. Mussels are sold raw; you will need to cook them for this dish.

What makes this recipe a life saver in an emergency is that you can substitute all or part of the fresh seafood with tinned. Don't try using frozen seafood, however, as it's too watery. For a real treat, substitute fresh scallops, especially the small ones known as queenies, for the mussels; if you've won the pools, use both. For instructions on how to cook scallops, see page 235.

Fresh dill, a fragrant feathery herb, is available in larger supermarkets. If you can't find it, use dried dill leaves, which are sold in little jars like other dried herbs. Failing that, you can use dill seeds, but you will need half the amount recommended below as they have a very strong flavour. If you do find fresh dill, reserve a little to decorate the salad.

Like other starters in this section, the salad can be partly made in advance and then finished off quickly just before serving.

For 4

150 ml (5 fl oz) vinaigrette (*see page 48*)
1 teaspoon dill
125 g (4 oz) mussels
125 g (4 oz) cooked prawns
125 g (4 oz) white crabmeat
2 tomatoes
1 small frisée lettuce
¼ cucumber
1 egg, hard-boiled
25 g (1 oz) capers, rinsed (optional)

1   Make the vinaigrette a few hours before you prepare the rest of the salad. Add the dill and leave to infuse.
2   Cook and shell the mussels (*see page 249*). Shell the prawns.
3   Put the crabmeat in one small bowl and the prawns and mussels in another. Pour a third of the vinaigrette over the crab and two thirds over the prawns and mussels. Stir each bowl so that the vinaigrette coats the seafood and acts as a marinade.
4   Meanwhile, peel the tomatoes (*see page 157*), deseed them and cut the flesh into 6 mm (¼ in.) dice. Leave to drain on kitchen paper.
5   Separate the lettuce leaves and wash and dry them.
6   Wash the cucumber. The following is a way of slicing it so that it looks attractive in the salad:

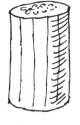

(a) Cut off the end, if necessary, and stand the cucumber upright.
(b) Slice it lengthways into 3 mm (⅛ in.) pieces.
(c) Discard the two curved outer pieces which are all peel. Lay the slices flat and cut into very thin matchsticks so that each end bears a little piece of green skin.

(d) Drain the cucumber pieces on kitchen paper.
7   Shell the hard-boiled egg and force the flesh through a sieve. Alternatively, chop it up into the smallest possible pieces.
8   All of the above can be done in advance; what follows is the final assembly. Arrange the salad on four large individual plates.
9   Place a small handful of lettuce in the centre of each plate. Spoon some of the vinaigrette from the seafood over the lettuce.
10 Sprinkle the crabmeat evenly over the lettuce. Follow with a sprinkling of cucumber, using it all up.
11 Spread the diced tomatoes on top of the cucumber and scatter the remaining seafood randomly on top of the tomato. Place a cluster of capers (if using) in the centre of each salad.
12 Sprinkle the hard-boiled egg over the plates and top with any remaining fresh dill.
13 Serve immediately.

As with all salads of this type, you can put in as little or as much effort as you want. Accordingly, you can omit the tomato and cucumber and just put the seafood on the lettuce. You don't have to peel the tomato before you dice it, though you should get rid of the seeds, and you can cut the cucumber in a different way from the one described. You can also omit the hard-boiled egg. The important elements of the dish are the seafood resting on a fresh salad flavoured with vinaigrette and dill.

Duck Liver Parfait with a Cointreau and Lime Jelly

Photograph on page 254

The term 'melt in the mouth' must have been invented for this dish. It's wonderfully luxurious . . . and very unhealthy! The whole recipe takes a little more time than other starters but requires no real skill. You could leave out the jelly if you were in a hurry – though this would be a pity. Needless to say, duck livers aren't particularly common; chicken livers are a perfectly good substitute.

You'll find that this recipe makes quite a large quantity, but it freezes very successfully.

For 4–6

For the Parfait:

300 g (10 oz) unsalted butter, softened, plus extra for greasing
125 g (4 oz) shallots or 1 medium onion, peeled and finely chopped
2 cloves garlic, peeled and finely chopped
½ teaspoon marjoram
50 ml (2 fl oz) brandy
75 ml (3 fl oz) madeira
50 ml (2 fl oz) port
500 g (1 lb) duck or chicken livers
Salt and pepper

For the Jelly:

375 ml (13 fl oz) white wine
300 ml (10 fl oz) Chicken Stock (*see page 147*)
75 ml (3 fl oz) Cointreau or another orange liqueur (not too sweet)
Juice 2 limes
1 × 24 g (1 oz) sachet aspic powder

For the Garnish:

Rind 2 limes
1 lettuce (oakleaf or frisée if possible)

To Make the Parfait:

1   Pre-heat the oven to 170°C (325°F, gas mark 3).
2   Grease a terrine dish or small loaf tin with butter.
3   Heat 50 g (2 oz) of the butter in a small frying pan over medium-low heat. When it melts, add the chopped shallots, garlic and marjoram and cook gently for 6–7 minutes. The shallots must not turn golden but should be soft and transparent.
4   Add the brandy, madeira and port and turn the heat up to medium-high. Boil, stirring occasionally, until the original volume has reduced by half.

You may find that it is easier to blend the liver in two batches, using the liquid from the frying pan to lubricate the blending.

5   Wash the livers and trim them of any membranes if necessary. If you have a sieve, push them through it so that they break up completely. This will give the parfait a smoother texture. Then put the minced liver into a blender or food processor.

6   Add the contents of the frying pan to the liver, plus the remaining butter, and blend until smooth. This will take a shorter time if you have already sieved the liver.

7   Stir in the salt and pepper. Pour the mixture into the terrine dish. Cover the dish with a lid if it has one; if not, cover it securely with two thickness of aluminium foil.

8   Boil a kettle of water.

9   Place the terrine in a roasting tin and pour the boiling water around the terrine until it comes half-way up the sides.

10   Place the roasting tin in the oven and cook for approximately 45 minutes or until the top feels firm.

11   Remove the terrine from the roasting tin and leave it to cool. When it has reached room temperature, it can be stored in the fridge until needed.

To Make the Jelly:

1   Pour the wine into a small saucepan and boil it over the highest heat until it is half its original volume.

2   Add the stock and bring back to the boil. Pour in the Cointreau and the lime juice and turn the heat down to a simmer.

You may find it easier to remove the rind from the limes (to use as a garnish) *before* extracting the juice.

3   Sprinkle the aspic powder over and stir until it has dissolved.

4   Pour the jelly into a shallow dish or bowl and leave it to cool. Then place it in the fridge to set. This will take at least 4 hours.

To Prepare the Garnish:

1   Bring a small pan of water to the boil. Meanwhile, scrape as much of the white pith as possible from the lime rind. Cut the rind into very thin strips, add to the boiling water and boil for 30 seconds. Drain on kitchen paper.

2   Separate the lettuce leaves and wash and dry them.

To Assemble the Dish:

1   Turn the jelly out of its dish and dice into 6mm (¼ in.) cubes.

2   Turn the parfait out of its mould on to a plate. Cut into thin slices.

3   Place two or three lettuce leaves on each plate at the 9 o'clock and 3 o'clock positions. Place a slice of the parfait on the upper part of the plate and a little heap of jellied cubes on the lower half.

4   Sprinkle some strips of lime rind on top of the parfait and serve.

Escalope of Pork with Marsala

This dish is often made with veal in Italy, where it originates. An escalope of veal is not only very expensive but, as it has such a delicate flavour, the Marsala – a sweet dessert wine – tends to overshadow it. Tender pork fillet is actually as good, and cheaper as well. The pork must be cut in slices 6 mm (¼ in.) thick; get the butcher to do this for you if necessary. You can also flatten the fillet further by beating it with a rolling pin. The thinner the meat is, the faster it will cook.

Marsala is widely available in off-licences and in supermarkets. It's also used to make an Italian pudding called zabaglione. As Marsala is so sweet, it often lingers in the back of people's drinks cabinets, with an infrequent minor starring role in the kitchen.

For 4

750 g (1½ lb) pork fillet, cut into 6 mm (¼ in.) slices
3 tablespoons vegetable oil
Salt and pepper
125 ml (4 fl oz) Marsala wine

1 Pre-heat the oven to 150°C (300°F, gas mark 2) and put a serving dish in to warm.
2 Wash and dry the pork fillet.
3 Pour the oil into a frying pan large enough to contain the meat in one layer and set the heat to medium-high. If you don't have a pan big enough to hold all the meat like this, cook it in two batches, using half the ingredients at a time. Because the meat takes such a short time to cook, it will not hurt to keep the first batch warm in the oven while the second batch cooks.
4 When the oil is hot but not smoking, put in the meat.
5 Cook the fillets on each side for 1 minute or until they turn golden brown.
6 Season with salt and pepper and pour in the Marsala. Stand back, as the liquid may spit a bit as the wine hits the hot oil.
7 Cook the meat for 3–5 minutes in the bubbling Marsala. The liquid should evaporate, leaving a thin syrupy sauce.
8 Transfer the meat to the warmed serving dish, pour the sauce over and serve immediately.

Fillet of Beef with Ginger and Garlic on a Bed of Creamed Spinach

Photograph on page 253

We know that the thought of starting a dish 24 hours in advance doesn't really appeal to the reluctant cook. But give this dish a try just once and then decide if it's worth the effort. Ginger and garlic, an oriental combination, actually complement most meats; here the use of beef makes for a really rich, luxurious taste. As beef fillet is expensive, save this dish for a special occasion.

To make the Creamed Spinach, follow the recipe on page 77. You can cook the spinach in advance up to the end of stage 2 and then simply add the butter and cream when you come to heat it just before serving with the beef. (You can omit the spinach from the recipe and serve the beef with another vegetable if you wish.) However, you cannot substitute powdered ginger for fresh in this recipe.

Like lamb, this beef tastes best served medium-rare, but obviously you can cook it longer if you prefer your meat well done. As the dish has such strong flavours, it needs only plain boiled potatoes and a green salad to accompany it, plus a glass of full-bodied wine.

For 4

750 g (1½ lb) fillet of beef, trimmed of fat
3 cloves garlic
1 × 2.5 cm (1 in.) cube root ginger
Salt and pepper
4 black peppercorns
1 bayleaf
1 sprig fresh thyme or 1 teaspoon dried thyme
125 ml (4 fl oz) red wine
2 tablespoons olive oil
1 quantity Creamed Spinach (*see page 77*)

For the Sauce:

2 tablespoons olive oil
½ tablespoon tomato purée
1 tablespoon French mustard
125 ml (4 fl oz) red wine
150 ml (5 fl oz) hot Beef Stock (*see page 148*)

1 Wash and dry the meat.
2 Peel the garlic cloves and slice in half lengthways. Peel the ginger cube and cut into 6 slices the same shape as the garlic slices. They will be inserted into the beef for flavour.
3 Using a thin sharp knife, make 12 small incisions all around the meat. Insert the garlic and ginger slices alternately into the incisions.

4   Season the meat all over with salt and pepper and place it in a deep dish with the peppercorns and herbs. Pour over the wine and oil. Cover the dish with clingfilm and place it in the fridge for at least 24 hours so that the flavour of the garlic and ginger have enough time to permeate the beef.

5   Allow 30–40 minutes to prepare the dish before serving, provided that the spinach has been prepared earlier. Otherwise, prepare the Creamed Spinach recipe up to the end of stage 2 before you take the meat out of the fridge.

6   Pre-heat the oven to 220°C (425°F, gas mark 7).

7   Take the meat out of the fridge, lift from the marinade and pat dry with a piece of kitchen paper. Discard the marinade.

8   Now make the sauce. Heat the olive oil over medium-high heat in a roasting tin on top of the stove.

9   When the oil is hot and you can see a faint blue haze above it, place the meat in the tin. Stand back as the oil may sputter. Brown the meat quickly on all sides, turning it over in the hot fat.

10 When all the sides are sealed, put the tin into the oven and roast the meat for 20–25 minutes. (If you like your meat well done, cook it for at least 30 minutes.)

11 Take the meat out of the oven, put it on a warmed serving dish and cover it. Turn the oven down to 170°C (325°F, gas mark 3). Place the meat in the oven to keep warm. Put four dinner plates in the oven to warm.

12 Put the roasting tin containing the cooking juices on the stove over a low heat and add the tomato purée and mustard, mixing them in well.

13 Pour in the red wine and gradually add the hot stock, mixing in thoroughly. Bring the sauce to the boil, then turn the heat down to medium.

14 Taste the sauce and add extra salt and pepper, if necessary. Cook the sauce until a quarter of it has evaporated.

15 Meanwhile, add the cream and butter to the cooked spinach and keep it warm in the oven.

16 Strain the sauce into a clean pan and return to the stove over a low heat.

17 Remove the beef from the oven and cut it into 12 slices (3 per person). As you carve, lots of juice will run out of the meat. Pour it into the sauce for added flavour.

18 In the centre of each warmed dinner plate put a portion of Creamed Spinach and then gently flood the surrounding area with the sauce.

19 Carefully place the slices of meat on top of the spinach and serve immediately.

Sautéed Calf's Liver in Bitter Orange Sauce with a Grape Salad

Photograph on page 255

This beautiful dish requires very careful attention only during the actual cooking of the meat; the rest is just assembly plus the fantastic combination of flavours. (For information on calf's liver, see page 180.) If you want a less formal dish, you can omit the salad and serve the liver on its own with boiled new potatoes and a green vegetable like beans.

The ingredients list may look daunting. Don't worry, however: you can make lots of substitutions – any other lettuce for frisée, olive oil for walnut oil, parsley for chervil, and you can omit the grapes if they're out of season (just give the dish a different name!).

When you serve the dish, make sure that you have all the elements ready before you start cooking. At the point when you want to cook the liver, the washed and prepared salad should be in the fridge and the sauce ingredients should be measured out. The dish can be spoilt by overcooking the liver, by keeping it warm for too long after cooking, or by overseasoning it, all of which can be easily avoided. The liver is actually meant to be pink inside when cooked, if you like it that way. However, don't be tempted to dress the salad until just before you serve it or it will become slimy.

The recipe below will make a sufficient quantity for a main course for four people. You can, however, serve the same amount as a starter between six, or halve the ingredients for a starter for four.

For 4

2 oranges
125 g (4 oz) butter
750 g (1½ lb) calf's liver, thinly sliced
Salt and pepper
1 clove garlic, peeled and crushed
1 teaspoon chopped chervil
125 ml (4 fl oz) white wine
175 ml (6 fl oz) single cream

For the Grape Salad:

1 small frisée lettuce
1 small bunch watercress
1 small carrot, peeled and grated
125 g (4 oz) small seedless red or white grapes
15 ml (½ fl oz) red or white wine vinegar
25 ml (1 fl oz) walnut oil
Salt and pepper

1   Start by preparing the salad. Carefully separate the lettuce and watercress leaves, discarding any that are discoloured. Wash and dry them and place them in a bowl. Add the grated carrot and gently mix together. Refrigerate the salad.

2   Separate the grapes and take off any remaining stems. Wash and dry the fruit and place them in a separate bowl in the fridge.

3   Put the vinegar into a small basin and slowly whisk in the walnut oil to form a vinaigrette. Leave in a cool place until required.

4   Now start preparing the sauce. Bring a small pan of water to the boil.

5   Remove the rind from one of the oranges. Select three wide slices of the rind and scrape off as much of the white pith from the inside as possible. Using a very sharp knife, cut the slices lengthways into very thin strips. Immerse the strips of rind into the boiling water for 30 seconds, then drain them on a piece of kitchen paper.

6   Separate the peeled orange into segments, removing as much of the pith as possible, and set aside.

7   Cut the other orange in half, squeeze the juice from it into a bowl and set aside.

8   From this point the dish should take about 15 minutes to cook from start to finish, provided that you have all the ingredients to hand.

9   Pour the dressing over the salad, season with salt and pepper and toss well so that the leaves are lightly coated with the dressing.

10 Place a handful of salad into the middle of each of four small plates and make a well in the centre of the leaves.

11 Place some grapes in the centre of each well and sprinkle a little of the orange rind over the grapes to highlight the colour. Put the plates in the fridge.

12 Melt 75 g (3 oz) of the butter in a frying pan over a medium-high heat. Put the remaining butter in the fridge to chill. When the butter in the pan foams, add as many liver slices as will fit in one layer. Season them with a tiny pinch of salt and pepper. Cook the liver for 2 minutes, moving it around very gently with a fish slice so that it doesn't stick to the pan.

13 Turn the liver over, season the other side very lightly with salt and pepper and cook for another 2 minutes. Then transfer the liver slices to a warmed serving dish and cover. Place in the oven at 110°C (225°F, gas mark ¼) to keep warm.

14 Repeat the process with the remaining liver slices.

15 To the empty (but unwiped) pan add the garlic, all but a pinch of the chervil and the remaining strips of orange rind and fry over medium-high heat for a few moments. Pour in the orange juice and white wine and turn the heat up. Boil the liquid until it reduces by about two thirds.

16 Add the cream and cook so that the sauce thickens slightly. Remove the pan from the heat.
17 Whisk in the chilled butter, a little at a time, to give the sauce a glossy sheen.
18 Remove the liver from the oven. Pour any of the juices which have exuded from the liver into the sauce and stir. Wipe any drips of juice off the serving plate with a piece of kitchen paper.
19 Pour the sauce over the liver and garnish with the orange segments. Sprinkle the reserved chervil on top.
20 Serve immediately, accompanied by the salad.

Rosettes of Lamb with a Lemon Mint and Honey Sauce

A new twist on the old theme of lamb and mint sauce, this is small tender rounds of lamb in a rich sour-sweet sauce, lightly flavoured with lemon mint. If you can't get lemon mint, substitute whatever mint is available. The lamb is cooked first and kept warm while the sauce is quickly prepared.

The rosettes are made by the butcher who bones out a best end of lamb and then rolls the flank over the eye of the meat. Once tied, it's cut into rosettes approximately 2.5 cm (1 in.) thick. Unfortunately, you can't buy this cut of meat in the supermarket; if you are unable to obtain rosettes, you can substitute loin chops, but the dish will look less elegant.

We prefer lamb cooked to a pink colour, as they do in France. Not only do you actually get the real taste of the lamb but the meat also remains moist. If you like your meat well done, cook it for longer than the time recommended below. The firmer the lamb is to the touch, the more well done it is.

For 4

8 lamb rosettes
75 g (3 oz) butter
1 teaspoon olive oil
Salt and pepper
2 stalks celery, finely diced
1 small onion, peeled and finely chopped
½ clove garlic, peeled and crushed
2 tablespoons chopped lemon mint, plus 4–8 whole leaves to garnish
1 tablespoon wine vinegar
3 tablespoons honey
75 ml (3 fl oz) hot Chicken Stock (*see page 147*)

1   Wash and dry the meat.

2   Put 50 g (2 oz) of the butter in a large frying pan. Cut the rest of the butter into 1 cm (½ in.) cubes and place in the freezer or the freezer compartment of the fridge.

3   Pre-heat the oven to 110°C (225°F, gas mark ¼). Place a serving dish and four dinner plates in the oven to warm.

4   Add the oil to the pan and turn the heat to medium-high. When the butter starts to foam, put the lamb rosettes in the pan and season them on both sides with salt and pepper. Fry the lamb gently for 5–8 minutes on each side, depending on whether you like your meat rare or well done.

5   Transfer the lamb to the warmed serving dish, cover with a lid or with foil to keep it moist and place it in the oven.

6   Discard two thirds of the fat remaining in the pan and then add the vegetables, garlic and chopped mint. Cook gently, stirring occasionally, for 5–8 minutes over medium heat or until the vegetables are soft.

7   Meanwhile, put the vinegar into a small non-aluminium saucepan and turn the heat up to high. Boil the vinegar rapidly until its volume has reduced by half. Set aside.

8   When the vegetables are soft, add the honey to the pan. As it cooks it will first turn slightly runny, then start to thicken and become 'bubbly'. At this point pour in the reduced vinegar and stock.

9   Turn the heat up to high. When the sauce boils, turn the heat down to medium and cook until it has reduced in volume by half.

10 Turn down the heat to medium-low and then whisk in the chilled butter cubes, one by one. Make sure that each cube has melted into the sauce and is well whisked in before adding the next one. Don't boil the sauce from this point onwards.

11 Take the warmed dinner plates and the lamb out of the oven. Place two lamb rosettes on each plate.

12 Taste the sauce and add extra salt or pepper if necessary. Strain it into a jug.

13 Pour the sauce around the lamb and decorate with the whole mint leaves. Serve immediately.

Spicy Charred Fish Steaks

This is the exception to the rule stated previously that fish should be treated gently. It's an American dish, though a relatively new one. The point is actually to burn the flavourings on to the fish: the butter will keep it moist.

Firm fish which would normally be sliced into steaks are good for this dish – cod, halibut, tuna, swordfish; but not salmon, as it has such a delicate flavour. If you don't like really spicy food, you can cut down on the cayenne pepper or omit it altogether, if you prefer.

Serve the dish with a cooling salad and boiled new potatoes.

For 4

4 × 1–2 cm (½–¾ in.) thick fish steaks
50 g (2 oz) butter
Juice 1 lemon
2 teaspoons paprika
1 teaspoon thyme
1 teaspoon ground black pepper
1 teaspoon dried basil or oregano
¼–½ teaspoon cayenne pepper
½ teaspoon salt

1   Wash and dry the fish.
2   Melt the butter over medium heat in small frying pan. Add the lemon juice, paprika, thyme, black pepper, dried basil or oregano, cayenne pepper and salt and stir well.
3   Turn the heat down to low and cook for 10 minutes.
4   Pour the mixture into a shallow dish. Dip both sides of each fish steak into the mixture, making sure that they're completely coated. Reserve the remaining mixture.
5   Place the fish steaks on a plate, cover with clingfilm and put in the fridge for 1 hour.
6   When you're ready to cook, pre-heat the grill to its highest setting.
7   Place the steaks on the grill rack and position them as close as possible to the heat source.
8   Grill for 3–4 minutes on each side. The top of the fish should turn reddish-black in colour. Don't worry if it chars: this adds to the flavour.
9   While the fish steaks are cooking, heat the remaining butter mixture over a low heat.
10 When the steaks are done, place them on individual warmed plates and pour the butter mixture over them. Serve immediately.

Moules Marinière (Steamed Mussels)

The most important thing is to buy and cook the mussels absolutely fresh. See opposite for information on buying and preparing these shellfish. Also, make sure that you have a pan – with a lid – large enough to hold the mussels. Many a cook has started the preparation for this dish only to find that the mussels couldn't all be cooked at once. You don't need a heavy thick-bottomed pan: an inexpensive thin metal one is perfectly all right, just so long as it's wide rather than deep.

Moules Marinière is a lunch or a light supper dish, made more luxurious with the addition of butter and cream to the sauce, though these are both optional for the faint-hearted.

For 4

75 g (3 oz) butter
1 clove garlic, peeled and crushed
1 medium onion, peeled and finely chopped
250 ml (8 fl oz) dry white wine
2.3–3.4 litres (4–6 pints) mussels, scrubbed and bearded
Juice ½ lemon
125 ml (4 fl oz) double cream
Salt and pepper
1 tablespoon chopped parsley

1   Pre-heat the oven to 150°C (250°F, gas mark ½). Put a large serving dish in the oven to warm.
2   Melt half the butter in a wide pan over medium heat. When it's melted, add the garlic and onion. Cook gently for 2–3 minutes. Do not let the vegetables brown.
3   Pour in the wine. When it's hot, put in the mussels and arrange them evenly over the bottom of the pan. Cover with a tight-fitting lid.
4   Cook the mussels over medium heat for 5–6 minutes. Using a slotted spoon remove the mussels which have opened. Discard any which have not opened, plus any half-shells.
5   Put the mussels in the warmed dish, cover with a plate or with foil and place in the oven.
6   Strain the cooking liquor through as fine a sieve as possible into a small saucepan. Place it over a high heat and boil the liquor until the volume has reduced by half.
7   Add the lemon juice and cream and bring back to the boil. Season with salt and pepper. Remove from the heat and whisk in the remaining butter.
8   Take the mussels out of the oven, pour the sauce over and sprinkle with the parsley. Serve immediately.

Buying and Preparing Mussels

Mussels are available in Britain from autumn through until spring. They're still usually sold by fishmongers in pints – that is, by volume instead of by weight. Allow 600–850 ml (1–1½ pints) per person, or 250 g (8 oz), as the shells are heavy.

Try to eat mussels on the day you buy them or within 48 hours at the outside. If you're not cooking the mussels immediately, you can keep them alive and fresh by covering them with cold water and sprinkling a handful of oatmeal (or flour) over them to feed them. Be sure to keep them refrigerated meanwhile. Mussels do need to be cooked alive; you must not cook dead ones because they'll make you ill.

Even though you're not going to eat the shells, they have to be cleaned because whatever drops off them will go into the sauce. You'll notice little tufts of hair, known as the beard, at the hinge of the mussel. This needs to be pulled off or cut away with a sharp knife. The beard isn't bad for you – it just gets in the way when you are eating the shellfish. After you've bearded the mussels, they need to be scrubbed clean of any slime, or bits of oatmeal or flour. This is best done with a stiff brush. The barnacles don't need to be scraped off; you'd be preparing the mussels for hours if they did! Once you've cleaned the mussels, the difficult bit is over.

As you clean the mussels, look out for any with broken shells or that seem heavy and full of mud or sand: discard these. The mussels should close when you tap their shells (but don't worry if they don't close completely).

All shellfish need very little cooking; overcooking makes them rubbery. Mussels do actually steam in their own juices, so you don't need a lot of liquid to cook them in. As soon as the steam has forced the shells open, they're done. You may find that some shells open wider than others, and that some don't open at all. At the end of the recommended cooking time, take all the open mussels out of the pan. Leave the unopened ones in for another 3 minutes. If some are still unopened after this, discard them.

Cooked mussels can be added to Tomato Sauce for spaghetti (*see page 114*), served as a starter with melted Garlic, Lemon and Parsley Butter (*see page 86*), or put into a potato salad (*see page 53*) for extra colour and flavour.

Desserts

Pink Grapefruit and Gin Granita

Italy specialises in different kinds of frozen dessert and this one is a sophisticated forerunner of the 'slush puppy', closer to crushed ice than to a sorbet. It's often served in expensive restaurants, not as a pudding but as a palate refresher between two heavy courses. If you're out to impress, this is an easy way of showing off.

Whether you serve it in the middle of a meal, at the end, or on a hot summer's afternoon, you can make it well in advance of the day you need it and store it successfully in the freezer compartment of your fridge. Serve it in glasses that you've chilled in the freezer beforehand for at least 15 minutes.

Making the sugar syrup, as in stage 1 of the recipe below, is a basic cooking technique. The sugar must completely dissolve in the water. Boiling it until it's thick enough to coat the back of a spoon will concentrate the flavour without the granita becoming insipid.

If pink grapefruit are unavailable, you can make the granita with the ordinary variety. You can omit stages 2 and 3 of the recipe and leave out the rind completely if you're in a hurry. The addition of egg white will give the granita a silky texture and a better appearance. However, the final result should not be smooth like a sorbet.

For 4

2 pink grapefruit
75 g (3 oz) sugar
150 ml (5 fl oz) water
Juice 1 lemon
2 tablespoons gin (or to taste)
1 egg white
Sprigs fresh rosemary to garnish

1   Squeeze the juice from one of the grapefruit. Place the sugar, water, lemon juice and grapefruit juice in a saucepan (do not use aluminium) and bring to the boil over the highest heat. When the mixture boils, turn the heat down to medium and simmer until it forms a thin syrup which will just coat the back of a spoon. This should take about 10–15 minutes. After cooking, set the syrup aside to cool to room temperature.

2   Meanwhile, put a small pan of water on to boil. Remove the outer rind thinly from the other grapefruit

with a potato peeler. Cut the rind into short narrow strands.

3   Put the strands of rind into the boiling water, return to the boil and leave for 30 seconds. Remove from the water and leave to drain on a piece of kitchen paper.

4   Now, with a sharp knife, remove the creamy white pith surrounding the rinded grapefruit and cut out the segments of fruit from between the membranes. Place them in a small basin and add the gin. Allow the grapefruit to marinate in the gin for 10 minutes.

5   Remove the grapefruit segments from the gin and set aside. Pour the gin into the cooled sugar syrup. Strain to remove any pips, if necessary.

6   Beat the egg white in a separate bowl with a fork or whisk until it's frothy but not stiff. Gradually pour the egg white into the sugar syrup, mixing all the time.

7   Pour the syrup into a container suitable for freezing, and place in the freezer compartment of the refrigerator.

8   Every 30 minutes for 2 hours, take the mixture out of the freezer and, using a fork, stir it to prevent it from becoming too solid. Scrape the ice crystals forming on the sides into the centre of the mixture to give it a uniform texture – the aim is to make it as flaky as possible, and to do this you must not let it freeze solid. If it has frozen too solidly, crush it with something hard. When you can see that the granita looks flaky throughout, you can stop stirring and leave it.

9   Before you serve the granita you may need to let it soften slightly in the fridge for 10 minutes so that you can get the serving spoon in. Spoon the granita into chilled glasses, garnish with the grapefruit segments and serve with a sprig of rosemary on the top.

Stuffed Apricots

Photograph on page 253

Apricots contain stones which can be easily removed, so they are ideal fruit for stuffing. Fresh apricots are essential for this recipe, which limits you to making it in the summer months. Ground almonds, the basis of the stuffing, are widely available. As for the sweet wine, you can use almost anything – though the rule is: never cook with something you wouldn't drink yourself!

The dish can be eaten either hot or cold, accompanied by cream or plain yoghurt.

For 4

Butter for greasing
750 g (1½ lb) apricots, or 4 per person
125 g (4 oz) ground almonds
125 g (4 oz) caster sugar
2–3 tablespoons sweet dessert wine (*see page 263*)

251

1   Pre-heat the oven to 180°C (350°F, gas mark 4). Grease a shallow baking tin big enough to hold the apricots in one layer.

2   Make a slit in each apricot lengthways to remove the stone but not so deep that you cut the apricot in half. Remove the stones.

3   Put the ground almonds in a bowl with the sugar. Add some of the wine.

4   Using your fingers, knead the ingredients into a stiff paste. You may need to add more wine to make it pliable.

5   Form the paste into small balls and press each one into an apricot.

6   Place the apricots in the baking tin and cover with foil.

7   Bake in the oven for 30 minutes or until the apricot flesh feels soft.

8   Serve hot or cold.

Tropical Fruit Platter

Photograph on page 256

It seems that we are the only nation disappointed if we're served fruit as a pudding. In other countries, especially where they grow a wide variety of fruit, it's treated with great love and care. In Middle Eastern and Asian restaurants (especially Japanese) fruit is given star treatment and often looks so wonderful that it seems almost too good to eat.

We can achieve the same standard here because of the sudden abundance of exotic fruit available in our shops. It may be expensive, but you can make one variety the centrepiece and surround it with more common but equally attractive fruit. Think about the colour combinations too – brightly coloured fruit looks very appetising. For example, you can place orange slices, watermelon and kiwi fruit on a plate and scatter a few strawberries about. If you grow mint, a few sprigs on the fruit plate look lovely. You could go completely over the top and decorate the plate with flowers, but there's not really much point in serving inedible decorations.

The word 'platter' in the title indicates that this is not a salad. The fruit, which must be very fresh and unbruised,

---

Opposite: Italian Chicken and Egg Soup (page 36), Fillet of Beef with Ginger and Garlic on a Bed of Creamed Spinach (page 241) and Stuffed Apricots (page 251).

Overleaf (left): Duck Liver Parfait with a Cointreau and Lime Jelly (page 238), Microwaved Fish Steaks (page 107) with Garlic Sautéed Courgettes (page 73) and Cabinet Pudding (page 258).

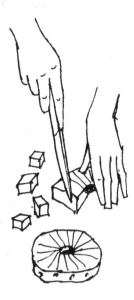

is cut up and arranged on a large flat plate with whatever creativity you possess. If you want to prepare the platter in advance and keep it fresh until you serve it, soak kitchen paper in water, squeeze it out and lay it over the fruit. Try to avoid types of fruit whose cut flesh goes brown in contact with the air, such as apples, pears, bananas. The more care you devote to preparing the fruit nicely – getting rid of seeds, pith and stones and cutting the flesh evenly without ragged edges – the better the dessert will look.

Choose from a selection of the following most common tropical fruit:

Pineapple – remove the rind and cut in horizontal round slices, then quarter these, discarding the woody core; or cut the fruit into long thin wedges like a melon.

Grapes – wash, dry and leave whole, still attached to the bunch.

Figs – leave whole; or cut in half.

Kiwi fruit – peel and slice horizontally into 6 mm (¼ in.) discs.

Fresh lychees – leave whole, leaving your guests to peel off the thin red skin.

Fresh dates – wash, dry and leave whole.

Pomegranate – (you don't need more than one fruit) cut in halves or quarters; alternatively, scoop out the seeds and scatter them about the platter.

Kumquats – wash and dry; they can be eaten whole, skin and all.

To one or more of these you can add sliced melon, oranges, peaches, nectarines, apricots. Small fruit, like berries, are best left whole.

Many of the larger supermarkets now stock even more exotic fruit, especially from south-east Asia. Don't be afraid to try them. A really lovely addition to a tropical fruit display is the star fruit, a yellow, waxy-skinned fruit with a slightly tart taste. If you slice it horizontally, you get yellow star shapes.

Previous page: New England Chowder (page 227), Sautéed Calf's Liver in Bitter Orange Sauce with a Grape Salad (page 243) and Berries with Fromage Frais (page 258).

Opposite: Glazed Goat's Cheese with a Chive and Yoghurt Dressing (page 230), Pork Cooked in Milk (page 175) and Tropical Fruit Platter (page 252).

Berries with Fromage Frais

Photograph on page 255

This remarkably simple and elegant way of serving fresh fruit uses fromage frais (also called fromage blanc) instead of the usual cream. A light cheese from France which has the consistency of yoghurt, fromage frais is sold in larger supermarkets.

Obviously, the more unusual the fruit, the more interesting the pudding. A real favourite is blueberries, but raspberries or loganberries, blackberries and strawberries (especially wild strawberries) are equally good.

For 4

500 g (1 lb) berries
250 g (8 oz) fromage frais
3–4 tablespoons caster sugar (or to taste)
1–2 teaspoons lemon juice (or to taste)

1 Pick over the berries and remove any bits of leaves, twigs and so on. Wipe the berries with a piece of moistened kitchen paper. Place in a serving bowl.
2 Put the fromage frais into a bowl. Add the sugar, 1 tablespoon at a time, and stir in, tasting constantly to find the level of sweetness you like.
3 Do the same with the lemon juice. You should end up with a perfect sweet/sharp balance.
4 Transfer the mixture to a clean serving dish and place on the table alongside the bowl of berries.

Cabinet Pudding

Photograph on page 254

If you're planning a meal with a light first and main course, you can enjoy something slightly more substantial to follow, in the form of this traditional pudding. Serving it attractively in small portions transforms it from British stodge to a dish worthy of an expensive restaurant.

The Apricot Sauce provides a touch of tartness. Turn the moulds out on to the plates and pour a little sauce around the puddings. The puddings can also be served with fresh cream or Custard (*see page 123*).

For 4–6

Butter for greasing
125 g (4 oz) sponge cake
25 g (1 oz) currants
25 g (1 oz) glacé cherries, cut in half
4 eggs
50 g (2 oz) caster sugar
½ teaspoon vanilla essence
600 ml (1 pint) milk

1 Pre-heat the oven to 170°C (325°F, gas mark 3).

2 Grease the moulds with butter.

3 Cut the cake into 6 mm (¼ in.) dice. Put it in a bowl with the currants and cherries and stir to mix.

4 Half-fill the moulds with this mixture.

5 Whisk the eggs in a large jug with the sugar and vanilla essence.

6 Pour the milk into a saucepan and place over a medium heat. When little bubbles start to appear around the sides and the milk is very warm, take the pan off the stove.

7 Pour the milk into the jug, whisking to blend the ingredients. Then pour the egg and milk mixture through a sieve into the moulds. Leave for 10–15 minutes so that the cake soaks up the liquid.

8 Meanwhile, boil a kettle of water.

9 Pour the hot water into a shallow roasting tin large enough to hold the moulds. Carefully place the moulds in the tin and pour boiling water around them. The water should come half-way up the side of the moulds.

10 Place the roasting tin in the oven and bake the puddings for 30–40 minutes or until they have set and their tops are firm to the touch. Take the roasting tin out of the oven and let it stand for 3–4 minutes.

11 If you are serving the puddings hot, turn the moulds out on to individual plates. Slide the thin blade of a knife around the outside of each pudding, place a plate on top, turn it upside down and shake so that the pudding falls out of the mould easily. Serve hot or at room temperature.

12 If you're serving the puddings at room temperature, leave them in their moulds till cool, then refrigerate until you need them. Turn them out of their moulds when you're ready to serve, allowing a little time for the puddings to come up to room temperature. In this instance serve the Apricot Sauce either hot or cold.

Apricot Sauce

For 4

4 tablespoons apricot jam
4 tablespoons or more water
¼ teaspoon lemon juice (if necessary)

1 Place the apricot jam and the water in a small saucepan over low heat. Stir with a wooden spoon until the jam has completely melted.

2 Cook for 1–2 minutes so that the consistency is thin but not watery.

3 Taste the sauce. If it's too sweet, add the lemon juice.

4 Pour the sauce through a sieve to get rid of any fruit pulp. Serve hot.

Cheese

Cheese has traditionally been served as part of a British meal right at the end, before the sleep-inducing port. The French serve it before the pudding. If you want a cheese course, you can serve it in either place.

Of greatest importance is the quality of the cheese, followed closely by the temperature at which it is served. Much cheese, whatever its provenance, is mass-produced and bland. If you don't have a great deal of money to spend, either don't serve cheese at all or buy just one or two good pieces. If you buy from a delicatessen, get the shopkeeper to recommend them.

If you find one really magnificent cheese, put a large piece of it in the middle of a plate and place it on the table in all its glory. Otherwise you can make up a small cheeseboard. A selection might consist of one blue-veined cheese, one goat's cheese, a soft French variety like Brie or Camembert, and one or two good-quality British cheeses, such as Cheshire, Double Gloucester or Lancashire.

Personal favourites for the cheeseboard include Gaperon, intensely garlic-flavoured and resembling a large white ball wrapped in a yellow ribbon; Cantal, the French version of Cheddar; the little round goat's cheeses called *crottins*; and Fourme d'Ambert, a tall, hat-shaped blue cheese.

Good cheeses from Italy include Dolcelatte, a rich, soft, blue cheese; Mascarpone, like fromage frais but full-fat; Pecorino, a salty white cheese made from ewe's milk; and fresh, crumbly Parmesan for cheese addicts.

Cheese must be served at room temperature, not straight from the fridge or you won't taste it. The French eat it on its own; we usually prefer it on bread or crackers. Make sure that the bread is good-quality. French cheeses, and British goat's cheese, go better with crusty white bread, while British cheeses are equally suited to a fresh loaf of wholemeal. A lovely combination is a hard British cheese with home-made Parkin (*see page 210*).

On their own cheeses can dry the palate, so you might like to accompany them with a bowl of fruit (this can also double as pudding, especially for a simple meal), some celery stalks or a bunch of grapes immersed in a bowl of iced water. Some people might think it criminal not to serve a glass of red wine with cheese. We'll leave that decision up to you . . .

Drinks

Alcoholic drinks are, for most people, part of entertaining and being entertained. You can fly in the face of convention and serve fruit juice throughout the meal, but it may raise a few eyebrows (except with children and pregnant women). This section offers just a few suggestions of what drinks to serve at various points of the meal.

You may want to accompany the drinks with something salty to eat. Crisps are messy, but nuts (especially the more unusual ones like pistachio and macadamia) and olives, black or green (but not the ones stuffed with strips of pimento), are popular.

Not-so-reluctant cooks, with plenty of time, serve *amuses-gueules* (a term you might come across in fashionable circles). These are very small hors d'oeuvres which, in restaurants, usually use up left-overs. You might like to spread gentleman's relish (Patum Peperium) on toast and cut it into small squares as an *amuse-gueule* if you're not feeling panicked, or if you're late with the starter!

Aperitifs

Aperitifs are either appetite whetters or ice breakers, depending on the situation. The following aperitifs are either trendy, or personal favourites, or both!

Sherry. Try *fino*, a dry sherry, and serve it chilled. Unless you particularly like sweet cream sherries, don't serve them as they are not as popular as they used to be.

Campari. This red bitter-flavoured Italian drink is usually teamed with soda (or orange juice for the uninitiated). Italy and France produce other exotic bitter drinks, like Punt e Mes or Fernet Branca.

Vermouths. These come dry and sweet white (for example, Noilly Prat and Cinzano Bianco) and red. They can be served with ice, mixed with soda and a slice of lemon, or combined with spirits.

Wine. A table wine makes a perfectly good aperitif, as long as it is fairly light, though not necessarily white. Try the following inexpensive whites: wine from Alsace (Gewürztraminer, Riesling or Tokay d'Alsace), Muscadet, Anjou or Touraine, *vinho verde* from Portugal, a German Mosel or a Riesling from Hungary or Yugoslavia. If you're serving red wine with the meal, and you've bought enough of it, try it as an aperitif. Otherwise, the famous Beaujolais – *nouveau* or otherwise – is a good light red.

Spritzer. Any of the dry white wines listed above (except the Portuguese) with either soda or fizzy mineral water added.

Sparkling wine. There is so much good-quality dry sparkling wine available that you need serve champagne only if you have money to burn. Prices vary, so shop around. Here's our choice: Blanquette de Limoux, Vouvray, Saumur, Crémant de Loire (all from France), Freixenet or another Spanish *cava*.

Kir. As supermarkets now stock Crème de Cassis, a blackcurrant flavouring, you can make this famous drink. It's dry white wine with a drop or more of Cassis. Kir Royale is the same but uses sparkling white wine (or champagne!) as the base.

Framboise. Similar to kir except that Framboise, a raspberry liqueur, is used instead of Cassis.

Buck's Fizz. The famous combination of orange juice (not tinned!) plus sparkling white wine or champagne. It's becoming better-known as a brunch drink.

Wine

We've all heard the jokes – 'it's an amusing little wine with no presumption' and so on – about winespeak, which means absolutely nothing to most people. So don't be intimidated by it. Some people regard wine as a hobby, like train spotting or stamp collecting, and their jargon happens to be better-known than that of the train spotters and stamp collectors, though it's just as specialised. The great thing about wine is that you don't have to know anything about it to drink it. Wine really does complement food; ignorance is no reason not to drink it.

The problem arises when you invite guests and you don't want to make a fool of yourself, which is perfectly understandable. The other consideration is cost. Luckily, a lot of very good acceptable drinking wine is affordable, around £3–4 a bottle.

If you want to try different wines from an off-licence or supermarket, stick to the inexpensive ones to begin with. However, there's no point in buying a wine labelled 'product of more than one EEC country' if you're trying to develop a taste. Supermarket chains buy wine in bulk. They are in the business of educating their customers, so you can rarely go wrong with one of their wines. They offer a large range, starting in price from just under £2 a bottle. If you're in a hurry, and don't have the time to saunter around the bins, get a white in as recent a vintage as possible, or a red in as old a vintage as possible. The years should be given on the label. Wine boxes, though unpopular with snobs, can be good value (though not always – check the price against single bottles) and they do dispense a glass at a time.

There used to be strict rules about food and wine. Nowadays all the rules seem to have been broken by the wine writers themselves, even the 'no fish with red wine' rule. Sweet wine still tends not to be served with savoury food and many people, having had their first unpleasant experience with it in their teens, still shun it.

Very generally speaking, it's usually white with the first course, no matter what you're serving, red with the main course (unless it's fish and you may want to continue with white), sweet wine with pudding if you can afford it and want to impress your guests, and a fortified wine, brandy or liqueur afterwards if you're greedy (and suicidal!). This is the convention at its most formal; you don't have to stick to it. Certainly, you can get by with serving one wine all the way through the first and second course and stopping there.

Limited space prevents us from giving you the caveats about what wine to serve with what specific food, let alone what wines we like. We offer here a very simple guide for people who don't necessarily want to be adventurous and who don't have a lot of money to spend, but who do want to serve a good drinkable wine.

France. As France produces so much wine, it would be ludicrous to start cataloguing the good inexpensive bottles. It's better to get recommendations from friends. Simply buy wines labelled 'Appellation Contrôlée', 'VDQS (Vin Délimité de Qualité Supérieure)' or 'Vin de Pays', all of which guarantee a certain quality. The latter wines are usually cheaper, often from co-operatives, and represent good value. Try the country wines from the south of France such as Buzet, Corbières, Côtes de Ventoux, and Côtes de Roussillon.

Italy. The term 'DOC' is the Italian equivalent of 'Appellation Contrôlée'. However, there are many good Italian wines which haven't been classified DOC. Valpolicella, Chianti, Bardolino and Barolo are widely available, reliable reds, with Barolo being the heaviest. Soave, Orvieto and Frascati are well-known whites which vary in quality. Try Verdicchio, Pinot Grigio and Tocai as less common whites.

Spain. Rioja, which often tastes of the oak in which it is stored, is the best-known Spanish wine, both red and white. Penedés, Navarre and Valdepeñas are also reliable.

Germany. Most German wine is white, medium-sweet and with varying amounts of flowery bouquet. It is not generally served with food in this country, except to people who don't like dry wine.

Other countries. If you don't have much money to spend, wines from Eastern Europe and Portugal are worth trying, especially the reds. The Cabernet Sauvignon and Chardonnay grape varieties make good rich wines in Bulgaria especially. Retsina, the resin-flavoured wine from Greece, is an acquired taste which is best served in the summer sun with an outdoor meal. Of course, Australian and Californian wines are often excellent, but as they have had to travel great distances they usually cost more than European wines of a similar quality.

Dessert wines. The best-known sweet French wine is Sauternes, though it is usually very expensive. Less costly ones are Beaumes-de-Venise, Muscat de Frontignan and Coteaux du Layon. Muscatels from Spain are good, as are most *amabile* or *dolce* Italian wines, like Vinsanto. Hungary produces the famous Tokay.

Port, brandy and liqueurs. If you can manage yet more alcohol at the end of the meal, good luck to you!

Serving Wine

How can you tell if a wine is off? Almost anyone can distinguish vinegar from wine, and that's basically all there is to it. Some wine tastes harsh and never improves with time, other wine needs to be opened a few hours in advance to bring out its best (this applies only to red). If you have a decanter or jug, you can pour your red wine into it beforehand. That way the wine breathes, the sediment sinks to the bottom and your guests need never know what you served them, if they don't ask.

White wine should generally be chilled. You can leave it to chill in the fridge for an hour before serving, but if you forget to do this, give it 20 minutes in the freezer (and don't forget about it) or stick it in a bucket surrounded by ice cubes and cold water for even more rapid chilling. Dessert wine should be served chilled.

As for wine paraphernalia, the new screwpull-type corkscrew is practically foolproof. Wine goes stale in contact with the air so if you have wine left over in the bottle, at least put the cork back in. You can buy devices which pump the excess air out of the bottle, thus guaranteeing a much longer life. Otherwise, left-over wine can be used for cooking.

Menu Planning

The most common occasions for entertaining are when you invite friends or family for dinner or lunch. Usually there is advance warning of this invasion so you have at least some time to plan and cook. Occasionally people drop round unexpectedly and you need to get food on the table quickly. Your guests, whether they regard you as a reluctant cook or not, usually have higher expectations of a meal if you have had time to cook. On the other hand, you can impress people much more easily if you produce tasty food, no matter how simple it is, at the drop of a hat.

Some people pore over cookbooks for weeks on end trying to decide what to serve at a dinner party. If this is the only cookbook you own, at least you won't be spoilt for choice! However, the right food for the occasion is fairly important, if you want to please your guests. Here are considerations to be taken into account:

Cost

It's generally true that the cheaper the dish, the more time it takes to make – for example, smoked salmon bunged on a plate is faster than home-made soup. Dishes produced from inexpensive ingredients are, however, just as delicious as luxuries bought from top food shops. You know your own budget. Decide what you can afford for the total meal. If you can afford, say, only one scallop per person for Mange-tout and Scallop Salad (*see page 235*), it won't matter so long as it tastes and looks good and it's followed by a more modest and filling main course, like a pasta dish or a stew that can be stretched with potatoes.

What can keep the price of a meal down is using ingredients that are in season, a point that cannot be overemphasised. Nobody will ever complain in mid-June that they're served strawberries and cream for the third time that week. If you're really concerned, do something slightly different with the strawberries, like pairing them with fromage frais (*see page 258*).

Vegetables are generally inexpensive. Nowadays, when lighter, healthier food is actually more fashionable, a large piece of meat is no longer the *pièce de résistance* at a dinner party. You can cook a vegetable dish as a starter (something like Braised Fennel – see page 156 – can be made in advance and be served at room temperature) and follow it with small portions of meat or fish with more cooked vegetables on the side.

Circumstances

First, the season. Obviously, people tend to want to eat lighter meals in summer than in winter, and with the wealth of summer fruit and salad vegetables it would be silly to serve swedes in July. When the days grow shorter and the warm sun is no longer beckoning you from the garden, you don't resent quite so much spending a little longer in the kitchen. Dishes like Garlic Sausage with Red Cabbage (*see page 171*) are slow-simmered winter dishes.

Do bear in mind the time of day at which you plan to serve the meal. Despite the custom of eating the Sunday roast joint at lunchtime, it's usually better to serve lighter food in the middle of the day so that your guests won't fall asleep before the last dish is cleared away! In fact, really heavy food is never a good idea: nobody likes to feel uncomfortable after a meal.

Perhaps the most important consideration is serving suitable food for the occasion. If you want to impress someone (for business or romantic reasons, or just for your own self-confidence), try using an unusual ingredient (like hazelnut oil for a salad dressing) or making something interesting out of conventional ingredients. There is snob value in simplicity. The aforementioned berries and *fromage frais*, or a Mozzarella and Tomato Salad (*see page 229*), though very easy and straightforward, look fantastic and make people think that you are confident enough not to cook. By the way, filling people up with stodge is not part of showing off, so avoid serving Chilli con Carne to your boss unless you have known him or her very well!

However, if you have a lot of people to feed (or a smaller number of hungry or greedy people), delicious stodge is both practical and appreciated. If the occasion is informal, don't feel obliged to serve three courses; but it doesn't have to be a large buffet for you to put more than one dish on the table. You can serve three different salads, one substantial main-course vegetable dish, a plate of cold meat, another of cheese and a loaf of good-quality bread, and have a magnificent feast.

What People Want, or Can Eat

In the late 1980s it's prudent always to ask your guests if they have any dietary restrictions, given the growing number of vegetarians. You may have friends who are Jews, Muslims or Hindus, or who may be diabetic or have various food allergies. Finding out this information – not to mention violent dislikes – before you plan your menu saves much embarrassment at the dinner table. Don't throw up your hands in despair; consider the meal a challenge. Once you've fed a vegetarian diabetic with an allergy to dairy products, no menu will ever be difficult again!

Ease of Preparation and Cooking

This is where most reluctant cooks come unstuck, so don't be too ambitious until you're confident. Entertaining in itself can be stressful, and you don't want to compound the problem by setting yourself a difficult menu.

Whether the meal is formal or informal, don't plan to serve more than two hot courses out of three. You can certainly get by with just one hot course, usually the main one, and in summer it's perfectly acceptable to have the entire meal cold. You can also serve a salad instead of an extra vegetable to save yourself work.

By the way, you can serve a salad at three different points in a meal – as a starter, American-style; with the main course; or between the main course and the pudding, as they do in France. If you choose the last option (our preference) you gain an extra course, the salad refreshes the palate and it looks sophisticated, especially if it's made with a variety of salad leaves, including a red-coloured type (*see page 42*). In fact, we think that salad should appear in every formal meal, both for health and presentation reasons.

If you are planning to serve a cold starter and pudding, you can make them ahead of time, preferably at least a few hours before, if not the preceding day. Soup is an ideal starter because it can be made in advance and then warmed up at the last minute. And starters which are bought (because you couldn't possibly make them at home) allow you to give more time to the rest of the meal. This includes food such as Antipasto (*see page 224*), Smoked Salmon and Gravadlax (*see pages 232–3*).

Vegetables can be pre-cooked briefly (blanched, then refreshed, *see page 157*), then dipped into boiling water or fried quickly to warm them up. Microwave ovens are useful for cooking many vegetables quickly between courses, so long as you don't mind your guests hearing the telltale 'pinging' noises!

If you are going to make something that requires last-minute cooking, you should either ensure that it's the starter so that you don't keep people waiting too long at the table, or make sure that your guests are good enough friends not to mind a delay. In fact, bear in mind, when planning a menu, how long it's going to take you to serve up between courses. If you're on your own, it's sensible to cook something you can manage to serve quickly without any help.

Many of the dishes in Section Three are easy and require little cooking – just quick assembly and an eye for presentation. Make sure that all elements of the dish are prepared beforehand, like chopped herbs, washed salad leaves and so on. Also, have all serving dishes or individual plates at hand so that you don't need to panic looking for clean crockery. (Incidentally, on the Continent you often keep your used cutlery between courses in restaurants. If you're short on knives and forks, you could ask your guests to do the same.)

Balance

A balance of textures, ingredients and colours within a meal is important. Even the most experienced cook will suddenly discover too late that all his or her courses are laden with cream, leaving the guests to stagger from the table.

(a) Texture

Try not to serve too many soft-textured dishes (usually egg-based foods, puréed vegetables, soups or cream puddings). Make sure that something crisp appears somewhere in the meal, whether it's a salad, a green vegetable or a piece of fruit. In restaurants the aforementioned cream is often found in a soup, forms the sauce of a main course and is then poured over the pudding. Avoid this at all costs.

(b) Ingredients

You should have a good variety of flavours in a meal, but you don't want to repeat a flavour or a main ingredient twice. So avoid serving tomato soup followed by spaghetti with tomato sauce, to use a very obvious example.

Although you should feel free to mix food of different cultures in a meal, think twice about following something like Curried Lentil Soup with Chinese Stir-fried Chicken and Vegetables. It may not be a felicitous combination.

Another consideration is the variety of protein in a meal. We advise against serving meat twice in a meal. It's usually expensive, and it weighs heavily upon the stomach. You can precede a meat main course with a vegetable soup, a salad or a small portion of fish. Alternatively, serve a meat starter like Duck Liver Parfait (*see page 238*) followed by a substantial cooked vegetable-dish course or a main-course salad.

If either the starter or the main course is heavy, end the meal with fruit, either within a salad or a platter (*see page 252*), or simply on its own. Your guests won't feel cheated; rather, they'll be grateful that you took pity on their digestion.

(c) Colour

If you have managed to compose a menu that takes into consideration texture, temperature and variety of ingredients, you will probably have a good combination of colours within the meal. However, colour within a course is sometimes neglected. For example, you end up with a pallid-looking plate if you serve grilled chicken with boiled potatoes and turnips. Try to combine a cooked green vegetable with a yellow, red or orange one for the main course.

Presentation

'. . . And for £30 all they gave me was three baby carrots, one broccoli spear and a piece of parsley arranged on a huge plate.' The horror stories about the excesses of Nouvelle Cuisine are becoming apocryphal. Nonetheless, the fashion for this style of eating has made everyone think about the presentation of food, and the relationship between the appearance and the taste of the dish. Luckily, you need neither spend hours in the kitchen creating the perfectly shaped carrot, nor spend a fortune on truffles to sprinkle on top of a fillet steak. There are a few tricks that anyone can use to transform a dish from the mundane into a visual delight.

(a) Dishing Up

Most food looks attractive on white plates. Restaurants have also discovered the trick of putting small amounts of food in the middle of big plates. White crockery can be bought very cheaply; a heavy plate is just as good as a piece of bone china. Even buying four or six large plates would be enough. However, plain plates of any shade enhance the appearance of the food, especially if you can choose food whose colour complements that of the plates. The deep vibrant colours of fresh fruit and vegetables, raw or cooked, jump out from a pale background.

The salads in Section Three are all *salades composées*, which means that the ingredients are carefully assembled on individual plates instead of being tossed in a bowl. Of course, this assembling takes time, so it's only worthwhile doing it for one course, ideally the starter. If you don't want to go to that amount of trouble, simply laying out food attractively on large serving dishes can look impressive (see Antipasto, *page 224*, and Mozzarella and Tomato Salad, *page 229*). In general, leave large empty spaces around the edge of the plate when serving individual portions, but fill serving dishes full.

Think about the shape of the food in the dish. If the food is flat, like slices of meat or tomatoes, you can overlap them slightly. However, you should serve round food, like radishes, piled up plentifully in a bowl instead of flat on a plate which might look mean and meagre.

(b) Decoration

There's a fine line between attractive decoration and fussiness. If in doubt, err on the side of caution. If you are using patterned plates, any decoration may look completely wrong, but you can experiment all you want when your dishes are plain. The most important thing about a garnish is that it should be edible, otherwise it looks contrived and ridiculous.

For savoury dishes especially, fresh herbs are the best decoration. They can be bought quite cheaply in most supermarkets, though they're cheaper still if you grow them at home. Parsley, in both the curly English and flat-leaved Continental varieties, is the herb most commonly used to decorate food. Great bunches of curly parsley have become a bit of a cliché so, if you have a choice, try to obtain the Continental type. However, if you're going to chop the parsley and sprinkle it over soups or salads, you can use either variety. The taste of parsley goes well with almost every dish. Other herbs have stronger, more distinctive tastes, so you have to match the herb with what you're serving. Whole leaves of a herb can be used as a garnish, especially if the same herb has already been used to flavour the dish. Mint leaves are traditionally used to decorate raw fruit puddings.

Ground spices can occasionally be used as decoration. A sprinkling of bright red paprika will liven up the appearance of a pale egg or cheese dish and its flavour is mild enough not to overpower. (Don't mistake cayenne or chilli pepper for paprika if you're in a hurry!) Ground nutmeg or cinnamon sprinkled on light-coloured puddings are fine as long as their flavour complements that of the dish. They should not be used gratuitously. Grated chocolate, powdered chocolate and sieved sugar are also used to decorate puddings.

Fruit and vegetables are often used as decoration. For example, if you've bought a sorbet, you could put a raw slice of the fruit flavouring the sorbet on each individual portion. Cherry tomatoes, mushrooms sliced into a fan, chopped spring onions – these are just a few ideas for garnishing an individual plate, or a larger serving dish. Don't even think about tomato or radish roses, or other grotesque tortured garnishes.

(c) Extras

Soup and other starters are often accompanied by bread. Serving a good bread, especially a slightly unusual one, starts the meal off well. If the bread has been heated through and is served in a basket covered with a paper or cloth napkin to keep it warm, it looks as though you've gone to a lot of trouble.

It's small things, like heating the bread, which often impress guests. You could serve a whole meal of food bought from a delicatessen, but if it's laid out nicely with some thought, people will go away thinking that you're a really good cook. Reluctant cooks can get away with very little effort in the kitchen if they give the impression of luxury on the table.

We mentioned the importance of using real Parmesan cheese. People often like to do things for themselves, whether it's grating their own cheese from a big hunk, slicing a loaf at the table or dunking raw vegetables into dips. Plates of cut lemons for grilled food, glass beakers of olive oil, bowls of shiny black olives – these all please the eye and require almost no work. You just have to use your imagination.

Postscript

By this point the world should be your oyster, as far as cooking is concerned. But where to next?

Instead of just giving you a holiday reading list, as most teachers would do, we're going to let you discover the enormous world of cookbooks for yourself. You should now be armed with enough knowledge not to be intimidated by horrible heavy tomes filled with dense text – and without pictures!

After mastering this book, you may wish to concentrate on certain kinds of cookery like different ethnic types, more difficult puddings, vegetarian food and so on. Hundreds of new cookbooks are published every year in this country alone, leaving aside the rest of the English-speaking world. Unless you have come across the author before, it's hard to know which book you'll find useful and enjoy using.

Here's a hint or two. First of all, try to get recommendations from friends. Also, selections of recipes from cookbooks often appear in magazines. Trying a recipe or two from these, or at least reading them, will help you decide if you want to buy the book.

When choosing a cookbook, ignore the cover: it rarely indicates the quality of the recipes. Photographs are useful to help you know what an unfamiliar finished dish is meant to look like, but they are not essential. After all, this book isn't crammed full of photos. Read the introduction to see if you get a feel of the writer's personality. Check whether the book is laid out in a way that's convenient to use. Also, if the book is very expensive and the photos too glossy, you may never want to use it for fear of getting it dirty. And unless you indulge in what's been termed 'gastro-porn' (slavering over books filled with luscious photos of even more luscious food), there's no point in spending the money.

Finally, look at the range of recipes in the table of contents and at specific recipes. If you think you'd like to eat a dish, you will probably want to cook it too. At this stage, a good suggestion might be to take a guess at the average number of ingredients in the recipes. If there are more than about twelve to fifteen (leaving aside the garnish), forget it!

Now we'll say it – good luck and even better eating!

Index